Saint Pope Paul VI

Matthew E. Bunson

# SAINT
# POPE PAUL VI

Celebrating *the* 262nd Pope
*of the* Roman Catholic Church

EWTN PUBLISHING, INC.
Irondale, Alabama

EWTN Publishing, Inc.
5817 Old Leeds Road, Irondale, AL 35210

Distributed by Sophia Institute Press, Box 5284, Manchester, NH 03108.

**Library of Congress Cataloging-in-Publication Data**
To come

First printing

*For BB*

*In virtue of our own charism as Successor of Peter,*
*we feel compelled to speak to you a word of challenge, exhortation*
*and encouragement. Permit us to open to*
*you our heart. Our sentiments are sentiments of*
*esteem, of interest and of love.*

Address on the Occasion of the Canonization
of St. John Neumann (June 20, 1977)

*I must bear witness to his name: Jesus is the Christ, the Son of the living God (Matt. 16:16). He reveals the invisible God, he is the firstborn of all creation, the foundation of everything created. He is the Teacher of mankind, and its Redeemer. He was born, he died, and he rose again for us. He is the center of history and of the world; he is the one who knows us and who loves us; he is the companion and the friend of our life. He is the man of sorrows and of hope. It is he who will come and who one day will be our judge and — we hope — the everlasting fullness of our existence, our happiness.*

Homily for Mass at Quezon Circle,
Philippines (November 29, 1970)

# Contents

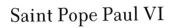

Saint Pope Paul VI

# Introduction

On June 19, 1963, eighty members of the Sacred College of Cardinals processed into the Sistine Chapel to vote in the conclave to choose the successor to Pope St. John XXIII, who had died from stomach cancer on June 5 at the age of eighty-three. The traditional drama of a conclave was heightened because John's death had come in the middle of the Second Vatican Council. John had convened the ecumenical council, the twenty-first in the Church's history, in 1962 to launch his vision of *aggiornamento*—that is, encouraging the Church to proclaim the unchanging truths of the Catholic Faith in a language that the modern world could understand.

With the council on hold for the election of a new pope, many bishops wondered if the cardinals would choose a new Holy Father who would continue the work of the council, one who would redirect its energies and focus, or perhaps even one who would bring it to a close after one session, as a project to be buried with Pope John. One name, however, was on everyone's mind.

There were, to be sure, several cardinals who could become the next pope—so-called *papabili*—but even before John's passing, one was seen as the logical, perhaps even inevitable, prelate to ascend to the Chair of Peter: Cardinal Giovanni Battista Montini, archbishop of Milan.

# Saint Pope Paul VI

On the afternoon of June 21, the Romans and the world watched for the results of the voting in the Sistine Chapel. Inside, beneath Michelangelo's *Last Judgment*, the cardinals completed the fifth ballot, on which Cardinal Montini was, in fact, elected. When asked by what name he wished to be called, he responded that he would be Paulus Sixtus, Paul VI, choosing the name to honor St. Paul and to emulate him in his desire to evangelize the world.

Nine days later, a large crowd gathered in St. Peter's Basilica for the formal installation Mass. Paul began his pontificate with a clear statement of his own humility, but also of certainty. He declared that he stood before the whole Church, trembling but confident, and accepted the keys of the Kingdom of Heaven—keys that were heavy, powerful, and mysterious.

Paul's reference to the heaviness of the keys is significant, for it can be argued that the weight of the papacy had begun for Montini not on June 21, but at the moment he had become a cardinal in 1958.

By agreeing to receive the red hat from Pope John—it was said that he had refused it from Pius XII in the 1950s—he knew that he would almost certainly become pope. He was the first cardinal named by John after his election in 1958, but Montini had long been a major figure in the Vatican. His transfer to Milan in 1956, where he earned immense praise for his pastoral style and his openness to renewal, only added to his reputation.

Indeed, it was said that he would have been elected pope in 1958 had he been in the College at the time of Pius's death. There had even been speculation that the 1958 conclave might choose him anyway, in what would have been the first instance since 1378 in which a pope had been chosen who was not a cardinal.

That didn't happen, but by 1963 the hour had come. Much like Cardinal Eugenio Pacelli (Pope Pius XII) in 1939 and Cardinal Joseph Ratzinger (Pope Benedict XVI) in 2005, Montini entered the conclave knowing that he would almost certainly be called to the Petrine Office. All three men were elected in moments of drama or danger for the Church. Pacelli was chosen as the globe was plunging into the maelstrom of World War II, and Ratzinger became pope at the end of one of the longest pontificates in history—one of a man already being called "the Great" and who would soon be canonized.

From the start, Paul had upon his shoulders not only the weight of years of expectation but the enormous task of bringing to a successful conclusion an era-defining council that he had not started. He would then have the duty of guiding the Church in its aftermath—a period of shocking social and political change, including the sexual revolution.

In 1968, he issued the encyclical *Humanae Vitae*, which reaffirmed the Church's teachings on contraception and family life in the face of pressure to embrace birth control. Paul would not budge, but the severity of the reaction and the open dissent took their toll. He never issued another encyclical.

The last years of his pontificate were a *via crucis* for him, and how best to understand those years remains the source of debate, controversy, and reflection. Through it all, he continued to defend the council, to speak on the implications of modernity for human life and the human person, and to call for Catholics to evangelize, to love the Eucharist, to be holy, and to be aware of the dangers of the age while understanding the signs of the times. He famously warned in a much misunderstood homily on the feast of Sts. Peter and Paul, on June 29, 1972, that in the face of "doubt, uncertainty, problems, restlessness, dissatisfaction, confrontation" in the Church, he had the terrible feeling that "the smoke of Satan entered the temple of God from some fissure." The phrase was soon seen as a kind of epigraph for both his final years and the condition of the Church seven years on from the Second Vatican Council.

# Saint Pope Paul VI

Paul died at the papal retreat of Castel Gandolfo, on August 6, 1978.

The late pope was vilified by some for seeming to have given up. Others called him a Hamlet for his apparent doubts and hesitation, especially in the face of the storm that ensued in the Church in the years after the council.

Assessments and reappraisals will continue, but certainly the teachings of Paul for the modern world are needed now more than ever, as, five decades after *Humanae Vitae*, we harvest the dread fruits of a contraceptive culture that Paul foresaw with such searing accuracy. Paul VI's pontificate produced an immense body of writings and teachings, but, sadly, much of it is already forgotten, overshadowed by his most famed works. One of the main purposes of this book is to bring those less celebrated, but often perceptive and beautiful, writings back into view.

The canonization of Pope Paul VI—forty years after the end of his papacy and fifty years after the promulgation of *Humanae Vitae*—is an opportunity not only to celebrate the life of a pontiff now honored as a saint of the Church but also to appreciate more fully the fullness of his teachings. Paul VI left us a body of work that is approachable and valuable for spiritual and theological reflection. Contrary to what is often said and written about Montini's papacy, he did not cease writing and teaching after *Humanae Vitae*, nor was the 1968 encyclical his only prophetic teaching. In truth, much of Paul VI's thought was visionary, and he presciently anticipated the labors of his successors. He meditated on the human condition, on atheism, on the isolation of young people in the modern world, on the risks of globalization, on the need for the dignity of the human person to be safeguarded in the face of technological and scientific breakthroughs, and on the risks of the Church's becoming too closed in on herself. He also spoke without doubt that the Second Vatican Council did not represent a rupture from Tradition, nor did it propose conformity with the passing and error-filled thinking of our age or any age. In all these concerns, he finds himself in continuity with St. John Paul II, Benedict XVI, and also Francis.

St. Paul VI was the Vicar of Christ. His words had significance in his time, and they remain incredibly valuable to us today. The timeless quality of his teachings was made clear in April 1968, when Archbishop Fulton J. Sheen wrote a defense of the pope that was published in the Vatican newspaper, *L'Osservatore Romano*, under the title of "The Voice of Peter."

We reaffirm our allegiance to the Voice of Peter in Paul VI, for we know that we share in Christ's prayer for His Church only to the extent that we are united with Peter. In these days when Satan has been given a long rope, we want above all things to share in the PRAYER OF CHRIST for the preservation of faith. But we know that we can do this only through our union with Peter. To Peter, and now to Paul VI, we look for the never failing faith, for the assurance that neither the pillars of the Church, nor its inferior parts will ever be severed from the Church's structure.[1]

---

[1] Archbishop Fulton Sheen, "The Voice of Peter." *L'Osservatore Romano*, weekly edition in English, April 11, 1968, archived at https://www.ewtn.com/library/Theology/PETRVOIC.HTM.

*Chapter 1*

# The Life and Holiness of Pope St. Paul VI

Shortly after Pope Paul VI's death in August 1978, Archbishop (later Cardinal) Jacques-Paul Martin, prefect of the Papal Household throughout Paul's pontificate, published a story about the late pope in the Vatican newspaper, *L'Osservatore Romano*. On the eve of the consistory to create him a cardinal in 1958, then-Archbishop Giovanni Battista Montini of Milan was received in private audience by Pope St. John XXIII, who had placed Montini's name at the top of the list of new members of the Sacred College. The cardinal-elect, Martin wrote, "with his customary humility, prostrated himself to kiss the new Pope's foot. 'Excellency, what are you doing?' exclaimed Pope John, compelling him to raise himself up, 'you know well that if you had received the purple some months earlier, it is you who would be here in my place today, and I who would kiss your foot!'"[2]

Pope John said this with his typically wry sense of humor, but he was also reminding the cardinal both that he should have been appointed years before, and that he should expect to succeed John as pope in short order. This moment is also indicative of the immense

[2] Most Rev. Jacques Martin, "Memories of Pope Paul VI," *L'Osservatore Romano*, weekly edition in English, August 31, 1978, archived at https://www.ewtn.com/johnpaul2/life/p6memories.htm.

weight Montini carried for much of his life: the expectation held by so many that he would eventually, even inevitably, become pope. The burden of expectations was only heightened by the specific circumstances that surrounded Paul's election. He succeeded one of the most outgoing, gregarious, and confident popes of the twentieth century. And he was chosen in the midst of an ecumenical council he did not convoke. Paul met the challenge—but for the intro-verted and thoughtful pontiff, being elected pope in 1963 was the next great task in a lifetime of duties and demands he had to face.

## Brescia's Child

The future pope was born on September 26, 1897, in the village of Concesio, near Brescia, Italy, in the family home of the Montinis. He was baptized Giovanni Battista Enrico Antonio Maria at the age of four days in the parish church of St. Antonio in Concesio. On the day of his baptism, St. Thérèse of Lisieux died in her con-vent in France.

He was the second of three brothers, between Lodovico and Francesco. His father, Giorgio Montini (d. 1943), was a lawyer, a member of the Italian Chamber of Deputies, and political editor of the Catholic paper *Il cittadina di Brescia*. His mother, Giuditta Alghisi (d. 1943), was a member of one of the local noble families and president of the Brescia chapter of Women's Catholic Action.

Giovanni grew up in the Faith, and both parents—his mother especially—imbued the children with a love of literature, art, mu-sic, philosophy, and political life. Giovanni was deeply prayerful from an early age, developing spiritually under the influence es-pecially of the Oratorians, who were in charge of the Church of Santa Maria della Pace in Brescia.

His schooling was complicated by his frail constitution, but he proved a very adept and talented student at the Jesuit-run Cesare

Arici Institute (1903–1914) and the Liceo Arnaldo da Brescia, a state school.

Giovanni discerned a call to the priesthood and entered the seminary of Brescia in 1916, but he studied mostly from home because of bouts of illness. He impressed the superiors of the seminary, however, and was ordained a priest on May 29, 1920, celebrating his first Mass in the Basilica della Santa Maria della Grazie in Brescia. The chasuble he wore for his first Mass was woven from his mother's wedding dress.

Father Montini was soon sent to Rome, where he studied philosophy and canon law at the Pontifical Gregorian University and literature at the University of Rome–La Sapienza. His intelligence, prudence, and temperament caught the eye of members of the Roman Curia, and in short order, the young priest was invited to study at the Accademia dei Nobili Ecclesiastici (the Academy of Noble Ecclesiastics, now the Pontifical Ecclesiastical Academy), the training center for Vatican diplomats. His letters provide a glimpse into his introverted personality and how studying and living in the midst of the socially demanding academic and ecclesiastical community in Rome was a cross for him to bear. At the time of his acceptance into the Accademia, he wrote his parents: "There is room ... for the possibility to have some solitude. That consoles me a bit, because solitude allows one to build up the energy to be in company with others."[3]

In 1922, only two years into his priesthood, he was appointed to the Vatican Secretariat of State. There he began a career of Vatican

---

[3] Quoted in Francis Phillips, "The Unseen Paul VI: An Introvert Who Wore Chains beneath His Robes," *Catholic Herald*. February 10, 2017, http://www.catholicherald.co.uk/commentandblogs/2017/02/10/the-unseen-paul-vi-an-introvert-who-wore-chains-beneath-his-robes/.

service that continued for more than three decades, even though it also meant that he never received an assignment in a parish.

## Sostituto Montini

In 1923, Montini was assigned to the Apostolic Nunciature (embassy) in Warsaw. It was a useful experience for the young priest, but he later commented that his time in Warsaw was not an especially happy one, given the political and economic problems in the country. After a year, he was called back to Rome, and in October 1924 he was named to the staff of the Vatican Secretariat of State, where he began earning a reputation for his tremendous work ethic and intelligence. After only a few months, he was promoted to the rank of *minutante* (secretary).

At the same time, Father Montini served as a chaplain to the Catholic students at the University of Rome and as spiritual moderator to the Federation of Italian Catholic University Students (Federazione Universitaria Cattolica Italiana, FUCI). He and Igino Righetti, president of FUCI, also launched a publishing company and a weekly newspaper, *La Sapienza*. Fluent in French, he translated several books into Italian, including *Three Reformers* (1928) by Jacques Maritain. From 1931 to 1937, Montini also taught the history of papal diplomacy at the Academy of Noble Ecclesiastics.

In 1930, the Secretariat of State was placed under the direction of the towering figure of Cardinal Eugenio Pacelli, who had been appointed by Pope Pius XI. Named a domestic prelate of His Holiness in 1931, Monsignor Montini emerged as one of Cardinal Pacelli's most trusted deputies. In December 1937, he was appointed to the post of *sostituto* (undersecretary) to the Secretary of State for ordinary Church affairs, and both Montini and Pacelli took part in the Thirty-Eighth International Eucharistic Congress in Budapest, Hungary, in May 1938.

## The Life and Holiness of Pope St. Paul VI

Pope Pius XI died on February 10, 1939, and Cardinal Pacelli was considered the heavy favorite to succeed him, especially with global war on the horizon. The next pope needed to be able to lead the Church and civilization in the face of the atheistic and diabolical regimes of Hitler in Nazi Germany and Stalin in the Soviet Union. Pacelli was indeed elected pope on March 2, 1939, after only three ballots; he took the name Pius XII.

The new pontiff named the seasoned diplomat Cardinal Luigi Maglione to the vacant post of Secretary of State, but he kept in place his two most trusted assistants, Montini and Msgr. Domenico Tardini, who was in charge of the external affairs (that is, diplomacy) of the Secretariat of State.

When Maglione died in 1944 with the globe in the grips of the Second World War, however, Pius took the unusual step of not naming a successor. Instead, Pius served as his own Secretary of State, with Montini and Tardini working directly under the pope and Montini continuing in his role as *sostituto* for internal affairs. Cardinal Martin remembered Montini's unceasing work habits during World War II:

> His capacity for work was astonishing. When we, simple employees, used leave the office about 8 p.m., having placed our work on the *Sostituto's* desk, our day was ended. For him, practically another was beginning, for he drove himself for long hours through the silence of the night. To the late stroller who found himself in St Peter's Square around midnight an interesting sight was to be seen: while the Vatican lay plunged in darkness and in sleep, along the immense facade of the apostolic palace only two windows emitted a ray of light: that of Pope Pius XII and that of the *Sostituto* Montini.[4]

---

[4] Ibid.

The herculean efforts were needed, as Montini's portfolio was enormous. Pius entrusted him not only with overseeing the daily needs of the Holy See but also with the overwhelming task of directing its war relief efforts. That meant aiding the millions of refugees displaced by the conflict, helping families find relatives, tracking prisoners of war, and trying to shield Jews from the Nazi regime. Montini was one of the unknown heroes in the Church in his work, especially in doing what he could to save Jews from arrest and deportation to the gas chambers. Cardinal Martin continued:

> It was alongside Pius XII that Monsignor Montini experienced the drama of the Second World War. The volumes published, through the care of the Secretariat of State, on "The Holy See and the World War" have revealed the breadth of action unfolded by the Holy See, both on the level of diplomacy and that of charity, in order to save so many innocents from death; in order to relieve so many who were starving (including Romans); in order to organise an immense system of exchange of news between prisoners and their families; in order to safeguard the impartiality of the Holy See between the pressures of the opposition between the "Allied" Countries and the "Axis" Powers; and in order successively to lodge their representatives on the narrow territory of The Vatican.[5]

## "Archbishop of the Workers"

With the end of the war, Montini and Tardini continued in their posts. By 1952, Pius XII had decided it was time to make a formal public statement of his esteem for his two closest collaborators:

---

[5]  Ibid.

He informed both Montini and Tardini that he wished to appoint them to the College of Cardinals. To his surprise, in an expression of humility, they both declined. Still determined to thank them for their service, on November 29, 1952, Pius named Montini Pro-Secretary of State for Ordinary Ecclesiastical Affairs and Tardini Pro-Secretary of State for Extraordinary Ecclesiastical Affairs.

Two years later came the surprising announcement that Pope Pius had appointed Montini to serve as archbishop of Milan. Montini was consecrated a bishop on December 12, 1954, in St. Peter's Basilica.

Why Pius sent him to Milan remains something of a mystery. Tardini stayed in service at the Vatican, while Montini was essentially removed from Rome during what many saw as the terminal period of the pontificate. It has been theorized that Montini had worn out his welcome within the Curia and that, by the end of 1953, Pius needed to make some changes to release some pressure. As it was, Montini was simply replaced by Msgr. (later Cardinal) Angelo Dell'Acqua, so the basic structure of the Secretariat of State was not completely remade. It has also been suggested that Pius was trying to provide Montini with additional pastoral experience in directly caring for the faithful. The pope knew well that because of his protégé's many years of service in the Vatican bureaucracy, Milan would be Montini's first pastoral assignment.

As archbishop of Milan, Montini gave himself completely to his flock. He was both intensely pastoral and deeply concerned with the pressing social and economic problems of his enormous see, one of the largest in the world, with more than three million Catholics and one thousand churches. He understood the need to repair the terrible physical and spiritual damage caused by the war, to respond to the intellectual foment of the time, and to reckon with the host of challenges facing workers in the industrialized society of the sprawling metropolis, many of whom were being drawn away from the Church by the promises of the communists.

Antonio Airò, a writer for the Milanese Catholic daily newspaper, witnessed Montini up close in the years before the council and wrote a 2009 remembrance called "Si rivolgeva anche ai 'lontani'" (He also spoke to the "far away") that was published for the Archdiocese of Milan.[6] He never forgot the archbishop telling him, "This Milan that is so modern, but also so distant, is the Milan that we must love and in which we must commit ourselves day by day; it is our cross, but also our great hopes."

Montini called himself "the archbishop of the workers" and launched a massive pastoral outreach across the archdiocese in November 1957. Joined by his priests, religious, and dedicated laypeople, thousands of events were held in parishes and factories to encourage Catholics in their Faith and to bring the fallen-away back to the Church. Montini issued two pastoral letters every year he was in Milan, one for the faithful and one—on Holy Thursday—for his priests.

Airò recalled the cardinal who went out to the camps of immigrants on the outskirts of Milan, who cried holding a handicapped child in his arms during a visit to the Little Cottolengo of Don Orione, a residence for handicapped and abandoned, and who displayed "an authentic evangelical compassion for man."

In these labors, Montini anticipated the concerns of the Council over the rise of atheism and a growing distance between man and God—the crisis of modernity, with the need for the Church

---

[6] See, in Italian, "Si rivolgeva anche ai 'lontani,'" Chiesa di Milano, March 3, 2015, http://www.chiesadimilano.it/arcivescovo/vescovi-precedenti/giovanni-battista-montini-1954-1963/si-rivolgeva-anche-ai-lontani-6195.html.

to speak to the modern world. It was in Milan that much of Paul's pontificate took shape.

## The Era of the Council

Most observers predicted that Pius XII would offer Archbishop Montini the red hat again within a short time of appointing him to Milan. But in the long pontificate of Pius XII, there were only two consistories, in 1946 and 1953. He named fifty-six cardinals in these two gatherings, but he died without ever convoking another. If he had planned to name Montini a cardinal, he never confirmed it publicly.

And so, at the death of the great Pope Pius XII on October 9, 1958, at the papal retreat of Castel Gandolfo, Montini was an archbishop and therefore excluded from participation in the conclave to elect Pius's successor. Montini's name was mentioned in the days leading up to the conclave, and some advanced the notion that he might be chosen despite not being a member of the College of Cardinals. The last time that happened was the papal 1378 election of Bartolomeo Prignano, the archbishop of Bari, who took the name Urban VI. Critics of the Montini idea pointed out immediately that Urban's difficult papacy led to the Great Western Schism, which divided the Church until 1417.

As it was, Montini reportedly received several votes in the early balloting, but a majority of the cardinals were not ready for such a bold step. On October 28, after eleven ballots, the cardinals elected Angelo Roncalli, patriarch of Venice, who took the name John XXIII. He was seventy-six years old.

John wasted no time in calling a new consistory for December 15, 1958, where he named twenty-three new cardinals. Montini's name, of course, was at the top of the list, but included among the new recipients of the red hat was also Domenico Tardini, whom John had appointed as his new Secretary of State.

# Saint Pope Paul VI

Barely more than a month later, on January 25, 1959, John announced his intention to convoke the Second Vatican Council, and Cardinal Montini was appointed to both the Central Preparatory Commission and the Technical-Organizational Commission. Montini became one of the most active supporters of John's plans for the council and also began preparing the Milan archdiocese. In 1962, in the days leading up to the opening of the council, Montini issued a pastoral letter to the archdiocese that expressed his support for John's project of *aggiornamento* for the Church to be able to speak directly and forthrightly to a world struggling with modernity.

While maintaining a discreet public presence in the preparations and conduct of the first session of the council, Cardinal Montini played a very significant role behind the scenes—along with Cardinal Leo-Joseph Suenens, archbishop of Mechelen-Brussels—in bringing order out of the looming chaos of debates, documents, and competing priorities of the council fathers. While John might tease Montini for being like Hamlet in deliberating too long before acting, the wearying pontiff leaned upon the archbishop of Milan for advice on navigating the complex theological waters of the council, as well as the diverse personalities among the council fathers.

On the floor of the council, Montini maintained his customary prudence during the first session. He spoke only twice, once on the proposed schema for the document on the liturgy (that became the Pastoral Constitution *Sacrosanctum Concilium*) and then on the schema for the document on the Church (that became the Dogmatic Constitution *Lumen Gentium*).

## Pope Paul VI

By the end of the first session, the signs were unmistakable that John did not have long to live. He had been diagnosed with stomach cancer in September of 1962, and in the following months, he grew more haggard with each passing week.

Upon his death on June 3, 1963, the council was suspended until a new pope was elected. To no one's surprise, Cardinal Montini was elected pope on June 21, 1963, and he took the name Paul VI.

The new pope declared his intention to emulate the apostle Paul, to be a "pilgrim pope" who would proclaim the gospel across the world. While he was crowned on June 30, 1963, with the triple tiara of the popes—a gift of his Milanese flock—he proved the last pope to be given such a coronation. As part of his simplification of papal government and ceremonial life, Paul sold the tiara to Cardinal Francis Spellman of New York. The money was given to the poor, and the tiara was eventually put on display at the Basilica of the National Shrine of the Immaculate Conception in Washington, D.C. All of the popes since then have been installed wearing a miter.

Paul's immediate order of business was thus to bring the council to a successful conclusion. He applied his organizational skills to the deliberations and the work of the various commissions, and so set right much of the disorder that had characterized the first session. It still required two more years and three more sessions—John had hoped for one—to conclude the massive amount of work. The years of the council were not without debate and controversy, especially over the liturgy, ecumenism, religious liberty, collegiality, and the Blessed Mother. He presided over every session and permitted the council participants to be heard—but he also took steps to clarify and to augment the documents when necessary. Some of his most notable actions during the council were to declare the Blessed Virgin Mother to be the Mother of the Church and to add to *Lumen Gentium* a note clarifying the statements concerning the collegiality of bishops.

Paul closed the council on December 8, 1965, with a call to all people everywhere, exemplifying the work and the purpose of the council:

> From this Catholic center of Rome, no one, in principle, is unreachable; in principle, all men can and must be reached. For the Catholic Church, no one is a stranger, no one is excluded, no one is far away. Every one to whom our greeting is addressed is one who is called, who is invited and who, in a certain sense, is present. This is the language of the heart of one who loves. Every loved one is present! And we, especially at this moment, in virtue of our universal pastoral and apostolic mandate, we love all, all men.[7]

## Implementing Reform

To give the work of the council its greatest possible spiritual support, Pope Paul VI declared an extraordinary jubilee (or Holy Year) to last from January 1 to May 29, 1966. It was his hope that during this celebration the faithful might be given extensive instruction in the reforms introduced by the council and that the Church might be thereby renewed and the changes greeted in a positive way.

Eager to bring reform also to the way the Vatican functioned, Paul reorganized the central administrative organs of the Church (the Roman Curia) in line with the provisions of his 1967 apostolic constitution, *Regimini Ecclesiae Universae*, streamlining

---

[7] Paul VI, Homily for the Feast of the Immaculate Conception and the Conclusion of the Second Vatican Council (December 8, 1965).

procedures for more effective service and giving the agencies a more international perspective by drawing officials and consultors from all over the world. Coupled with curial reorganization was the simplification of papal ceremonies. Paul reduced the size of the court and abolished many centuries-old traditions, such as the Noble Guard, a papal guard that had protected the Holy Father since 1801.

Other reforms included financial reorganization, fixing the retirement age at seventy-five for priests and bishops, and confirming the Secretariats for the Promotion of Christian Unity, Nonbelievers, and Non-Christian Religions. He also set up a large number of commissions and promulgated many documents that led to the introduction of the new Mass in 1969 and the reform of the Church calendar in 1970.

Continuing the process of the broadening of the College of Cardinals, he created 144 cardinals and gave the Sacred College a more international complexion than it ever had before. He also made the memorable decision to limit participation in papal elections to 120 cardinals under the age of eighty—a rule that stands to this day. Cardinals over eighty years of age were to retire, give up all curial offices, and be ineligible to participate in papal elections.

Faithful to the deliberations of the council, Paul chartered the synod of bishops in 1965 with the decree *Apostolica Sollicitudo*, "to encourage close union and valued assistance between the Sovereign Pontiff and the bishops of the entire world; to insure that direct and real information is provided on questions and situations touching upon the internal action of the Church and its necessary activity in the world of today; to facilitate agreement on essential points of doctrine and on methods of procedure in the life of the Church." The first synod of bishops was held from September to October 1967, for "the preservation and strengthening of the Catholic faith, its integrity, its force, its development, its doctrinal and historical coherence." Further synods were held on such topics as enhancing participation by bishops with the pope and each other in the governance of the Church, the ministerial priesthood and justice in the world, and evangelization of the modern world.

All of these were intended to advance the work of the council, but from the start, Paul faced opposition from prelates who resisted the changes and others who accelerated the process to such a degree that serious disorientation began to occur, especially in Europe and in the United States. The process of implementation was also buffeted by tempestuous cultural shifts—including the sexual revolution—and the crisis of dissent within the Church that used the "spirit of the council" to justify liturgical aberrations and rejection of proper authority.

To bolster the faithful in this time of crisis, the pope declared a special Year of Faith from 1967 to 1968 dedicated to the apostles Peter and Paul, marking the nineteenth centenary of their martyrdom. The Year of Faith ended in St. Peter's Square, on June 30, 1968, with a solemn profession of faith, titled the "Credo of the People of God." Only weeks later, Paul promulgated the encyclical *Humanae Vitae*.

Yet, for those who lived during the years after the council and then the last years of Pope Paul VI, there seemed at times an astounding contradiction between the enthusiasm and hope that greeted the end of the council and the dissent, disappointment, and frustration that often dominated the discussions and atmosphere.

Seminaries in the late 1960s closed at an alarming rate, replaced by "theological institutes" that were staffed in many places by ex-priests and ex-nuns who promoted dissent and the rejection of traditional Catholic thought. The decline of vocations and the departure of priests and men and women religious struck like an earthquake. Just as shocking was the decline in Mass attendance. In 1962, Mass attendance was 80 percent in the Netherlands; this sank to 64 percent in 1966 and 31 percent by 1976. Modern historians have lamented the failure of some bishops to move with alacrity in dealing with the crisis that ensued. The orthodox bishops struggled against a liberal and dissenting Catholic leadership in chanceries, parishes, and especially universities that blocked efforts to implement the council in a faithful way. In this way, the Dutch Church's tragedy of dissent, exemplified by the monstrous and heresy-filled 1966 Dutch Catechism, anticipated the problems that were soon reproduced across Europe, the United States, and Canada.

## A World in Crisis

Pope Paul did not see a Church in dire need of surrendering to the world but a world in need more than ever of the eternal truths of the Church — truths that needed to be communicated in ways most meaningful to the modern mind. His concerns stemmed from the shattering changes in the world in the modern era, but especially the nuclear age, the rise of communism, and the spread of the destructive philosophies of atheism, secularism, materialism, and sexual "freedom."

The year that epitomized the social upheaval was 1968. Riots and other shocking events swept France, the United States, West Germany, and England. Sen. Robert Kennedy and Reverend Martin Luther King were assassinated; Vietnam War protests gathered steam; radical cultural benchmarks emerged; and liberals in the West were all but silent while Warsaw Pact forces crushed the Prague Spring and the aspirations of the Czech people for democracy. In France, students revolted in May, demanding greater freedoms in education, art, and sex.

These storms struck the Church from outside, even as the internal tumult after the council continued unabated. To be sure, the confluence of events was not entirely unrelated. Some Catholic theologians, clergy, and laypeople used the confusion in the immediate aftermath of the council to unleash in Catholic teaching the same radical ideas that were being propagated in the streets and classrooms of the wider world. This was apparent in the Dutch Church's struggles and the demands for "academic freedoms" from Catholic professors, but above all it was epitomized by the controversy over *Humanae Vitae*.

## *Humanae Vitae*

One of the most important developments of the era was the proliferation of artificial contraception across the developed world. There was a general expectation that the Church would issue a definitive statement on the matter. To this end, Pope John XXIII had established a Papal Commission for the Study of Problems of the Family, Population, and Birth Rate in 1963, comprising bishops, theologians, and other recognized experts in the field of family life. Pope Paul VI then expanded the commission's membership.

Rather than surrender to the demands and expectations of the media and dissenting Catholics, the pontiff reaffirmed the Church's unwavering teachings, especially Pope Pius XI's 1930 encyclical, *Casti Connubii*, and issued *Humanae Vitae* on July 25, 1968, in which he taught:

> Therefore We base Our words on the first principles of a human and Christian doctrine of marriage when We are obliged once more to declare that the direct interruption of the generative process already begun and, above all, all direct abortion, even for therapeutic reasons, are to be absolutely

excluded as lawful means of regulating the number of children.[8] Equally to be condemned, as the magisterium of the Church has affirmed on many occasions, is direct sterilization, whether of the man or of the woman, whether permanent or temporary.[9]

Similarly excluded is any action which either before, at the moment of, or after sexual intercourse, is specifically intended to prevent procreation—whether as an end or as a means.[10]

Neither is it valid to argue, as a justification for sexual intercourse which is deliberately contraceptive, that a lesser evil is to be preferred to a greater one, or that such intercourse would merge with procreative acts of past and future to form a single entity, and so be qualified by exactly the same moral goodness as these. Though it is true that sometimes it is lawful to tolerate a lesser moral evil in order to avoid a greater evil or in order to promote a greater good, it is never lawful, even for the gravest reasons, to do evil that

---

[8]  See Council of Trent Roman Catechism, pt. II, chap. 8; Pius XI, encyclical letter *Casti Connubii* (December 31, 1930); Pius XII, address to Medico-Biological Union of St. Luke (1944); address to midwives (1951); address to Family Campaign and other family associations (1951); John XXIII, encyclical letter *Pacem in Terris* (April 11, 1963); Vatican Council II, Pastoral Constitution on the Church in the Modern World *Gaudium et Spes* (December 7, 1965), 51.

[9]  See Pius XI, *Casti Connubii*; Decree of the Holy Office, February 22, 1940; Pius XII, address to midwives; Piux XII, address to the Society of Hematology (1958).

[10]  See Council of Trent Roman Catechism, pt. 2, chap. 8; Pius XI, *Casti Connubii*; Pius XII, address to midwives; address to the Society of Hematology; John XXIII, encyclical letter *Mater et Magistra* (May 15, 1961).

good may come of it (see Rom. 3:8) — in other words, to intend directly something which of its very nature contradicts the moral order, and which must therefore be judged unworthy of man, even though the intention is to protect or promote the welfare of an individual, of a family or of society in general. Consequently, it is a serious error to think that a whole married life of otherwise normal relations can justify sexual intercourse which is deliberately contraceptive and so intrinsically wrong. (14)

The pope anticipated the violent reaction that was to come, warning in the encyclical:

It is to be anticipated that perhaps not everyone will easily accept this particular teaching. There is too much clamorous outcry against the voice of the Church, and this is intensified by modern means of communication. But it comes as no surprise to the Church that she, no less than her divine Founder, is destined to be a "sign of contradiction" (Luke 2:34). She does not, because of this, evade the duty imposed on her of proclaiming humbly but firmly the entire moral law, both natural and evangelical.

Since the Church did not make either of these laws, she cannot be their arbiter — only their guardian and interpreter. It could never be right for her to declare lawful what is in fact unlawful, since that, by its very nature, is always opposed to the true good of man.

In preserving intact the whole moral law of marriage, the Church is convinced that she is contributing to the creation of a truly human civilization. She urges man not to betray his personal responsibilities by putting all his faith in technical expedients. In this way she defends the dignity of husband and wife. This course of action shows that the

Church, loyal to the example and teaching of the divine Savior, is sincere and unselfish in her regard for men whom she strives to help even now during this earthly pilgrimage "to share God's life as sons of the living God, the Father of all men."[11] (18)

*Humanae Vitae* was the last encyclical of Paul's papacy, although he continued to speak, to write, and to teach the truth until his death ten years later.

## The Labors of Paul

Even as all these events were unfolding, Paul embarked upon an unprecedented series of journeys. Until the globe-trotting pontificate of Pope John Paul II, Paul was the most prolific traveler in the history of the Church, more than living up to his desire to be a "pilgrim pope" in the spirit of the missionary labors of St. Paul.

As a cardinal, Montini had visited the United States, Ireland, and parts of Africa. After his election, Paul focused the early years of his pontificate on traveling to countries across the globe.

He began by making a trip to Jerusalem in 1964, becoming the first pope in many centuries to walk in the Holy City. While there, he stunned the world by meeting with Ecumenical Patriarch Athenagoras I of the Orthodox churches. The next year, he journeyed to the United States and spoke at the United Nations to plead for peace, issuing the memorable call, "No more war. War, never again." He also attended the Eucharistic Congresses in Bombay, India (1964) and Bogota, Colombia (1968); undertook a pilgrimage to Fátima (1967); and visited Uganda (1969), Australia (1970),

---

[11] See Paul Vl, encyclical letter *Populorum Progressio* (March 26, 1967).

the Philippines (1970), and many other far-flung places. In the Philippines, he was nearly assassinated by a knife-wielding assailant.

Paul continued the policy of his predecessor in reaching out to the world diplomatically. He met with many world leaders, including Soviet President Nikolai Podgorny in 1967, Marshal Tito of Yugoslavia in 1971, and President Nicolai Ceausescu of Romania in 1973, and worked constantly to reduce tension between the Church and the intransigent regimes of Eastern Europe by means of a sometimes controversial policy of détente called *Ostpolitik* that sought to reach a rapprochement with the communists. In all, more than forty countries established diplomatic relations with the Vatican during Paul's pontificate.

Finally, on New Year's Day 1968, Paul VI instituted the annual World Day of Peace to address a regular message of peace to the world's political leaders and the peoples of all nations. The Day of Peace, along with its annual papal messages, continues to this day.

Paul was also sincerely devoted to the cause of Christian unity and ecumenism. Building on his Jerusalem trip, on December 7, 1965, he read a joint statement with Patriarch Athenagoras expressing regret over the mutual excommunications that had been pronounced in 1054, causing the schism that still divided the Eastern and Western churches. In a moment full of symbolism, he exchanged an embrace with the envoy of the patriarch. He then met with Michael Ramsey, archbishop of Canterbury, in March 1966, and with the patriarch again in July 1967 in Istanbul. Later, in April 1977, he and Donald Coggan, archbishop of Canterbury, released a joint pledge of continued effort toward reunion.

For too many Catholic commentators, it has seemed that Pope Paul issued only one encyclical, *Humanae Vitae*. In fact, he issued seven, including *Sacerdotalis Caelibatus* (Priestly Celibacy), in which he reaffirmed the strict observance of priestly celibacy throughout the Western Church at a time when dissenting voices were calling for its end. In the 1967 enyclical *Populorum Progressio* (Development of Peoples), he appealed to wealthy countries to take "concrete action" to promote human development and to remedy imbalances between richer and poorer nations; this encyclical, coupled with other documents and related actions, launched the Church into a new depth of involvement as a public advocate for human rights and for humanizing social, political, and economic policies. In Pope Benedict XVI's 2009 encyclical *Caritas in Veritate*, he stressed the prophetic and influential role of Paul's encyclical in the history of Catholic social teaching. Benedict wrote:

> In 1967, when he issued the Encyclical *Populorum Progressio*, my venerable predecessor Pope Paul VI illuminated the great theme of the development of peoples with the splendour of truth and the gentle light of Christ's charity. He taught that life in Christ is the first and principal factor of development[12] and he entrusted us with the task of travelling the path of development with all our heart and all our intelligence,[13] that is to say with the ardour of charity and the wisdom of truth. It is the primordial truth of God's love, grace bestowed upon us, that opens our lives to gift and makes it possible to hope for a "development of the whole man and of all men,"[14] to hope for progress "from less human conditions to those which are more human,"[15] obtained by overcoming the difficulties that are inevitably encountered along the way. (8)

---

[12] See John XXIII, encyclical letter *Pacem in Terris*, 16.
[13] See ibid., 82.
[14] Ibid., 42.
[15] Ibid., 20.

## Paul's Last Years

Because Paul VI issued no further encyclicals after *Humanae Vitae*, there has been a perception that he simply gave up. In truth, the pope continued to teach and to try to provide clarity in a confused time, even in the final years of his pontificate.

In 1970, he issued a decree on mixed marriages, *Matrimonia mixta*, which was an effort to help Catholics understand the issues related to marrying outside the Church. In 1975, the Congregation for the Doctrine of the Faith promulgated the Declaration on Certain Questions Concerning Sexual Ethics, *Persona Humana*, a stern, albeit belated effort to stem the tide of the sexual revolution. In the decree, Paul's prefect for the Congregation, Cardinal Franjo Seper, wrote:

> In the present period, the corruption of morals has increased, and one of the most serious indications of this corruption is the unbridled exaltation of sex. Moreover, through the means of social communication and through public entertainment this corruption has reached the point of invading the field of education and of infecting the general mentality.... As a result, in the course of a few years, teachings, moral criteria and modes of living hitherto faithfully preserved have been very much unsettled, even among Christians. There are many people today who, being confronted with widespread opinions opposed to the teaching which they received from the Church, have come to wonder what must still hold as true.[16] (I)

And in 1976, the Congregation also issued the declaration *Inter Insigniores*, "On the Question of Admission of Women to the

---

[16] Franjo Cardinal Seper, "Declaration *Persona Humana* on Certain Questions Concerning Sexual Ethics" (December 29, 1975), pt. I.

Ministerial Priesthood," reiterating, "the Church, in fidelity to the example of the Lord, does not consider herself authorized to admit women to priestly ordination."[17]

Though Paul ceased to issue encyclicals after *Humanae Vitae*, he regularly used another form of papal writing to encourage the faithful: the apostolic exhortation, a papal writing that carries less magisterial weight than an encyclical and that typically calls upon the faithful to undertake some action. These included *Signum Magnum*, on "the traditional doctrine of the Church regarding the function of the Mother of God on the plane of salvation and her relations with the Church"; *Evangelica Testificatio*, on "the renewal of the religious life according to the teaching of the Second Vatican Council"; *Marialis Cultus*, on "the right ordering and development of devotion to the Blessed Virgin Mary"; *Gaudete in Domino*, on Christian joy; and especially *Evangelii Nuntiandi*, on proclaiming the Gospel in the modern world, which became a kind of blueprint for the New Evangelization of Pope John Paul II and Pope Benedict XVI.

Pope Paul also urged Catholics to remember the universal call to holiness, offering encouragement in the pursuit of sanctity in an age that seemed to have forgotten the heroic life of virtue. He canonized eighty-four saints, including a group of twenty-two Ugandan martyrs and the forty martyrs of England and Wales. Two Americans were also added: Elizabeth Ann Bayley Seton and John Nepomucene Neumann. He likewise proclaimed two new Doctors of the Church, both women: Sts. Teresa of Ávila and Catherine of Siena.

Paul continued to travel and to proclaim hope to the world, but he was deeply troubled by crises in the Church, both the rampant

---

[17] Ibid.; "Declaration *Inter Insigniores* on the Question of the Admission of Women to the Ministerial Priesthood" (October 15, 1976), prologue.

misinterpretations of and dissent from the council and the stand of some in the Church who rejected the reforms of the council in areas such as liturgy, collegiality, and religious liberty.

On June 29, 1972, on the feast of Sts. Peter and Paul, he delivered a homily that remains even today one of the most debated of his entire papacy. The homily itself has never been officially translated into English and is available from the Vatican only in a summarized version.[18] Speaking of the crisis in the Church, Paul expressed the feeling that "the smoke of Satan entered the temple of God from some fissure," adding that an atmosphere of doubt, uncertainty, problems, restlessness, dissatisfaction, and confrontation had emerged in the Church. He lamented that the faithful had often ceased to trust the Church. Rather, he added, that trust was given to the first profane prophet who comes our way, and we chase him down to ask for the formula of life. Instead of a new bright sunny day for the Church, we are now facing clouds and storms and uncertainty.

Although most observers focus on the frightening comments of the pope, what is not much discussed in this famous homily is Paul's proposed answer to the crisis. He said that he would like to fulfill the function given him by Peter and confirm all in the Faith, what he termed a "charism of the certainty that the Lord." He reminded the Church that faith grants certainty and that believing with simplicity and humility helps us to feel that we are on the right track.

It was a remarkable statement of faith and fortitude that did not at all support the perception that the pope had given up.

Nevertheless, Paul's health declined slowly over the next years, and it was long speculated that he had considered resignation. In

---

[18] The Italian summary can be found on the Vatican website, http://w2.vatican.va/content/paul-vi/it/homilies/1972/documents/hf_p-vi_hom_19720629.html.

fact, Paul did write a resignation letter on May 2, 1965. The letter was first revealed to the public in the 2018 book *The Boat of Paul*, edited by the regent of the Papal Household, Father Leonardo Sapienza, and published in *L'Osservatore Romano* in May 2018, along with a commentary by Pope Francis.

Paul wrote the letter barely two years after his election and presented it to the dean of the College of Cardinals, Cardinal Tisserant, who filed it away until it might become necessary to invoke it in the event of Paul's incapacitation.

It was then to be the task of the dean of the College and the other curial leaders to accept the resignation and begin the process for a conclave. Pope Francis, in his comment on the letter, expressed astonishment at the documents, "which seem to me a humble and prophetic witness of love for Christ and his Church; and a further proof of holiness of this great Pope.... What matters to him are the needs of the Church and of the world. And a Pope prevented by a serious illness, could not exercise with sufficient effectiveness the apostolic ministry."

Paul, however, never executed the letter, despite his growing list of infirmities. Instead, he decided that his health could last and that he could serve effectively until the end.

By the start of 1978, Pope Paul VI was looking frail. He missed most of the liturgies of Eastertide because of the flu, adding to his deep sadness over the violent state of Italian politics—especially the March 1978 kidnapping of the Italian Christian Democrat leader Aldo Moro by the communist Red Brigades. Paul and Moro had been friends since the early days of the Federation of Catholic University Students, when Moro had been a university student. *L'Osservatore Romano*, the Vatican newspaper, published a handwritten note from Paul to the kidnappers: "I am writing to you, men of the Red Brigades ... you, unknown and implacable adversaries of this deserving and innocent man, I pray to you on my knees, liberate Aldo Moro simply and without any conditions."[19] The Communists instead murdered Moro and left his body in a car in the middle of Rome.

Paul continued on for three months, but a quiet death watch began—especially after he was taken to the papal retreat at Castel Gandolfo in the middle of July to escape the heat of Rome. He died there on August 6, 1978, from a heart attack.

## A Papacy in a Time of Turbulence

The passing of Paul VI marked the end of an era in the Church. With Pope St. John XXIII, Paul VI had presided over the Second Vatican Council and had then carried the awesome burden of implementing it in the shattering period from 1965 onward. It was the first era of the postconciliar Church, and it proved at times confusing and even disheartening for many Catholics. Pope Paul seemed to carry that weight alone, and it has been remarked by photographers and painters that no image of him was without that pain clearly imprinted in his eyes.

Pope Benedict XVI gave a fitting testament to his predecessor when he spoke on the 110th anniversary of Paul's birth:

> Paul VI ... rendered a particularly precious service to the Church and the world in times far from easy and in social conditions marked by profound cultural and religious changes.
>
> Let us pay homage to the spirit of evangelical wisdom with which my beloved Predecessor was able to guide the Church during and after the Second Vatican Council. With prophetic intuition, he perceived the hopes and anxieties of the people of that time; he strove to make the most of the positive

---

[19] *L'Osservatore Romano*, April 23, 1978.

experiences, seeking to illuminate them with the light of the truth and love of Christ, the one Redeemer of humanity. Yet, his love for humanity with its progress, marvellous discoveries, benefits and the facilitation of science and technology did not prevent him from highlighting the contradictions, errors and risks of a scientific and technological programme that is not anchored by a sound reference to ethical and spiritual values. So it is that his teaching still remains timely today and is a source on which to draw for a better understanding of the conciliar texts and an analysis of the ecclesial events that characterized the second part of the 1900s.

Paul VI was cautious and courageous in guiding the Church with realism and Gospel optimism, nourished by indomitable faith. He looked forward to the coming of the "civilization of love", convinced that evangelical charity is an indispensable element for building an authentic universal brotherhood. Only by recognizing God as Father, who in Christ revealed his love to all, can human beings truly become and feel like brothers and sisters. Only Christ, true God and true man, can convert the human soul and enable it to contribute to achieving a society based on justice and solidarity. The Successors of Paul VI have gathered in the spiritual inheritance of the Servant of God and have walked on the same path. Let us pray that his example and teachings will be an encouragement and incentive to us to love Christ and the Church more and more, motivated by that indomitable hope which supported Pope Montini to the very end of his life.[20]

---

[20] Benedict XVI, address at the end of the concert offered on the occasion of the 110th anniversary of the birth of Pope Paul VI (September 26, 2007).

Paul was all of these things, but coming between the beloved "Good Pope John" and the colossus Pope St. John Paul II the Great, his legacy seemed for many years to be in eclipse. His pontificate was dominated by the council (and the problems that came with its implementation) and the controversy over *Humanae Vitae*. Paul held together the Church during a difficult era and handed to his successors the Barque of Peter, battered from the storms of the age but still sailing in the direction intended by the Holy Spirit.

Some charged him with being too cautious, lacking courage, and being at times overwhelmed by events and the very change—social, ecclesiastical, political, and economic—that the Second Vatican Council pledged to confront. Still, Pope Paul held to the frequently difficult road of authentic reform and therefore suffered spiritual torment in the face of opposition from all sides. He can today be seen as a valiant figure who prophetically anticipated many of the problems that have plagued the world since his death.

## A Saint

From the time of his passing, there was a movement to promote Paul's canonization. While criticized in some quarters for his response to the crises after the council and vilified by dissenting theologians for *Humanae Vitae*, Paul nevertheless was loved and respected by those who knew him for his intellect, his gentle courtesy, his humility and, above all, his personal holiness.

With his canonization, Paul has become the latest in a series of modern popes to be raised to the altars, including Sts. Pius X, John XXIII, and John Paul II. There are also the ongoing causes for Venerable Pius XII and Servant of God John Paul I.

The Church has been blessed with a long line of good popes, arguably dating back to the middle of the sixteenth century and the election of Pope Paul III, who launched in full vigor the renewal of the Church in the face of the Protestant Reformation. But the last century has been especially marked by saintly pontiffs, and now Paul has taken his place among them.

As with these other popes, Paul VI's canonization is not a judgment on his pontificate as much as it is the holiness of Giovanni Battista Montini. While many have criticized his administration of the papal office, the holiness of Pope Paul is indisputable. His confessor, the Jesuit (and later cardinal) Paolo Dezza, was quoted in Peter Hebblethwaite's 1993 biography of Paul:

> If Paul VI was not a saint, when he was elected Pope, he became one during his pontificate. I was able to witness not only with what energy and dedication he toiled for Christ and the Church but also and above all, how much he suffered for Christ and the Church. I always admired not only his deep inner resignation but also his constant abandonment to divine providence.[21]

The cause for canonization for Pope St. Paul began officially in March 1993 with the declaration by the Congregation for the Causes of Saints that a formal investigation could proceed. The pontiff thus received the title "Servant of God" fifteen years after his death.

The Diocese of Rome subsequently opened the diocesan phase of the cause, which took five years and required the careful study of all the pope's writings, speeches, and letters from a theological and historical perspective. The committees completed their work in March 1998.

The cause was then transferred to the Congregation for the Causes of Saints. The officials of the congregation examined all

---

[21] Peter Hebblethwaite, *Paul VI: The First Modern Pope* (Mahwah, NJ: Paulist Press, 1993), p. 600.

the documentation from the diocesan phase and validated the cause, meaning it was canonically permitted to proceed. The *positio*—the formal documents and other information gathered from the diocesan process that makes the argument for the heroic virtue of a candidate—was presented to the congregation in 2011. A year later, the officials and experts of the congregation agreed unanimously to affirm the heroic virtue of Pope Paul. This meant that the first major hurdle to canonization had been cleared. On December 20, 2012, Pope Benedict XVI signed the official decree that granted the late pope the title "Venerable."

There remained the validation of two miracles, one for beatification and another for canonization, a long and painstaking process involving both theological and medical experts.

The miracle for Paul's beatification occurred in the most fitting way imaginable. In the 1990s, an unborn child in California suffered from ruptured organs that doctors declared would lead to severe birth defects and likely death. They encouraged the mother to have an abortion, but she refused. Instead, she heeded the counsel of an Italian nun, who suggested that she pray for the intercession of Pope Paul. The baby was born healthy and showed no sign of any defects.

The healing was not initially reported to the postulator of Paul's cause. He learned of it from media reports and then took steps to secure the details. The case was presented to both theological and medical commissions for a thorough review, and in 2013, after years of investigations, the Vatican medical board concluded that the healing of the child could not be explained naturally. They were soon joined by the theological commission's approval in early 2014, followed by that of the Congregation for the Causes of Saints. Pope Francis gave his enthusiastic sanction to the miracle, and on October 19, 2014, Pope Paul VI was declared blessed in St. Peter's Square at the end of the Extraordinary Synod of Bishops on the Family.

## The Life and Holiness of Pope St. Paul VI

While there were brief rumors that Francis would canonize Pope Paul without the traditionally required second miracle—as he did for Pope John XXIII in 2014—a second miracle was ultimately approved. As with the miracle for beatification, it involved an unborn child, this time in Verona, Italy. Amanda Maria Paola was diagnosed with a ruptured placenta, and on October 29, 2014—just a week after Paul's beatification—her parents journeyed to the Santuario delle Grazie in Brescia to ask for Paul's intercession. Despite the belief of doctors that the child could not survive, she was born alive and miraculously flourished. The miracle was subsequently approved by the theological and medical commissions assisting the Congregation for the Causes of Saints at the end of 2017. Pope Francis confirmed the canonization and set a date of October 21, 2018, for the formal announcement, during the Synod of Bishops on Youth.

In the beatification homily in 2014, Pope Francis said:

When we look to this great Pope, this courageous Christian, this tireless apostle, we cannot but say in the sight of God a word as simple as it is heartfelt and important: thanks! Thank you, our dear and beloved Pope Paul VI! Thank you for your humble and prophetic witness of love for Christ and his Church!

In his personal journal, the great helmsman of the Council wrote, at the conclusion of its final session: "Perhaps the Lord has called me and preserved me for this service not because I am particularly fit for it, or so that I can govern and rescue the Church from her present difficulties, but so that I can suffer something for the Church, and in that way it will be clear that he, and no other, is her guide and saviour."[22] In

---

[22] Fr. Pasquale Macchi, *Paolo VI nella sua parola* (Paul VI in his words) (Brescia, 2001), pp. 120–121.

this humility the grandeur of Blessed Paul VI shines forth: before the advent of a secularized and hostile society, he could hold fast, with farsightedness and wisdom — and at times alone — to the helm of the barque of Peter, while never losing his joy and his trust in the Lord.

Paul VI truly "rendered to God what is God's" by devoting his whole life to the "sacred, solemn and grave task of continuing in history and extending on earth the mission of Christ,"[23] loving the Church and leading her so that she might be "a loving mother of the whole human family and at the same time the minister of its salvation."[24]

A final word must be given to the pope who followed Paul as the successor of St. Peter and Vicar of Christ: Pope St. John Paul II. "A strong and mild Apostle," John Paul said in 2003, twenty-five years after the pope's passing,

> Paul VI loved the Church and worked for her unity and to intensify missionary action. In this perspective, one understands fully the innovative initiative of the *Apostolic Journeys* that today make up an integral part of the ministry of the Successor of Peter. He desired that the ecclesial Community open itself to the world, without, however, surrendering to the spirit of the world. With prudent wisdom he knew how to resist the temptation of "ceding" to the modern mentality, sustaining difficulties and misunderstandings, and in some cases even hostility, with Gospel fortitude.

[23] Paul VI, homily for the Rite of Coronation (1963).

[24] Francis, homily for the closing Mass of the Extraordinary Synod on the Family and Beatification of the Servant of God Paul VI (October 19, 2014), quoting Paul VI, encyclical letter *Ecclesiam Suam* (August 6, 1964), prologue.

Even in the most difficult moments, he always gave his illuminating word to the People of God. At the end of his days, the entire world came to know his greatness and embraced him lovingly.[25]

*Chapter 2*

# Jesus Christ

At the time of his election in 1963, Cardinal Montini was asked by what name he wished to be called as pope. He declared to the assembled cardinals who had just elected him that he wished to be known as Paul (*Paulus vocabatur*). He was the first pontiff to take that name since Paul V, a member of the house of Borghese, in 1605.

He said he chose Paul because he intended to emulate St. Paul of Tarsus, who journeyed across the Roman Empire proclaiming Jesus Christ. As pope, Paul VI wanted to be a pilgrim, going out and helping all the corners of the globe to come to know Jesus Christ. He proved good to his word: He set a new standard for papal traveling that was taken up by his successor, Pope St. John Paul II.

He made nine trips away from Italy, including those to the Holy Land in 1964, Eucharistic Congresses in India and Colombia, the United States in 1965, Portugal in 1967, Africa in 1969, and Asia and the Pacific in 1970.

As pope, he spoke frequently about Jesus Christ, of course, but some of his most emphatic and profound teachings about Christ took place when he was visiting countries around the world. His zeal was exemplified by his proclamation to newly consecrated bishops in India in 1964: "We cannot remain silent; We must exclaim: Glory to Thee, O Lord! Thanks to Thee, O Friend of men!

# Saint Pope Paul VI

O Master! O Bread of Life! O Savior! We humbly acknowledge
Thee! We believe in Thee! We love Thee!"[26]

And Paul also expressed—in words that anticipated Pope Francis's emphasis on joy—the importance of joy in the life of the
Christian that comes with the understanding of Jesus Christ as
Savior. In his largely forgotten 1975 apostolic exhortation, *Gaudete
in Domino* (Joy in the Lord), Paul wrote, "In essence, Christian joy
is the spiritual sharing in the unfathomable joy, both divine and
human, which is in the heart of Jesus Christ glorified."[27]

\* \* \*

For a Christian, no man is excluded from the possibility of being
saved by Christ and of enjoying the same destination in the Kingdom of God. It is therefore inconceivable for those who accept
the gospel message, even taking into account physical, intellectual
or moral differences, to deny fundamental human equality in the
name of the alleged superiority of a race or ethnic group.

—Address to the Diplomatic Corps (January 14, 1978)

The Christian is no stranger among his own people. He shares with
them all their honorable customs. As a good citizen should, he
loves his native land. And yet the faith he professes is Catholic, the
same faith as is professed by Africans, Americans and Europeans.
How can this be? It is because the historical man called Jesus of
Nazareth was also the Son of God. It is because man was created
by God and for God, and in his very being he is drawn by the
One who called him to life. This is so personal and so essential an

---

[26] Paul VI, address to new bishops, Bombay, India (December 3,
1964).

[27] Paul VI, apostolic exhortation *Gaudete in Domino* (May 9, 1975),
pt. 2.

element of man that the person who drives God out of his life soon runs the risk of refusing to accept his fellowmen as his brothers.

—Homily for Mass in Jakarta, Indonesia (December 3, 1970)

What must stimulate the faithful even more to follow the examples of the most holy Virgin is the fact that Jesus Himself, by giving her to us as our Mother, has tacitly indicated her as the model to be followed. It is, in fact, a natural thing that the children should have the same sentiments of their mothers and should reflect their merits and virtues.

—*Signum Magnum*, II, 5 (May 13, 1967)

I must bear witness to his name: Jesus is the Christ, the Son of the living God.[28] He reveals the invisible God, he is the firstborn of all creation, the foundation of everything created. He is the Teacher of mankind, and its Redeemer. He was born, he died and he rose again for us. He is the center of history and of the world; he is the one who knows us and who loves us; he is the companion and the friend of our life. He is the man of sorrows and of hope. It is he who will come and who one day will be our judge and—we hope—the everlasting fullness of our existence, our happiness.

—Homily for Mass at Quezon Circle,
Philippines (November 29, 1970)

Imitation of Jesus Christ is undoubtedly the regal way to be followed to attain sanctity and reproduce in ourselves, according to our forces, the absolute perfection of the heavenly Father. But while the Catholic Church has always proclaimed a truth so sacrosanct, it has also affirmed that imitation of the Virgin Mary, far

[28] Matt. 16:16.

from distracting the souls from the faithful following of Christ, makes it more pleasant and easier for them.

—*Signum Magnum*, II, 2 (May 13, 1967)

Paschal joy is not just that of a possible transfiguration: it is the joy of the new presence of the Risen Christ dispensing to His own the Holy Spirit, so that He may dwell with them. The Holy Spirit is given to the Church as the inexhaustible principle of her joy as the bride of the glorified Christ. He recalls to her mind, through the ministry of grace and truth exercised by the successors of the apostles, the very teaching of the Lord. The Holy Spirit stirs up in the Church divine life and the apostolate. And the Christian knows that this Spirit will never be quenched in the course of history.

—*Gaudete in Domino*, III (May 9, 1975)

Jesus Christ comes into our lives in answer to the call whose seeds were placed by God in each one's heart.[29] His Word, which is the revelation of a loving God, and his grace, which is the sharing of God's very life through his Holy Spirit and in the sacraments, build up the community of God's People which is called the Church. It is a community united by one baptism, one faith and one Lord, and living for "one God who is Father of all, over all, and within all."[30]

—Homily for Mass in Jakarta, Indonesia (December 3, 1970)

This, dear sons and daughters, is what We came here to proclaim: Jesus Christ. He is our Savior, and at the same time he is the Teacher for all of us. He is "the Way, the Truth and the Life."[31]

---

[29] Cf. Vatican Council II, Decree on the Mission Activity of the Church *Ad Gentes* (December 7,1965), 11.

[30] Cf. Eph. 4:5–6.

[31] John 14:6.

Anyone who follows him will not be walking in the dark.[32] That is the memory We would like to engrave on your souls forever.

—Homily for Mass in Jakarta, Indonesia (December 3, 1970)

Even after Christ had ascended to heaven she remained united to Him by a most ardent love while she faithfully fulfilled the new mission of spiritual Mother of the most beloved of the disciples and of the nascent Church. It can be asserted that the whole life of the humble handmaid of the Lord, from the moment when she was greeted by the Angel, until her assumption in body and soul to heavenly glory, was a life of loving service.

—*Signum Magnum*, I (May 13, 1967)

God is necessary, just as the sun is. And if we moderns have to bring ourselves to such a pass to become aware of this, it is a sign that we must clear up the common false notion we often have of the divinity and must make an unceasing effort to give to the name of God the boundless richness of his unfathomable transcendence and the ineffable sweetness, replete with reverence and love, of his universal presence. We must "believe in God."

—General Audience (June 12, 1968)[33]

In the Virgin Mary everything is relative to Christ and dependent upon Him. It was with a view to Christ that God the Father from all eternity chose her to be the all-holy Mother and adorned her with gifts of the Spirit granted to no one else. Certainly genuine Christian piety has never failed to highlight

---

[32] Cf. John 8:12.

[33] Paul VI, "A World in Need of Faith," *L'Osservatore Romano*, weekly edition in English, June 20, 1968, archived at http://www.ewtn.com/library/PAPALDOC/P6WRLDFA.HTM.

the indissoluble link and essential relationship of the Virgin to the divine Savior.[34]

—*Marialis Cultus*, 25 (February 2, 1974)

What is "sacred history" but the identification of a divine thought, of a transcendent "economy", in the course of the events that lead to Christ and are derived from Christ? But this discovery is a subsequent one. It is a synthesis, the formulations of which are sometimes questionable, made by the scholar when the events are past and can be considered in an overall perspective, and sometimes placed deductively in an ideological background derived from other doctrinal sources, not from the inductive analysis of the events themselves. Now, on the contrary, modern thought is invited to decipher in historical reality, particularly the present, the "signs," that is the indications of a meaning that goes further than the one recorded by the passive observer.

—General Audience (April 16, 1969)[35]

In a mysterious way, Christ Himself accepts death at the hands of the wicked[36] and death on the cross, in order to eradicate from man's heart the sins of self-sufficiency and to manifest to the Father a complete filial obedience. But the Father has not allowed death to keep Him in its power. The resurrection of Jesus is the seal placed by the Father on the value of His Son's sacrifice: it is the proof of the Father's fidelity.

—*Gaudete in Domino*, III (May 9, 1975)

---

[34] Cf. Vatican Council II, Dogmatic Constitution on the Church *Lumen Gentium* (November 21, 1964), 66.

[35] Paul VI, "Signs of the Times," *L'Osservatore Romano*, weekly edition in English, April 24, 1969, archived at http://www.ewtn.com/library/PAPALDOC/P6SIGNS.HTM.

[36] Cf. Acts 2:23.

# Jesus Christ

Neither the grace of the divine Redeemer, nor the powerful intercession of His Mother and our spiritual Mother, nor yet her sublime
sanctity, could lead us to the port of salvation if we did not respond
to them by our persevering will to honor Jesus Christ and the Holy
Virgin with our devout imitation of their sublime virtue.

—*Signum Magnum*, II, 1 (May 13, 1967)

The mastery over natural things and forces, the primacy accorded
to practical and utilitarian activity, the totally new organization of
life resulting from the many forms in which technical know-how
is employed, these take away from man the remembrance of God
and quench in him the need for faith and religion.

—General Audience (June 12, 1968)

Then is the realm of the divine revealed in all its clarity, and
far from depreciating the realm of nature and the science which
explores that realm or the technology which controls it, these
stupendous values are illumined with a new beauty which gives
freedom to the world of technology and takes away from it that
sense of oppressive organization and consequent frustration, resulting from the very limitations of the materialist roundabout,
and now in these days is breaking out into violent and irrational
rebellion, as if in denunciation of the basic insufficiency of our
desacralized civilization to satisfy the inalienable demands of the
human spirit.

—General Audience (June 12, 1968)

Jesus Christ. He Who is the eternal and consubstantial Son of God;
Who is also the Son of Mary, true man, our Brother.

He is here in the Eucharistic Mystery which this Congress
celebrates. He is really present, not merely represented, not only
invoked remembered. He Himself is here, real and unique; only

under the sacramental appearances is He multiplied. And He is multiplied in order to be communicated to each of us.

—Address to new bishops, Bombay, India (December 3, 1964)

No one is excluded from the joy brought by the Lord. The great joy announced by the angel on Christmas night is truly for all the people,[37] both for the people of Israel then anxiously awaiting a Savior, and for the numberless people made up of all those who, in time to come, would receive its message and strive to live by it.

—*Gaudete in Domino*, III (May 9, 1975)

As the kernel and center of His Good News, Christ proclaims salvation, this great gift of God which is liberation from everything that oppresses man but which is above all liberation from sin and the Evil One, in the joy of knowing God and being known by Him, of seeing Him, and of being given over to Him.

—*Evangelii Nuntiandi*, 9 (December 8, 1975)

It would be illusory to build a Church inconsistent with its established traditions, designed according to arbitrary structures and improvised by unauthorized reformers, as though the Church could ignore what is derived from the constitutional principles established by Christ Himself. It would be illusory, on the other hand, if the reform, even though promoted by sincere spirituality, should fall into the mold of secular life heedless of the requirements proper to faith and devoted attachment to the cross of the Lord.

—General Audience (August 7, 1968)[38]

---

[37] Cf. Luke 2:10.

[38] Paul VI, "The Ideal Concept of Christian Life," *L'Osservatore Romano*, weekly edition in English, August 15, 1968, archived at http://www.ewtn.com/library/PAPALDOC/P6IDEAL.HTM.

Think it over carefully. You are the Church, which means that you belong to the Church, to the holy Church of God, to the great assembly called together by Christ, to the living community of His word and His grace, to His Mystical Body. This consciousness of belonging to the Church must grow ever clearer in us. It is a consciousness of our dignity, for in the Church we are truly adopted sons of God and brothers of Christ, living through Him in the Holy Spirit. It is a consciousness of our good fortune.

—General Audience (June 1, 1966)[39]


Jesus Christ: you have heard him spoken of; indeed the greater part of you are already his: you are Christians. So, to you Christians I repeat his name, to everyone I proclaim him: Jesus Christ is the beginning and the end, the Alpha and the Omega; he is the king of the new world; he is the secret of history; he is the key to our destiny. He is the mediator, the bridge, between heaven and earth. He is more perfectly than anyone else the Son of Man, because he is the Son of God, eternal and infinite. He is the son of Mary, blessed among all women, his mother according to the flesh, and our mother through the sharing in the Spirit of his Mystical Body.

Jesus Christ is our constant preaching; it is his name that we proclaim to the ends of the earth[40] and throughout all ages.[41] Remember this and ponder on it: the Pope has come here among you and has proclaimed Jesus Christ!

—Homily for Mass at Quezon Circle,
Philippines (November 29, 1970)


[39] Paul VI, "Voi Forse Sapete," *The Pope Speaks* (Fort Wayne, IN: Our Sunday Visitor, 1966), archived at http://www.ewtn.com/library/ PAPALDOC/P6VOI.HTM.

[40] Cf. Rom. 10:18.

[41] Rom. 9:5.

And what is the response that we the members of his holy people must give? We must respond to God's grace by our fidelity to the saving Word, by a conduct worthy of new men. The infinite holiness of God communicated to us calls for a response in the form of our finite holiness modelled on that of Jesus Christ. Then everything is transformed and illuminated: the life of individuals, that of families, the use of this world's goods, our relationships with others, all the life of society; for it is the whole man that Christ frees, raises up, and saves.

—Homily for Mass in Jakarta, Indonesia (December 3, 1970)

This kingdom and this salvation, which are the key words of Jesus Christ's evangelization, are available to every human being as grace and mercy, and yet at the same time each individual must gain them by force—they belong to the violent, says the Lord,[42] through toil and suffering, through a life lived according to the Gospel, through abnegation and the cross, through the spirit of the beatitudes. But above all each individual gains them through a total interior renewal which the Gospel calls metanoia; it is a radical conversion, a profound change of mind and heart.[43]

—*Evangelii Nuntiandi*, 10 (December 8, 1975)

In essence, Christian joy is the spiritual sharing in the unfathomable joy, both divine and human, which is in the heart of Jesus Christ glorified. As soon as God the Father begins to manifest in history the mystery of His will, according to His purpose which He set forth in Christ as a plan for the fullness of time,[44] this joy is

[42] Cf. Matt. 11:12; Luke 16:16.
[43] Cf. Matt. 4:17.
[44] Cf. Eph. 1:9–10.

mysteriously announced in the midst of the People of God, before its identity has been unveiled.

—*Gaudete in Domino*, II (May 9, 1975)

Christ is here.

He is here through the reality, ever repeated: a gathering in his name.[45] He is here through the faith that makes him live in each one of us.[46] He is here also through the coming of Our humble person, to whom, as a lowly successor of Peter, is applied in a very special way the title of Vicar of Christ. And Christ our Lord is here through the apostolic ministry entrusted to each of us,[47] and through the collegial relationship that joins us together.[48] We, the successors of the Apostles and the pastors of the Church of God, are invested with the power not only of representing Christ, but also of making present on earth and in time his voice[49] and his saving action.[50] Christ is here. Let us take notice of this mysterious reality, with an act of faith both conscious and strong.

—Address to the bishops of Asia, Manila, and
the Philippines (November 28, 1970)

Animated by the power of the Spirit of Jesus Christ, the Savior of mankind, and upheld by hope, the Christian involves himself in the building up of the human city, one that is to be peaceful, just and fraternal and acceptable as an offering to God.[51]

—*Octogesima Adveniens*, 37 (May 14, 1971)

---

[45] Matt. 18:20.
[46] Eph. 3:17.
[47] Cf. *Lumen Gentium*, 21.
[48] Ibid., 22.
[49] Luke 10:16.
[50] Matt. 28:19.
[51] Cf. Rom. 15:16.

# Saint Pope Paul VI

This is the paradox of the Christian condition which sheds particular light on that of the human condition: neither trials nor sufferings have been eliminated from this world, but they take on a new meaning in the certainty of sharing in the redemption wrought by the Lord and of sharing in His glory. This is why the Christian, though subject to the difficulties of human life, is not reduced to groping for the way; nor does he see in death the end of his hopes.

—*Gaudete in Domino*, III (May 9, 1975)

"Behold the handmaid of the Lord; be it done to me according to thy word." From that moment, she consecrated all of herself to the service not only of the heavenly Father and of the Word Incarnate, who had become her Son, but also to all mankind, having clearly understood that Jesus, in addition to saving his people from the slavery of sin, would become the King of a messianic Kingdom, universal and eternal.

—*Signum Magnum*, III (May 13, 1967)

Although he was the Son of God, Jesus Christ wished for the sake of our redemption to become one of us. He shared our human condition, making himself part of the world of his time, speaking the language of his country, and drawing on local life for the examples with which to illustrate his teaching of justice, truth, hope and love. Today his teaching has spread throughout the world. It adapts itself in its expression to all languages, and to all traditions and civilizations. No book has been translated into so many tongues as the Gospel. No prayer is said in so many languages as the Our Father, taught by Jesus himself.

—Homily for Mass in Jakarta, Indonesia (December 3, 1970)

Even sinners can belong to the Church. This is a doctrine opposed by those who claim that the Church on earth is composed only of saints. Sin interrupts union with God, but if it doesn't interrupt adherence to the communion of salvation which is the Church (as does a sin that is expressly directed against belonging to the Church—heresy, schism, apostasy—or that implies separation from the community, which means excommunication), then it can find its redemption in this institution which was established specifically in order to save men.

—General Audience (June 1, 1966)

*Chapter 3*

# The Church

Even as the Second Vatican Council continued its work in August 1964 — including completing its deliberations on the Dogmatic Constitution on the Church *Lumen Gentium* — Pope Paul VI chose to issue his first encyclical of his pontificate, *Ecclesiam Suam*. It seemed a curious choice given that the council over which he was presiding was poised to issue an authoritative document on the Church and that the entire ecumenical council was discussing in great detail the nature, mission, and renewal of the Church. Paul, however, was making a very clear statement in his decision to focus his attentions on the Church in his teaching. In fact, *Ecclesiam Suam* can be seen as a kind of program for his pontificate, which encompassed the meditation of the council on the reform of the Church and the immense task of implementing reform and renewal in an age of crisis.

For Paul, the Church remains the hope of all humanity. This he made clear in the very opening words of *Ecclesiam Suam*: "The Church was founded by Jesus Christ," he wrote, "to be the loving mother of the whole human family and minister to its salvation. All through the centuries, therefore, whenever men have yearned for the glory of Almighty God and the eternal salvation of souls, they have naturally made the Church the special object of their devotion and concern."

# Saint Pope Paul VI

Paul's vision of the Church is made clear in his encyclical. In a 2004 article for the Vatican newspaper, *L'Osservatore Romano*, marking the encyclical's fortieth anniversary, Professor Andrea Riccardi wrote:

> The Encyclical is divided into three parts: the "Self-Awareness" of the Church and of Christians; "The Renewal" which challenges their vocation; relations with "others", which thus leads to "The Dialogue" … Parts I and II of *Ecclesiam Suam* are fundamental: without self-awareness and renewal there can be no serious relationship with the world. Living the Christian identity leads to understanding the "*distinction*"—the Pope's word—"between the Christian and the worldly life". It means living "in the world but not as the world lives." … The Gospel is a mission to carry out, a proclamation to spread abroad: this was Paul VI's programme.
>
> Grace is not a jealously guarded privilege but is poured out and communicated. This is where "dialogue" fits in. For Paul VI, dialogue is the maturation of an inheritance, that of his Predecessors, starting with Leo XIII. Thus, the Pope says, "the Church has something to say, a message to give, a communication to make." The purpose of this dialogue is therefore "to inject the Christian message into the stream of modern thought." Paul VI did not want a Church estranged from the world (or which condemned it), reduced as it were to a proud minority; but he did not believe in a Church which is diluted in the world. There was a message to communicate and a dialogue to revive.[52]

[52] Andrea Riccardi, "40th Anniversary of *Ecclesiam Suam* by Pope Paul VI: An Encyclical that Defines a Pontificate," *L'Osservatore Romano* weekly edition in English, September 1, 2004, archived at https://www.ewtn.com/library/CHISTORY/40ECSUP6.HTM.

In the years that followed, echoes of the encyclical resonated in his teachings. He urged the faithful to deepen their love and their knowledge of the Church. He reminded them to be faithful to their vocation. And he implored them to proclaim the gospel to the modern world. He said in his 1975 exhortation *Evangelii Nuntiandi* something that Pope Francis has embraced in his own teachings:

> The Christian community is never closed in upon itself. The intimate life of this community—the life of listening to the Word and the apostles' teaching, charity lived in a fraternal way, the sharing of bread this intimate life only acquires its full meaning when it becomes a witness, when it evokes admiration and conversion, and when it becomes the preaching and proclamation of the Good News. (15)

Paul also taught in *Octogesima Adveniens* that the Gospel will always be relevant and necessary:

> The Gospel is not out-of-date because it was proclaimed, written and lived in a different sociocultural context. Its inspiration, enriched by the living experience of Christian tradition over the centuries, remains ever new for converting men and for advancing the life of society. It is not however to be utilized for the profit of particular temporal options, to the neglect of its universal and eternal message.[53] (4)

By 1972, the pope was aware of the depths of the postconciliar problems for many Catholics. On June 29, 1972, he gave his reply, describing in stark imagery his feeling that "the smoke of Satan entered the temple of God from some fissure," adding that the Church was struggling in an atmosphere of "doubt, uncertainty, problems,

---

[53] *Gaudium et Spes*, 10.

restlessness, dissatisfaction, confrontation." Even so, Paul remained hopeful and concluded the harrowing homily with a call to the faithful to be confirmed in the Faith, for that leads to certainty.

He never gave up proclaiming the final words of *Ecclesiam Suam*: "The Church today is more than ever alive. But it seems good to consider that everything still remains to be done; the work begins today and never comes to an end. This is the law of our temporal, earthly pilgrimage."[54]

\* \* \*

The "full, supreme and universal power"[55] which Christ gives to His Vicar for the pastoral government of His Church is this especially exercised by the Pope in the activity of preaching and causing to be preached the Good News of salvation.

In union with the Successor of Peter, the bishops, who are successors of the apostles, receive through the power of their episcopal ordination the authority to teach the revealed truth in the Church. They are teachers of the faith.

— *Evangelii Nuntiandi*, 67–68 (December 8, 1975)

The Church has the firm conviction that all temporal liberation, all political liberation—even if it endeavors to find its justification in such or such a page of the Old or New Testament, even if it claims for its ideological postulates and its norms of action theological data and conclusions, even if it pretends to be today's theology—carries within itself the germ of its own negation and fails to reach the ideal that it proposes for itself whenever its profound motives are not those of justice in charity, whenever its zeal

---

[54] Paul VI, encyclical letter *Ecclesiam Suam* (August 6, 1964), 117.
[55] *Lumen Gentium*, 22.

lacks a truly spiritual dimension and whenever its final goal is not salvation and happiness in God.

—*Evangelii Nuntiandi*, 35 (December 8, 1975)

A vivid and lively self-awareness on the part of the Church inevitably leads to a comparison between the ideal image of the Church as Christ envisaged it, His holy and spotless bride,[56] and the actual image which the Church presents to the world today. This actual image does indeed, thank God, truly bear those characteristics impressed on it by its divine Founder; and in the course of the centuries the Holy Spirit has accentuated and enhanced these traits so as to make the Church conform more and more to the original intention of its Founder and to the particular genius of human society which it is continually striving to win over to itself through the preaching of the gospel of salvation. But the actual image of the Church will never attain to such a degree of perfection, beauty, holiness and splendor that it can be said to correspond perfectly with the original conception in the mind of Him who fashioned it.

—*Ecclesiam Suam*, 10 (August 6, 1964)

Preaching, the verbal proclamation of a message, is indeed always indispensable. We are well aware that modern man is sated by talk; he is obviously often tired of listening and, what is worse, impervious to words. We are also aware that many psychologists and sociologists express the view that modern man has passed beyond the civilization of the word, which is now ineffective and useless, and that today he lives in the civilization of the image. These facts should certainly impel us to employ, for the purpose of transmitting the Gospel message, the modern means which this civilization has produced.

—*Evangelii Nuntiandi*, 42 (December 8, 1975)

[56] Cf. Eph. 5:27.

# Saint Pope Paul VI

Founded to build the kingdom of heaven on earth rather than to acquire temporal power, the Church openly avows that the two powers—Church and State—are distinct from one another; that each is supreme in its own sphere of competency.[57] But since the Church does dwell among men, she has the duty "of scrutinizing the signs of the times and of interpreting them in the light of the Gospel."[58] Sharing the noblest aspirations of men and suffering when she sees these aspirations not satisfied, she wishes to help them attain their full realization. So she offers man her distinctive contribution: a global perspective on man and human realities.

—*Populorum Progressio*, 13 (March 26, 1967)

The more an individual Church is attached to the universal Church by solid bonds of communion, in charity and loyalty, in receptiveness to the Magisterium of Peter, in the unity of the *lex orandi* which is also the *lex credendi*, in the desire for unity with all the other Churches which make up the whole—the more such a Church will be capable of translating the treasure of faith into the legitimate variety of expressions of the profession of faith, of prayer and worship, of Christian life and conduct and of the spiritual influence on the people among which it dwells. The more will it also be truly evangelizing, that is to say, capable of drawing upon the universal patrimony in order to enable its own people to profit from it, and capable too of communicating to the universal Church the experience and the life of this people, for the benefit of all.

—*Evangelii Nuntiandi*, 64 (December 8, 1975)

We would add that this cardinal principle of holy Church is not a supremacy of spiritual pride and a desire to dominate mankind,

---

[57] Cf. Leo XIII, encyclical letter *Immortale Dei* (November 1, 1885).
[58] *Gaudium et Spes*, 4.

but a primacy of service, ministration, and love. It is no vapid rhetoric which confers on Christ's vicar the title: "Servant of the servants of God."

—*Ecclesiam Suam*, 110 (August 6, 1964)

The Holy Spirit is the soul of the Church. It is He who explains to the faithful the deep meaning of the teaching of Jesus and of His mystery. It is the Holy Spirit who, today just as at the beginning of the Church, acts in every evangelizer who allows himself to be possessed and led by Him. The Holy Spirit places on his lips the words which he could not find by himself, and at the same time the Holy Spirit predisposes the soul of the hearer to be open and receptive to the Good News and to the kingdom being proclaimed.

—*Evangelii Nuntiandi*, 75 (December 8, 1975)

Who is this pilgrim? What are his motives and his intentions? We reply, We are a servant and messenger of Jesus Christ, placed by Divine Providence at the Head of His Church as the successor of Saint Peter, Prince of the Apostles. Messenger of Jesus and Head of the Church are in reality one function only, since the Church's reason for existing is to proclaim and spread the teaching of Jesus, and to continue His ministry on earth. This is Our identity and Our mission.

—Homily for Mass in Bombay, India (December 4, 1964)

For the Christian community is never closed in upon itself. The intimate life of this community—the life of listening to the Word and the apostles' teaching, charity lived in a fraternal way, the sharing of bread[59] this intimate life only acquires its full meaning when it becomes a witness, when it evokes admiration and

---

[59] Cf. Acts 2:42–46; 4:32–35; 5:12–16.

conversion, and when it becomes the preaching and proclamation of the Good News....

The Church is an evangelizer, but she begins by being evangelized herself. She is the community of believers, the community of hope lived and communicated, the community of brotherly love, and she needs to listen unceasingly to what she must believe, to her reasons for hoping, to the new commandment of love.

—*Evangelii Nuntiandi*, 15 (December 8, 1975)

While the Church does indeed hand on to her children the inviolable conditions laid down by God's law, she is also the herald of salvation and through the sacraments she flings wide open the channels of grace through which man is made a new creature responding in charity and true freedom to the design of his Creator and Savior, experiencing too the sweetness of the yoke of Christ.[60]

—*Humanae Vitae*, 25 (July 25, 1968)

The Church is the depositary of the Good News to be proclaimed. The promises of the New Alliance in Jesus Christ, the teaching of the Lord and the apostles, the Word of life, the sources of grace and of God's loving kindness, the path of salvation—all these things have been entrusted to her.

—*Evangelii Nuntiandi*, 15 (December 8, 1975)

The split between the Gospel and culture is without a doubt the drama of our time, just as it was of other times. Therefore every effort must be made to ensure a full evangelization of culture, or more correctly of cultures. They have to be regenerated by an

---

[60] See Matt. 11:30.

encounter with the Gospel. But this encounter will not take place if the Gospel is not proclaimed.

—*Evangelii Nuntiandi*, 20 (December 8, 1975)

The Church openly admits the values peculiar to temporal realities. She recognizes that the world possesses goods, carries out enterprises, expresses thoughts and arts, deserves praise, etc. in its being, in its becoming, in its own kingdom, even if the latter is not baptized, that is, profane, lay, secular. Even if it is pluralistic, that is diversified and divided in itself to the point of threatening ruin,[61] she recognizes under the safeguard of certain principles (which we must not ignore and forget), its right to freedom in its individual members and in its collective expressions.

—General Audience (March 5, 1969)[62]

The Church, in fact, travels forward with humanity and shares its lot in the setting of history. At the same time that she announces to men the Good News of God's love and of salvation in Christ she clarifies their activity in the light of the Gospel and in this way helps them to correspond to God's plan of love and to realize the fullness of their aspirations.

—*Octogesima Adveniens*, 1 (May 14, 1971)

Must the Church be European, Latin, Oriental ... or must she be African? This seems a difficult problem, and in practice may be so, indeed. But the solution is rapid, with two replies. First, your

---

[61] Cf. Luke 11:17.
[62] Paul VI, "The Church's Presence in the World of Today," *L'Osservatore Romano*, weekly edition in English, March 13, 2001, archived at http://www.ewtn.com/library/PAPALDOC/P6TODAY. HTM.

# Saint Pope Paul VI

Church must be first of all Catholic. That is, it must be entirely founded upon the identical, essential, constitutional patrimony of the self-same teaching of Christ, as professed by the authentic and authoritative tradition of the one true Church. This condition is fundamental and indisputable. We must, all of us, be both jealous and proud of that Faith of which the Apostles were the heralds, of which the Martyrs, that is, the Witnesses, were the champions, of which the Missionaries were scrupulous teachers. You know that the Church is particularly tenacious, we may even say conservative, in this regard. To make sure that the message of revealed doctrine cannot be altered, the Church has even set down her treasure of truth in certain conceptual and verbal formulas. Even when these formulas are difficult, at times, she obliges us to preserve them textually. We are not the inventors of our Faith; we are its custodians. Not every religious feeling is good; but only that religious sentiment which interprets the thought of God, according to the apostolic teaching authority established by the sole Master, Jesus Christ.

—Homily for Mass in Kampala, Uganda (July 31, 1969)

The history of the Church, from the discourse of Peter on the morning of Pentecost onwards, has been intermingled and identified with the history of this proclamation. At every new phase of human history, the Church, constantly gripped by the desire to evangelize, has but one preoccupation: whom to send to proclaim the mystery of Jesus? In what way is this mystery to be proclaimed? How can one ensure that it will resound and reach all those who should hear it? This proclamation—kerygma, preaching or catechesis—occupies such an important place in evangelization that it has often become synonymous with it; and yet it is only one aspect of evangelization.

—*Evangelii Nuntiandi*, 22 (December 8, 1975)

# The Church

It is up to these Christian communities, with the help of the Holy Spirit, in communion with the bishops who hold responsibility and in dialogue with other Christian brethren and all men of goodwill, to discern the options and commitments which are called for in order to bring about the social, political and economic changes seen in many cases to be urgently needed. In this search for the changes which should be promoted, Christians must first of all renew their confidence in the forcefulness and special character of the demands made by the Gospel.

—*Octogesima Adveniens*, 4 (May 14, 1971)

There is of course a wide diversity among the situations in which Christians — willingly or unwillingly — find themselves according to regions, socio-political systems and cultures. In some places they are reduced to silence, regarded with suspicion and as it were kept on the fringe of society, enclosed without freedom in a totalitarian system. In other places they are a weak minority whose voice makes itself heard with difficulty. In some other nations, where the Church sees her place recognized, sometimes officially so, she too finds herself subjected to the repercussions of the crisis which is unsettling society, some of her members are tempted by radical and violent solutions from which they believe that they can expect a happier outcome.

—*Octogesima Adveniens*, 3 (May 14, 1971)

Granted this first reply, however, we now come to the second. The expression, that is, the language and mode of manifesting this one Faith, may be manifold; hence, it may be original, suited to the tongue, the style, the character, the genius, and the culture, of the one who professes this one Faith. From this point of view, a certain pluralism is not only legitimate, but desirable. An adaptation of the Christian life in the fields of pastoral, ritual, didactic and spiritual activities is not only possible, it is even favored by the Church.

—Homily for Mass in Kampala, Uganda (July 31, 1969)

The most profound pastoral understanding, the deepest human compassion exist only in fidelity to God's word. There is no division, no dichotomy, no opposition between God's commands and our pastoral service. If all the exigencies of the Christian message are not preached, our apostolic charity is incomplete.

—Address on the Occasion of the Canonization of St. John Neumann (June 20, 1977)

The Church, as the People of God on pilgrimage towards the future kingdom, must be able to perpetuate herself, and therefore renew herself down succeeding human generations. For her this is a condition for fruitfulness, and even simply for life itself. It is therefore necessary that at each moment of her history the rising generation should in some way fulfill the hope of the preceding generations, the very hope of the Church, which is to transmit without end the gift of God, the Truth and the Life. This is why in every generation young Christians justly ratify, with full consciousness and unconditionally, the covenant entered into by them in the sacrament of Baptism and reinforced in the sacrament of Confirmation.

—*Gaudete in Domino*, VI (May 9, 1975)

We must love and serve the Church as it is, wisely seeking to understand its history and to discover with humility the will of God who guides and assists it, even when He permits human weakness to eclipse the splendor of its countenance and the holiness of its activity. It is precisely this holiness and splendor which we are endeavoring to discover and promote.

—*Ecclesiam Suam*, 47 (August 6, 1964)

# The Church

We are sure that grace will not fail the Christian people, and we hope that they themselves will not fail grace, or reject—as some today are gravely tempted to do—the inheritance of truth and holiness handed down to this decisive moment in the history of the world. And this is the point—we think that we have every reason to have confidence in Christian youth: youth will not fail the Church if within the Church there are enough older people able to understand it, to love it, to guide it and to open up to it a future by passing on to it with complete fidelity the Truth which endures. Then new workers, resolute and fervent, will in their turn enter upon spiritual and apostolic work in the fields which are white and ready for the harvest. Then the sower and the reaper will share the same joy of the kingdom.[63]

—*Gaudete in Domino*, VI (May 9, 1975)

But let Us repeat once again for our common admonition and profit: the Church will rediscover its youthful vitality not so much by changing its external legislation, as by submitting to the obedience of Christ and observing the laws which the Church lays upon itself with the intention of following in Christ's footsteps. Herein lies the secret of the Church's renewal, its *metanoia*, to use the Greek term, its practice of perfection.

—*Ecclesiam Suam*, 51 (August 6, 1964)

In a word, the Bishops are ministers, they are servants; they are not for themselves but for others. They are yours; they exist for you, faithful people hearing Our words![64] They exist for the Church. It is for the Church that the Bishops have the right and duty to exercise the functions of Teachers, Priests and

[63] Cf. John 4:35–36.
[64] Cf. Luke 22:26; Rom. 1:14; *Lumen Gentium*, 20.

Shepherds.[65] They are for the Church, and to the Church they offer all their life.[66]

—Homily at Episcopal Ordination,
Kololo, Uganda (August 1, 1969)

The Church has always been the same; it is the family of those who believe in Christ, "composed of every nation under heaven."[67] The scene at Pentecost comes to mind and from our hearts there arises and finds expression on our lips the invocation to the Holy Spirit: *"Veni Sancte Spiritus."*

—Address to the bishops of Asia in Manila,
Philippines (November 28, 1970)

Let us be very careful not to conceive of the universal Church as the sum, or, if one can say so, the more or less anomalous federation of essentially different individual Churches. In the mind of the Lord the Church is universal by vocation and mission, but when she puts down her roots in a variety of cultural, social and human terrains, she takes on different external expressions and appearances in each part of the world.

—*Evangelii Nuntiandi*, 62 (December 8, 1975)

We remind you of all this, brothers, that your confidence may be great in Christ's assistance for you and your labors, for your sufferings and your hopes. You must be aware of your vocation, the fact of your having been chosen and of your responsibility. You must

---

[65] Cf. 1 Pet. 4:2; *Pontificale Romanum* (Roman Pontifical), 18; Vatican Council II, Decree Concerning the Pastoral Office of Bishops in the Church *Christus Dominus* (1965), 12–16.

[66] 2 Cor. 12:15.

[67] Acts 2:5.

ever hear re-echoing in the depths of your souls the words of Saint Paul: "Be on your guard for yourselves and for all the flock of which the Holy Spirit has made you the overseers, to feed the Church of God which he bought with his own blood."[68] Be strong, be patient. You have before you an immense field for your apostolate; its very geographical vastness and the enormous multitudes that inhabit it would suffice to fire your apostolic zeal.

—Address to the bishops of Asia in Manila, Philippines (November 28, 1970)

In the ordinary divine economy of salvation, men do not save themselves by themselves. The Church is the visible sacrament of the saving love of God.[69] The ministerial Priesthood is indispensable,[70] and finds its full expression in the Episcopate. There must, in fact, be someone who brings men the Word of God;[71] there must be someone who distributes to them the mysteries of grace;[72] there must be someone who guides them in the paths of the Lord;[73] there must be someone who unites them in Christ through the Gospel.[74]

—Homily at Episcopal Ordination, Kololo, Uganda (August 1, 1969)

Above all the Gospel must be proclaimed by witness. Take a Christian or a handful of Christians who, in the midst of their own community, show their capacity for understanding and acceptance,

---

68 Acts 20:28.
69 Cf. *Lumen Gentium*, 9.
70 Ibid., 10.
71 Cf. Vatican Council II, Dogmatic Constitution on Divine Revelation *Dei Verbum* (November 18, 1965), 10.
72 Cf. 1 Cor. 4:1–2.
73 Cf. John 21:15; *Lumen Gentium*, 19–20.
74 Rom. 10:8; 1 Cor. 4:1–2; Titus 1:7; 1 Pet. 4:10; etc.

their sharing of life and destiny with other people, their solidarity with the efforts of all for whatever is noble and good. Through this wordless witness these Christians stir up irresistible questions in the hearts of those who see how they live: Why are they like this? Why do they live in this way? What or who is it that inspires them? Why are they in our midst? Such a witness is already a silent proclamation of the Good News and a very powerful and effective one. Here we have an initial act of evangelization.

—*Evangelii Nuntiandi*, 21 (December 8, 1975)

For it is to you, Beloved Brothers, Bishops of newborn or very young Churches, that pastoral love is imposed in a superior degree, rather than elsewhere. It might be said that you have to found your local Churches; you have to build them up, in a way analogous to that which Christ indicated to Peter.[75] You have to seek out, and call to the Faith, new Christians—a great task, this, and one which meets with difficulties of every kind, thus demanding from the Bishop and his collaborators self-denial, courage, constancy, wisdom and sacrifice. Moreover, you must work in poverty, and often against opposition. And your hearts are open wide to the children, to youth, to the poor, and to all who suffer.

—Homily at Episcopal Ordination,
Kololo, Uganda (August 1, 1969)

Evangelization loses much of its force and effectiveness if it does not take into consideration the actual people to whom it is addressed, if it does not use their language, their signs and symbols, if it does not answer the questions they ask, and if it does not have an impact on their concrete life. But on the other hand, evangelization risks losing its power and disappearing altogether if one empties

75 Cf. Matt. 16:16.

or adulterates its content under the pretext of translating it; if, in other words, one sacrifices this reality and destroys the unity without which there is no universality, out of a wish to adapt a universal reality to a local situation.

—*Evangelii Nuntiandi*, 63 (December 8, 1975)

From the beginning, the tradition of the Church—is it perhaps necessary to recall it?—presents us with this privileged witness of a constant seeking for God, of an undivided love for Christ alone, and of an absolute dedication to the growth of His kingdom. Without this concrete sign there would be a danger that the charity which animates the entire Church would grow cold, that the salvific paradox of the Gospel would be blunted, and that the "salt" of faith would lose its savor in a world undergoing secularization.

—*Evangelica Testificatio*, 3 (June 29, 1971)

It is certainly fitting to recall this fact at a moment like the present one when it happens that not without sorrow we can hear people—whom we wish to believe are well-intentioned but who are certainly misguided in their attitude—continually claiming to love Christ but without the Church, to listen to Christ but not the Church, to belong to Christ but outside the Church. The absurdity of this dichotomy is clearly evident in this phrase of the Gospel: "Anyone who rejects you rejects me."

—*Evangelii Nuntiandi*, 16 (December 8, 1975)

Dear sons and daughters, you have wished by means of the practice of the evangelical counsels to follow Christ more freely and to imitate Him more faithfully, dedicating your entire lives to God with a special consecration rooted in that of Baptism and expressing it with greater fullness: could you but understand all

the esteem and the affection that We have for you in the name
of Christ Jesus!

—*Evangelica Testificatio*, 4 (June 29, 1971)

We must not ignore the fact that many, even generous Christians who are sensitive to the dramatic questions involved in the
problem of liberation, in their wish to commit the Church to the
liberation effort are frequently tempted to reduce her mission to
the dimensions of a simply temporal project. They would reduce
her aims to a man-centered goal; the salvation of which she is the
messenger would be reduced to material well-being. Her activity,
forgetful of all spiritual and religious preoccupation, would become
initiatives of the political or social order. But if this were so, the
Church would lose her fundamental meaning. Her message of liberation would no longer have any originality and would easily be
open to monopolization and manipulation by ideological systems
and political parties.

—*Evangelii Nuntiandi*, 32 (December 8, 1975)

It is the Spirit of Pentecost who today leads very many followers of
Christ along the paths of prayer, in the cheerfulness of filial praise,
towards the humble and joyous service of the disinherited and of
those on the margins of society. For joy cannot be dissociated from
sharing. In God Himself, all is joy because all is giving.

—*Gaudete in Domino*, Conclusion (May 9, 1975)

The Church links human liberation and salvation in Jesus Christ,
but she never identifies them, because she knows through revelation, historical experience and the reflection of faith that not
every notion of liberation is necessarily consistent and compat-
ible with an evangelical vision of man, of things and of events;
she knows too that in order that God's kingdom should come it

# The Church

is not enough to establish liberation and to create well-being and development.

—*Evangelii Nuntiandi*, 35 (December 8, 1975)

Nevertheless this universal Church is in practice incarnate in the individual Churches made up of such or such an actual part of mankind, speaking such and such a language, heirs of a cultural patrimony, of a vision of the world, of an historical past, of a particular human substratum. Receptivity to the wealth of the individual Church corresponds to a special sensitivity of modern man.

—*Evangelii Nuntiandi*, 45 (December 8, 1975)

Behold, then, set upon your shoulders, the weight of numberless duties, of responsibilities and of sorrows! As We said, you must build up the Church; but We may add that, almost by the very nature of your ministry, you must also lend your service to help build up civil society, while remaining free from political engagements and temporal interests. For you must make generous contribution towards the education of the people, towards the honesty of their customs.

—Homily at Episcopal Ordination,
Kololo, Uganda (August 1, 1969)

Now, only a Church which preserves the awareness of her universality and shows that she is in fact universal is capable of having a message which can be heard by all, regardless of regional frontiers....

As history in fact shows, whenever an individual Church has cut itself off from the universal Church and from its living and visible center—sometimes with the best of intentions, with theological, sociological, political or pastoral arguments, or even in the desire for a certain freedom of movement or action—it has escaped only with great difficulty (if indeed it has escaped) from two equally serious dangers. The first danger is that of a withering isolationism, and then, before long, of a crumbling away, with each of its cells breaking away from it just as it itself has broken away from the central nucleus. The second danger is that of losing its freedom when, being cut off from the center and from the other Churches which gave it strength and energy, it finds itself all alone and a prey to the most varied forces of slavery and exploitation.

—*Evangelii Nuntiandi*, 63–64 (December 8, 1975)

The fact that we are distinct from the world does not mean that we are entirely separated from it. Nor does it mean that we are indifferent to it, afraid of it, or contemptuous of it. When the Church distinguishes itself from humanity, it does so not in order to oppose it, but to come closer to it. A physician who realizes the danger of disease, protects himself and others from it, but at the same time he strives to cure those who have contracted it. The Church does the same thing. It does not regard God's mercy as an exclusive privilege, nor does the greatness of the privilege it enjoys make it feel unconcerned for those who do not share it. On the contrary, it finds in its own salvation an argument for showing more concern and more love for those who live close at hand, or to whom it can go in its endeavor to make all alike share the blessing of salvation.

—*Ecclesiam Suam*, 3 (August 6, 1964)

We live in the Church at a privileged moment of the Spirit. Everywhere people are trying to know Him better, as the Scripture reveals Him. They are happy to place themselves under His inspiration. They are gathering about Him; they want to let themselves be led by Him. Now if the Spirit of God has a preeminent place in the whole life of the Church, it is in her evangelizing mission that He is most active. It is not by chance that the great inauguration of evangelization took place on the morning of Pentecost, under the inspiration of the Spirit.

It must be said that the Holy Spirit is the principal agent of evangelization: it is He who impels each individual to proclaim the Gospel, and it is He who in the depths of consciences causes the word of salvation to be accepted and understood.[76] But it can equally be said that He is the goal of evangelization: He alone stirs up the new creation, the new humanity of which evangelization is to be the result, with that unity in variety which evangelization wishes to achieve within the Christian community. Through the Holy Spirit the Gospel penetrates to the heart of the world, for it is He who causes people to discern the signs of the times—signs willed by God—which evangelization reveals and puts to use within history.

—*Evangelii Nuntiandi*, 75 (December 8, 1975)

The development, desired by us, of devotion to the Blessed Virgin Mary is an indication of the Church's genuine piety. This devotion fits—as we have indicated above—into the only worship that is rightly called "Christian," because it takes its origin and effectiveness from Christ, finds its complete expression in Christ, and leads through Christ in the Spirit to the Father. In the sphere of worship this devotion necessarily reflects God's redemptive plan, in which a special form of veneration is appropriate to the singular place which Mary occupies in that plan.[77] Indeed every authentic development of Christian worship is necessarily followed by a fitting increase of veneration for the Mother of the Lord.

—*Marialis Cultus*, Introduction (February 2, 1974)

[76] Cf. *Ad Gentes*, 4.
[77] Cf. *Lumen Gentium*, 66.

# Saint Pope Paul VI

Techniques of evangelization are good, but even the most advanced ones could not replace the gentle action of the Spirit. The most perfect preparation of the evangelizer has no effect without the Holy Spirit. Without the Holy Spirit the most convincing dialectic has no power over the heart of man. Without Him the most highly developed schemas resting on a sociological or psychological basis are quickly seen to be quite valueless.

—*Evangelii Nuntiandi*, 75 (December 8, 1975)

The Church's reflection today on the mystery of Christ and on her own nature has led her to find at the root of the former and is a culmination of the latter the same figure of a woman: the Virgin Mary, the Mother of Christ and the Mother of the Church.

—*Marialis Cultus*, introduction (February 2, 1974)

Do you know the meaning of "Catholic Church"? It means that the Church is for the entire world, that she is for all, that nowhere is she an alien. Each man, whatever his country, his race, his age or his education has a place in the Church. How can I say such an astonishing thing? Because that is what Jesus Christ, the first-born of all men, has wanted. He is the Son of God, our Father, in heaven, and at the same time he is the Son of Mary, our sister, a human being like ourselves. It is he who saves us, it is he who is our teacher. He has sent me just as he sent your missionaries.

—Homily for Mass in Leulumoega, Western Samoa (November 30, 1970)

The individual Churches, intimately built up not only of people but also of aspirations, of riches and limitations, of ways of praying, of loving, of looking at life and the world, which distinguish this or that human gathering, have the task of assimilating the essence of the Gospel message and of transposing it, without the slightest

betrayal of its essential truth, into the language that these particular people understand, then of proclaiming it in this language.
—*Evangelii Nuntiandi*, 63 (December 8, 1975)

Merely to remain true to the faith is not enough. Certainly we
must preserve and defend the treasure of truth and grace that we
have inherited through Christian tradition. As St. Paul said, "keep
that which is committed to thy trust."[78] But neither the preservation nor the defense of the faith exhausts the duty of the Church
in regard to the gifts it has been given. The very nature of the
gifts which Christ has given the Church demands that they be
extended to others and shared with others. This must be obvious
from the words: "Going, therefore, teach ye all nations,"[79] Christ's
final command to His apostles. The word apostle implies a mission
from which there is no escaping.
—*Ecclesiam Suam*, 63 (August 6, 1964)

The Church must enter into dialogue with the world in which it
lives. It has something to say, a message to give, a communication
to make.
—*Ecclesiam Suam*, 65 (August 6, 1964)

And so I have a favour to ask of you. It is this. Let us together send
a message, I mean a letter, an invitation, to all the Catholics of
the whole world. Let us tell them that there are still many people,
many peoples indeed, who have not yet received missionaries, or
else have received too few of them. Let us say that they must send
new men and women missionaries here and to all the islands and
all parts of the world that still do not know Jesus Christ. They

[78] 1 Tim. 6:20.
[79] Matt. 28:19.

are needed to preach the Gospel, and to baptize all who desire to become Christians. They are also needed to educate the people, to teach the children, to instruct the youth in what is good and beautiful, to labor, and to give your life the chance to grow and develop. They are to come in order to proclaim to all the duty to respect every human being, to show to all the way to live well, in justice and peace, and to recall to all who the Risen Christ is, and that we must love God and love all men. Do you like this idea?

— Homily for Mass in Leulumoega, Western Samoa (November 30, 1970)

Thus each individual Church that would voluntarily cut itself off from the universal Church would lose its relationship to God's plan and would be impoverished in its ecclesial dimension. But, at the same time, a Church *toto orbe diffusa* would become an abstraction if she did not take body and life precisely through the individual Churches. Only continual attention to these two poles of the Church will enable us to perceive the richness of this relationship between the universal Church and the individual Churches.

— *Evangelii Nuntiandi*, 62 (December 8, 1975)

It seems to us useful to add to this mention of the Christological orientation of devotion to the Blessed Virgin a reminder of the fittingness of giving prominence in this devotion to one of the essential facts of the Faith: the Person and work of the Holy Spirit. Theological reflection and the liturgy have in fact noted how the sanctifying intervention of the Spirit in the Virgin of Nazareth was a culminating moment of the Spirit's action in the history of salvation.

— *Marialis Cultus*, 26 (February 2, 1974)

The Spirit of the Lord, who animates man renewed in Christ, continually breaks down the horizons within which his understanding likes to find security and the limits to which his activity would willingly restrict itself; here dwells within him a power which urges him to go beyond every system and every ideology. At the heart of the world there dwells the mystery of man discovering himself to be God's son in the course of a historical and psychological process in which constraint and freedom as well as the weight of sin and the breath of the Spirit alternate and struggle for the upper hand.

—*Octogesima Adveniens*, 37 (May 14, 1971)

To reveal Jesus Christ and His Gospel to those who do not know them has been, ever since the morning of Pentecost, the fundamental program which the Church has taken on as received from her Founder. The whole of the New Testament, and in a special way the Acts of the Apostles, bears witness to a privileged and in a sense exemplary moment of this missionary effort which will subsequently leave its mark on the whole history of the Church.

—*Evangelii Nuntiandi*, 51 (December 8, 1975)

It is sometimes said that many spiritual writings today do not sufficiently reflect the whole doctrine concerning the Holy Spirit. It is the task of specialists to verify and weigh the truth of this assertion, but it is our task to exhort everyone, especially those in the pastoral ministry and also theologians, to meditate more deeply on the working of the Holy Spirit in the history of salvation, and to ensure that Christian spiritual writings give due prominence to His life-giving action.

—*Marialis Cultus*, 27 (February 2, 1974)

She carries out this first proclamation of Jesus Christ by a complex and diversified activity which is sometimes termed "pre-evangelization" but which is already evangelization in a true sense, although at its initial and still incomplete stage. An almost indefinite range of means can be used for this purpose: explicit preaching, of course, but also art, the scientific approach, philosophical research and legitimate recourse to the sentiments of the human heart.

—*Evangelii Nuntiandi*, 51 (December 8, 1975)

This is how the Lord wanted His Church to be: universal, a great tree whose branches shelter the birds of the air,[80] a net which catches fish of every kind[81] or which Peter drew in filled with one hundred and fifty-three big fish,[82] a flock which a single shepherd pastures.[83] A universal Church without boundaries or frontiers except, alas, those of the heart and mind of sinful man.

—*Evangelii Nuntiandi*, 61 (December 8, 1975)

The Church can regard no one as excluded from its motherly embrace, no one as outside the scope of its motherly care. It has no enemies except those who wish to make themselves such. Its catholicity is no idle boast. It was not for nothing that it received its mission to foster love, unity and peace among men.

—*Ecclesiam Suam*, 94 (August 6, 1964)

---

[80] Cf. Matt. 13:32.
[81] Cf. Matt. 13:47.
[82] Cf. John 21:11.
[83] Cf. John 10:1–16.

*Chapter 4*

# Mary

On March 3, 2018, Pope Francis officially declared that, on the Monday after Pentecost, the Church would henceforth honor the Blessed Virgin Mary under the title "Mother of the Church." The purpose of the new feast was to help the faithful to deepen their devotion to the Blessed Virgin Mary and to encourage genuine Marian piety, especially with regard to her role in the Church. This new day on the Church's calendar builds upon the legacy of Pope Paul, a truly Marian pontiff.

Pope Paul VI's deep Marian devotion has over the years been seriously underestimated. The Blessed Mother had always been central to his spirituality—from his childhood, when his mother introduced him to the Rosary; to his first Mass, celebrated at an altar dedicated to Mary; to his time as archbishop of Milan, when he visited on foot the fourteen chapels of the Via delle Cappelle in the mountainous northern Italian city of Varese while reciting the Rosary. Later, in 1967, he became the first pope to visit Fátima. But perhaps most significant, in 1964, he bestowed on Mary the title "Mother of the Church."

The title can be traced at least as far back as St. Ambrose of Milan (337–397), but it was officially sanctioned by Pope Paul at the close of the third session of the Second Vatican Council in 1964. He declared on that day:

# Saint Pope Paul VI

For the glory of the Virgin Mary and for our own consolation, *we proclaim the Most Blessed Mary Mother of the Church*, that is to say of all the people of God, of the faithful as well as of the pastors, who call her the most loving Mother. And we wish that the Mother of God should be still more honored and invoked by the entire Christian people by this most sweet title.[84]

For Pope Paul, the title made explicit what the council had declared implicitly in the Dogmatic Constitution on the Church *Lumen Gentium*, in its eighth chapter. While there had been discussion by the council of a separate document on the Blessed Mother, a close vote by the council fathers decided to attach their teaching on Mary to *Lumen Gentium*, focusing on the role of the Blessed Mother in the economy of salvation and on the relationship between the Blessed Virgin and the Church.

In the time after the council, some in the Church falsely claimed that the council fathers had deemphasized the Blessed Mother or, on the other hand, that the love, devotion, and veneration (*hyperdulia*) given to the Mother of God was somehow anachronistic. Paul rejected any such misleading interpretations. In 1967, he issued the exhortation *Signum Magnum*, building on the proclamation of Mary as Mother of the Church and urging personal consecration to the Blessed Mother:

The first truth is this: Mary is the Mother of the Church not only because she is the Mother of Christ and His most intimate associate in "the new economy when the Son of God took a human nature from her, that He might in the

---

[84] Paul VI, address on the close of the third session of the Second Vatican Council, November 21, 1964; translation found at https://www.ewtn.com/fatima/papal-documents/pope-paul-VI/1964Paul6.htm.

mysteries of His flesh free man from sin,"[85] but also because "she shines forth to the whole community of the elect as a model of the virtues."[86] (I)

At a general audience on May 29, 1969, Paul addressed what the council had tried to accomplish in its reflections on the Blessed Mother:

> The Council had no wish to expound new doctrines concerning her, just as it did not aim to say everything possible about her; but it did present Mary most holy in such a way and with such rules that everyone who is faithful to the Council teachings must not only feel strengthened in professing that Marian devotion which has always been held in such great honor and with such great intensity in the Catholic Church, but must also feel drawn to model his devotion in accordance with the broad, authentic, enchanting visions which the magnificent and meaningful conciliar pages offer for the meditation and devotion of the thus well-provided Catholic.[87]

Then, in 1974, he issued the exhortation *Marialis Cultus*, clarifying the Church's devotion to Mary while reiterating its theological and importance:

> The Church's devotion to the Blessed Virgin is an intrinsic element of Christian worship. The honor which the Church has always and everywhere shown to the Mother of the Lord,

---

85 Cf. *Lumen Gentium*, 55.
86 Ibid., 65, 63.
87 Paul VI, "The Vatican Council on Our Blessed Mother." *L'Osservatore Romano*, weekly edition in English, June 6, 1968, archived at http://www.ewtn.com/library/PAPALDOC/P6VAT-MAR.HTM.

from the blessing with which Elizabeth greeted Mary[88] right up to the expressions of praise and petition used today, is a very strong witness to the Church's norm of prayer and an invitation to become more deeply conscious of her norm of faith. And the converse is likewise true. The Church's norm of faith requires that her norm of prayer should everywhere blossom forth with regard to the Mother of Christ. (56)

\* \* \*

From the moment when we were called to the See of Peter, we have constantly striven to enhance devotion to the Blessed Virgin Mary, not only with the intention of interpreting the sentiments of the Church and our own personal inclination but also because, as is well known, this devotion forms a very noble part of the whole sphere of that sacred worship in which there intermingle the highest expressions of wisdom and of religion[89] and which is therefore the primary task of the People of God.

—*Marialis Cultus*, introduction (February 2, 1974)

The first of the redeemed, immaculate from the moment of her conception, the incomparable dwelling-place of the Spirit, the pure abode of the Redeemer of mankind, she is at the same time the beloved Daughter of God and, in Christ, the Mother of all. She is the perfect model of the Church both on earth and in glory.

—*Gaudete in Domino*, IV (May 9, 1975)

Look down with maternal clemency, Most Blessed Virgin, upon all your children. Consider the anxiety of bishops who fear that their flocks will be tormented by a terrible storm of evils. Heed the

---

[88] Cf. Luke 1:42–45.
[89] Cf. Lactantius, *Divinae Institutiones*, IV, 3, 6–10.

anguish of so many people, fathers and mothers of families who are uncertain about their future and beset by hardships and cares. Soothe the minds of those at war and inspire them with "thoughts of peace." Through your intercession, may God, the avenger of injuries, turn to mercy. May He give back to nations the tranquility they seek and bring them to a lasting age of genuine prosperity.

—*Christi Matri*, 13 (September 15, 1966)

It was the Holy Spirit who filled Mary with grace in the very first moment of her conception, thus redeeming her in a more sublime way in view of the merits of Christ, the Savior of mankind, and making her the Immaculate One.[90] It was the Holy Spirit who descended upon her, inspired her consent in the name of mankind to the virginal conception of the Son of the Most High and made her womb fruitful so that she might bring forth the Savior of her people and Lord of an imperishable kingdom.[91] It was the Holy Spirit who filled her soul with jubilant gratitude and moved her to sing the *Magnificat* to God her Savior.[92] It was the Holy Spirit who suggested to the Virgin that she faithfully remember the words and events connected with the birth and childhood of her only Son, events in which she played such an intimate, loving part.[93]

—Letter to Cardinal Léon Jozef Suenens for the International Marian Congress (May 13, 1975)[94]

[90] See Pius IX, Apostolic Constitution *Ineffabilis Deus* (December 8, 1854).

[91] Cf. Luke 1:35–38.

[92] Cf. Luke 1:45–55.

[93] Cf. Luke 2:19, 33, 51.

[94] Paul VI, "The Holy Spirit and the Blessed Virgin: Letter to Cardinal Léon Jozef Suenens," *The Pope Speaks* (Fort Wayne, IN: Our Sunday Visitor, 1975), archived at http://www.piercedhearts.org/hearts_jesus_mary/heart_mary/holyspirit_mary_paulvi.htm.

# Saint Pope Paul VI

May the Immaculate Heart of Mary shine before the eyes of all Christians as the model of perfect love toward God and toward our fellow beings; may it lead them toward the Holy Sacraments by virtue of which souls are cleansed from the stains of sin and are preserved from it. May it also stimulate them to make reparation for the innumerable offenses against the Divine Majesty. Lastly, may it shine like a banner of unity and a spur to perfect the bonds of brotherhood among all Christians in the bosom of the one Church of Jesus Christ.

—*Signum Magnum*, II, 7 (May 13, 1967)

Nothing seems more appropriate and valuable to Us than to have the prayers of the whole Christian family rise to the Mother of God, who is invoked as the Queen of Peace, begging her to pour forth abundant gifts of her maternal goodness in midst of so many great trials and hardships.

—*Christi Matri*, 8 (September 15, 1966)

What is necessary for presenting ourselves to God, is pointed out to us by Mary. She teaches us simply, in a masterly way and exceedingly well how to use material things and our daily experiences. In Our Blessed Mother we see a purity without an equal. What exquisite whiteness! The world has lost the concept of an immaculate conception because men bear within the imbalance, the weakness, the inertia and disharmony of original sin.

—Homily for the Assumption (August 15, 1968)[95]

---

[95] Paul VI, "The Mother of God in the Mission of Salvation." *L'Osservatore Romano*, weekly edition in English, August 29, 1968, archived at https://www.ewtn.com/library/PAPALDOC/P6MTHGD. HTM.

# Mary

Truly, the reality of the Church is not exhausted in its hierarchical structure, in its liturgy, in its sacraments, in its juridical ordinances. The intimate, the primary source of its sanctifying effectiveness are to be sought in its mystic union with Christ; a union which we cannot conceive as separate from her who is the Mother of the Word Incarnate and whom Jesus Christ Himself wanted closely united to Himself for our salvation. Thus the loving contemplation of the marvels worked by God in His Holy Mother must find its proper perspective in the vision of the Church. And knowledge of the true Catholic doctrine on Mary will always be a key to the exact understanding of the mystery of Christ and of the Church.

— Address on the close of the third session of the
Second Vatican Council (November 21, 1964)

If evils increase, the devotion of the People of God should also increase. And so, venerable brothers, we want you to take the lead in urging and encouraging people to pray ardently to our most merciful mother Mary by saying the Rosary during the month of October, as We have already indicated. This prayer is well-suited to the devotion of the People of God, most pleasing to the Mother of God and most effective in gaining heaven's blessings.

— *Christi Matri*, 9 (September 15, 1966)

This ideal of Christian perfection that We have set before you — a lofty, yet a lowly one — puts Us in mind of Mary, the holiest of Virgins, who reflects the ideal most perfectly and most wonderfully in her own person. Her life on earth was in fullest accord with this ideal, and now in heaven she enjoys its glory and blessedness. Devotion to the Mother of God is happily flourishing in the Church in this day and age, and We gladly take this opportunity of expressing Our admiration for Mary, the Holy Virgin Mother of Christ, the

# Saint Pope Paul VI

Mother of God and men, the model of Christian perfection, the mirror of true virtue, the pride of our humanity.

—*Ecclesiam Suam*, 38 (August 6, 1964)

Every time we behold Our Lady, whether in action or in silence, she displays innumerable virtues. We try with great pains to acquire and practice them, but in Her they show forth in a perfect degree. Poverty, obedience, sweetness, meekness, and above all, love: all these are present, and yet there is another singular gift, one which was particularly emphasized by the Council. That is faith. Mary believed.

—Homily for the Assumption (August 15, 1968)

With Christ, she sums up in herself all joys; she lives the perfect joy promised to the Church: *Mater plena sanctae laetitiae*. And it is with good reason that her children on earth, turning to her who is the mother of hope and of grace, invoke her as the cause of their joy: *Causa nostrae laetitiae*.

—*Gaudete in Domino*, IV (May 9, 1975)

We find ourselves, each one of us, in the order of creation and of grace, in definite relationships with the divine; in Mary, however, those relationships rose to their fullest level which we cannot describe. The words in which they are enunciated bear so weighty a meaning as to plunge them in mystery.

—General Audience (May 29, 1968)

We wish to emphasize the fact that the veneration which the universal Church today accords to blessed Mary is a derivation from and an extension and unceasing increase of the devotion that the Church of every age has paid to her, with careful attention to truth and with an ever watchful nobility of expression.

—*Marialis Cultus*, 15 (February 2, 1974)

# Mary

Therefore, while we are celebrating Her glory, let us strive to approach this perfect model given to us for our own everyday living. Even those who assume a worldly attitude often feel a longing for an ideal beauty; this happens especially when the idols we took for masterpieces turn out to be miserable phantasms. Newspapers, books, literature, the theater are full of them. It is then that we must lift up our eyes, as Christians have always done, and look for the Madonna to draw from her the lessons we need.

— Homily for the Assumption (August 15, 1968)

Mary is also the Virgin in prayer. She appears as such in the visit to the mother of the precursor, when she pours out her soul in expressions glorifying God, and expressions of humility, faith and hope. This prayer is the Magnificat,[96] Mary's prayer par excellence, the song of the messianic times in which there mingles the joy of the ancient and the new Israel.

— *Marialis Cultus*, 18 (February 2, 1974)

From what we have been illustrating in the light of the holy Gospel and of Catholic tradition, it appears evident that the spiritual motherhood of Mary transcends space and time and belongs to the universal history of the Church, since she has always been present in the Church with her maternal assistance. Likewise the meaning of the affirmation appears clear, which is so often repeated: our era may well be called the Marian era.

— *Signum Magnum*, II, 6 (May 13, 1967)

At Cana, Mary appears once more as the Virgin in prayer: when she tactfully told her Son of a temporal need she also obtained an

---

[96] Cf. Luke 1:46–55.

effect of grace, namely, that Jesus, in working the first of His "signs," confirmed His disciples' faith in Him.[97]

—*Marialis Cultus*, 18 (February 2, 1974)

Mary is, finally, the Virgin presenting offerings. In the episode of the Presentation of Jesus in the Temple,[98] the Church, guided by the Spirit, has detected, over and above the fulfillment of the laws regarding the offering of the firstborn[99] and the purification of the mother,[100] a mystery of salvation related to the history of salvation. This union of the Mother and the Son in the work of redemption reaches its climax on Calvary, where Christ "offered himself as the perfect sacrifice to God"[101] and where Mary stood by the cross,[102] "suffering grievously with her only-begotten Son. There she united herself with a maternal heart to His sacrifice, and lovingly consented to the immolation of this victim which she herself had brought forth and also was offering to the eternal Father."

—*Marialis Cultus*, 20 (February 2, 1974)

In truth, all periods of the Church's history have benefited and will benefit from the maternal presence of the Mother of God because she will remain always indissolubly joined to the mystery of the Mystical Body, of whose Head it was written: "Jesus Christ is the same, yesterday and today, yes, and forever."[103]

—*Signum Magnum*, II, 6 (May 13, 1967)

---

[97] Cf. John 2:1–12.
[98] Cf. Luke 2:22–35.
[99] Cf. Ex. 13:11–16.
[100] Cf. Lev. 12:6–8.
[101] Heb. 9:14.
[102] Cf. John 19:25.
[103] Heb. 13:8.

# Mary

For the glory of the Virgin Mary and for our own consolation, *we proclaim the Most Blessed Mary Mother of the Church*, that is to say of all the people of God, of the faithful as well as of the pastors, who call her the most loving Mother. And we wish that the Mother of God should be still more honored and invoked by the entire Christian people by this most sweet title.

—Address on the close of the third session of the Second Vatican Council (November 21, 1964)

One cannot contemplate Our Lady without seeing and adoring the divine trinitarian setting in which she is placed; the divine transcendence shines before our eyes which rejoice to be able in some degree to contemplate her, this daughter of "the race of Adam" which is our own. It is this ability to approach her that explains, perhaps, the priority in practice which devotion to Mary often assumes in the religious life of many devout souls for whom it is an instinctive comfort to stay there where Mary is, rather than to fly on, that being a place which belongs to our own history and one which fits in better with the range of our human and religious experience. But it is Mary herself who then draws us along with her in her transcendent flight towards God: remember the Magnificat.

—General Audience (May 29, 1968)

Then Our Lady—Who does not know this?—belongs wholly to Christ: in Him, through Him, with Him. We cannot, even for an instant, forget this other relationship which defines Mary, Mother of Jesus, animated and living by his Word and the companion of his Passion. It is this relationship that gives reason for her every prerogative, for her every grandeur, for her every title to our unbounded veneration, to our love, to our trust.

—General Audience (May 29, 1968)

No human creature has come nearer to Christ, none have been more his and more filled with grace than she; no-one has been so closely united to Christ as his Mother, and no-one has been so loved by Christ as she who gave Him virginal birth by the power of the Holy Spirit, she who heard his Word with a "fiat" which marked Our Lady's whole life, she who was the willing participant in every mystery of Christ's salvific mission.[104]

—General Audience (May 29, 1968)

No-one has had so great a trust as she in the beneficent goodness of Christ.[105] No-one, if is easy to believe, had so great a love for Christ as had his Mother, not only because of the ever incomparable love-relation that a mother has with the fruit of her womb, but also because of the Charity of the Holy Spirit which was in her a vivifying and loving principle of her divine maternity, which associated her with the Passion of her Son, and which, at Pentecost, overflowed in her heart and so dilated it as to make her the spiritual mother of the new-born Church, and indeed of the Church throughout the centuries; and we who belong to this Church rejoice in being able to address her with that title which she prophesied would be hers: "All generations shall call me blessed."[106]

—General Audience (May 29, 1968)

Mary is not only an example for the whole Church in the exercise of divine worship but is also, clearly, a teacher of the spiritual life for individual Christians. The faithful at a very early date began to look to Mary and to imitate her in making their lives an act

---

[104] Cf. *Lumen Gentium*, 61.
[105] Cf. John 2:5.
[106] Luke 1:48.

of worship of God and making their worship a commitment of their lives.

—*Marialis Cultus*, 21 (February 2, 1974)

Our Lady, then, represents the ideal towards whom our thoughts, our devotion, and our will likewise must be directed, in order to receive the gifts of mercy from her. For what do we ask Our Lady? The grace to make us understand her sublime sanctity, the privileges which God has conferred on her, her experiences in the Gospel story, and that we may be able to imitate and absorb even a part of such great riches. In a word, we desire that this same light may be reflected in us that we may become, like her, an example in the Church.

—Homily for the Assumption (August 15, 1968)

All this can be realized if we consider two things—first of all, the Blessed Virgin is the exemplar in the Church, because all that flourishes in the Church is summed up in Mary. In her we find the plenitude of grace and perfection. Secondly, Our Lady contains in herself all sanctity, all beauty, all the acts of Divine Providence that we will find by studying the Church. To our amazement we can trace in the history of the Church the chain of events Our Lord has willed so that her work as redemptrix might continue. What is called the Mystery, the design of God, the plan which the Lord had in our salvation is found in its highest degree in Mary, the Holy Virgin.

—Homily for the Assumption (August 15, 1968)

What, in fact, does the Church accomplish through the example of Our Lady? What has Our Lady done? She has given birth to Christ; she has given Christ to the world. And what must the Church do? It must bring forth new Christians, and make men sons and brothers of Christ. What the Church does in every Man, Our Lady has done in her Son. Thus we call her Mother of the Church, because she gives birth to us in the supernatural order in the same way in which she brought forth Christ the Lord into being. The saints have asserted this with compelling force.

—Homily for the Assumption (August 15, 1968)

The piety of the faithful and their veneration of the Mother of God has taken on many forms according to circumstances of time and place, the different sensibilities of peoples and their different cultural traditions.

—*Marialis Cultus*, 24 (February 2, 1974)

Mary is our *type*, our model. Her virtues, her earthly experiences, as told us in the Gospels, give her to us as our Exemplar. It is enough to look at but a few of the events which the Gospels record of the Mother of Jesus; and for this We do not need a magnifying glass—only the exacting lens of Christian piety.

—Homily for the Assumption (1968)

Just as, in fact, the divine maternity is the basis for her special relationship with Christ, and for her presence in the economy of salvation brought about by Jesus Christ, thus it also constitutes the principal basis for the relations between Mary and the Church, since she is the mother of Him who, right from the time of His Incarnation in her virginal bosom, joined to Himself as head His Mystical Body which is the Church. Mary, then as mother of Christ, is mother also of all the faithful and of all the pastors.

—Address on the close of the third session of the
Second Vatican Council (November 21, 1964)

The most holy Mary is our Mother and our teacher. If in all the events of life, we look at once to Mary, we can hear the inspiration:

# Mary

Be good, be patient and charitable, act in this manner, suffer cheerfully and present your pains to the Lord as I also have done. Always hope; always love; give to your life the real meaning of dedication to Christ—and thus you will receive salvation.

—Homily for the Assumption (August 15, 1968)

Although adorned by God with the riches of admirable prerogatives, to make her a worthy Mother of the Word Incarnate, she is nevertheless very close to us. Daughter of Adam, like ourselves, and therefore our sister through ties of nature, she is, however, the creature who was preserved from original sin in view of the merits of the Savior, and who possesses besides the privileges obtained the personal virtue of a total and exemplary faith, thus deserving the evangelical praise, *beata quae credidisti* (blessed art thou who believed). In her earthly life, she realized the perfect image of the disciple of Christ, reflected every virtue, and incarnated the evangelical beatitudes proclaimed by Christ. Therefore in her, the entire Church, in its incomparable variety of life and of work, attains the most authentic form of the perfect imitation of Christ.

—Address on the close of the third session of the
Second Vatican Council (November 21, 1964)

It was the Holy Spirit who urged the compassionate Mary to ask her Son for that miraculous change of water into wine at the wedding feast of Cana, which marked the beginning of Jesus' activity as a wonder worker and led his disciples to believe in him. It was the Holy Spirit who strengthened the soul of the Mother of Jesus as she stood beneath the cross, and inspired her once again, as he had at the Annunciation, to consent to the will of the heavenly Father who wanted her to be associated as a mother with the sacrifice her Son was offering for mankind's redemption. It was the

# Saint Pope Paul VI

Holy Spirit who filled the Sorrowful Mother with immense love, widening and deepening her heart, as it were, so that she might accept as a last testament from the lips of her Son her maternal mission with regard to John, the beloved disciple: a mission which, "as the Church has always understood it," prefigured her spiritual motherhood toward mankind as a whole.

> —Letter to Cardinal Léon Josef Suenens for the
> International Marian Congress (May 13, 1975)

The Madonna is not only our Mother and Queen; she is a sister, a companion. Once she was a citizen of this world; she passed along the same paths and, more than anyone else, knows the burdens of life, the seriousness of existence in the vast human family struck by so much illness. But it is destined to do penance, to suffer sanctifying pain, to learn detachment from exterior things, to hope until those higher things come to be loved.

> —Homily for the Assumption (August 15, 1968)

The Holy Father wishes all those who are listening to him to have a true devotion to Our Lady. Always think of her with an earnest attention: what would Mary do? what does she teach me? plan for me? We shall see an illimitable light of goodness, faith and joy guiding our steps. Try to say the "Salve Regina" with such sentiments. Stop a bit at the prayer which makes this trustful appeal: "...our life, our sweetness, and our hope, Hail!" O Mary, our life, our sweetness, and our hope, we salute you!

> —Homily for the Assumption (August 15, 1968)

The faithful will be able to appreciate more easily Mary's mission in the mystery of the Church and her preeminent place in the communion of saints if attention is drawn to the Second Vatican Council's references to the fundamental concepts of the nature of the Church as the Family of God, the People of God, the Kingdom of God and the Mystical Body of Christ.[107] This will also bring the faithful to a deeper realization of the brotherhood which unites all of them as sons and daughters of the Virgin Mary.

—*Marialis Cultus*, 28 (February 2, 1974)

Above all, we desire that it should be made clear that Mary, the humble handmaid of the Lord, exists only in relation to God and to Christ, our sole Mediator and Redeemer. And likewise, may the true nature and the aims of the Marian veneration in the Church be illustrated, particularly where there are many separated brothers, so that those who are not part of the Catholic community may understand that devotion to Mary, far from being an end in itself, is instead a means essentially ordained to orient souls to Christ and thus unite them with the Father in the love of the Holy Ghost.

—Address on the close of the third session of the Second Vatican Council (November 21, 1964)

In contemplating Mary and her mission these different generations of Christians, looking on her as the New Woman and perfect Christian, found in her as a virgin, wife and mother the outstanding type of womanhood and the preeminent exemplar of life lived in accordance with the Gospels and summing up the most characteristic situations in the life of a woman. When the Church considers the long history of Marian devotion she rejoices at the continuity of the element of cult which it shows, but she does not bind herself to any particular expression of an individual cultural epoch or to the particular anthropological ideas underlying such expressions.

—*Marialis Cultus*, 36 (February 2, 1974)

[107] *Lumen Gentium*, 6, 7–8, 9–11.

# Saint Pope Paul VI

The Madonna was both Mother and Virgin. The Church is also a Mother who brings forth all of us—not by human power, but by the exalted gift of the Holy Spirit; we might say, by a virginity of service.

—Homily for the Assumption (August 15, 1968)

The modern woman will note with pleasant surprise that Mary of Nazareth, while completely devoted to the will of God, was far from being a timidly submissive woman or one whose piety was repellent to others; on the contrary, she was a woman who did not hesitate to proclaim that God vindicates the humble and the oppressed, and removes the powerful people of this world from their privileged positions.[108]

—*Marialis Cultus*, 37 (February 2, 1974)

Again we might consider in what way the Church is united to Christ. It is united in Him. It must be just as Our Lady was united to Christ. She, the all-holy Virgin, had but one ideal, one love, one plan: during her whole life she was interested only in offering her homage to God; she was absorbed in consecrating herself immeasurably to Jesus, the Church, likewise, has no other purpose, no other end than, that of bringing Christ to the world. The comparison might go on, but it is all very clear when we remember that the Holy Virgin from her place in heaven, near the heart of the Savior pours out on us the light of her example.

—Homily for the Assumption (August 15, 1968)

The mysteries of Our Lady's life become the mysteries of our life when we participate in that of the Church. If we are truly faithful

---

[108] Cf. Luke 1:51–53.

to the Church, we shall obtain something of the beauty and of the mission of the Most Holy Virgin.

—Homily for the Assumption (August 15, 1968)

The Virgin Mary has always been proposed to the faithful by the Church as an example to be imitated, not precisely in the type of life she led, and much less for the socio-cultural background in which she lived and which today scarcely exists anywhere. She is held up as an example to the faithful rather for the way in which, in her own particular life, she fully and responsibly accepted the will of God,[109] because she heard the word of God and acted on it, and because charity and a spirit of service were the driving force of her actions.

—*Marialis Cultus*, 35 (February 2, 1974)

Before such splendor of virtue, the first duty of all those who recognize in the Mother of Christ the model of the Church, is to unite themselves to her in giving thanks to the Most High for working great things in Mary for the benefit of all mankind. But this is not enough. It is also the duty of all the faithful to pay as tribute to the most faithful handmaid of the Lord, a veneration of praise, of gratitude and of love because, by a wise and mild divine provision, her free consent and her generous cooperation in the designs of God had, and still have, a great influence in the attainment of human salvation.[110]

—*Signum Magnum*, I (May 13, 1967)

There are certain persons concerned with the care of souls who scorn a priori, devotions of piety which, in their correct forms have

---

[109] Cf. Luke 1:38.
[110] Cf. *Lumen Gentium*, 56.

been recommended by the magisterium, who leave them aside and in this way create a vacuum which they do not fill. They forget that the Council has said that devotions of piety should harmonize with the liturgy, not be suppressed. Secondly there are those who, without wholesome liturgical and pastoral criteria, mix practices of piety and liturgical acts in hybrid celebrations. It sometimes happens that novenas or similar practices of piety are inserted into the very celebration of the Eucharistic Sacrifice. This creates the danger that the Lord's Memorial Rite, instead of being the culmination of the meeting of the Christian community, becomes the occasion, as it were, for devotional practices.

—*Marialis Cultus*, 31 (February 2, 1974)

## PRAYER OF PAUL VI AT THE CLOSE OF THE THIRD SESSION OF THE SECOND VATICAN COUNCIL, NOVEMBER 21, 1964

O, Virgin Mary, Mother of the Church, to you we recommend the entire Church and our ecumenical council!

You, *auxilium Episcoporum,* aid of bishops, protect and assist the bishops in their apostolic mission, and all those priests, Religious and laymen, who help them in their arduous work.

You who were presented by your Son Himself, at the moment of His redeeming death, as Mother to His best-loved disciple, remember the Christian people who entrust themselves to you.

Remember all your sons; support their prayers to God, preserve their faith, strengthen their hope, increase their charity.

Remember those who are in tribulation, in need, in danger and particularly those who suffer persecution and who are in prison because of their faith. For these, O Virgin, obtain fortitude and hasten the desired day of just freedom.

Look with benign eyes on our separate brothers and condescend to unite us, you who brought forth Christ as a bridge of unity between God and men.

O, temple of light without shadow and without blemish, intercede with your only Son, mediator of our reconciliation with the Father[111] that He may have mercy on our shortcomings and may dispel any difference between us, giving us the joy of loving.

To your Immaculate Heart, O Mary, we finally recommend the entire human race. Lead it to the knowledge of the sole

[111] Cf. Rom. 5:11.

and true Savior, Jesus Christ; protect it from the scourges provoked by sin, give to the entire world peace in truth, in justice, in liberty and in love.

And let the entire Church, by celebrating this great ecumenical assembly, raise to the God of mercy the majestic hymn of praise and thanksgiving, the hymn of joy and of exultation, because the Lord has worked great things through you, O clement, O loving, O sweet Virgin Mary.

*Chapter 5*

# The Second Vatican Council

On January 12, 1966, Pope Paul used one of his general audiences to speak about the legacy of the Second Vatican Council. The audience was significant because it included a passionate defense of the council soon after it had concluded its work. The pope not only tried to defend its place in the patrimony of the Church but also provided a framework, or hermeneutic, for understanding it.

In the years that followed the council, there were many who claimed that the "spirit" of the council should guide us to interpretations that were far removed from the authentic teachings of the council and the Sacred Tradition to which it contributed. The pope declared, however, in the immediate aftermath of the council, that it would not be true to think that the council somehow represented a detachment, a rupture, or a liberation from the traditional teaching of the Church. He also warned that no one should think that it permits conformity to the thinking of our time.

The idea of a hermeneutic of continuity and reform for understanding and fulfilling the work of the council became one of the great legacies of Popes John Paul II and Benedict XVI, but it finds its roots in Paul VI's words in this general audience and in many other speeches and homilies in which he placed the council in faithful continuity with the patrimony of the Church. It is one of the tragedies of modern Church history that more Catholics—and bishops in particular—did not listen more attentively to Paul's words.

The general audience also gives a clear indication of the degree to which Paul had become the voice of the council. This is extraordinary, given that he had not convoked it but, rather, had been bequeathed the unenviable task of bringing John XXIII's project to a successful close.

Pope John XXIII had announced his intention to convoke the Twenty-First Ecumenical Council in January 1959. As archbishop of Milan, Cardinal Montini had been one of the earliest and most public supporters of the decision. In private, though, he had concerns about the scale of the problems that might be encountered and famously declared, "This old boy doesn't realize what a hornets' nest he is stirring up."[112]

Montini became a key figure in the preparation for the council and during the first session that began in October 1962. He then inherited the hornets' nest in June 1963, knowing full well both the enormity of the mission ahead of him and the fact that he had been elected in part because of the role he had played during John's preparations.

History has always attached the Second Vatican Council to the legacy and the vision of Pope St. John. It was Paul, however, who guided the majority of its sessions and promulgated all of its documents. He bore the weight of the intense deliberations and then assumed the even greater task of implementing the results for the Church. The remaining years of his pontificate were largely consumed by the controversies and crises of the times, both in the world and in the Church, but to the very end, he was steadfast in his commitment to the council. He spoke about it often and he defended it until his death in 1978.

[112] Hebblethwaite, *Paul VI*, p. 284.

# The Second Vatican Council

\* \* \*

We are confident that the great work of the Council will continue to enjoy the help and light of the Holy Spirit, and will be brought to a successful conclusion through our readiness to follow His divine inspirations, our eagerness to inquire more fully and more deeply into the genuine teaching of Christ and its legitimate and necessary development in the course of history, and our earnest resolve to make of divine truth an argument for union, understanding, and harmony among men and not a reason for dividing them in sterile discussions and regrettable rivalries. Thus may the Council be a source of glory for God, joy for His Church, and edification for the world.

—*Ecclesiam Suam*, 32 (August 6, 1964)

Let us make an effort to take as our guide the teaching of the recent Ecumenical Council. This teaching sums up and ratifies the heritage of Catholic tradition and opens the way for a renewal of the Church according to the needs and possibilities of modern times. This adherence to the teachings of the Council can establish a wonderful harmony throughout the Church, and this harmony can enhance the effectiveness of our pastoral activity and preserve us from the errors and weaknesses of the present time. This is especially true in one particular field, the field of faith.

—Address to the bishops of Asia in Manila, Philippines (November 28, 1970)

We believe that when the Ecumenical Council comes to deal with the problems relating to the Church's activity in the modern world, it will give the doctrinal and practical rules needed for the proper conduct of our dialogue with our contemporaries. We believe too that in matters relating to the Church's actual apostolic mission and the many changing circumstances in which it is exercised, the supreme authority of the Church will in every instance determine wise, effective and clear aims, principles, and methods, so that a lively and effective dialogue may be assured and lasting.

—*Ecclesiam Suam*, 89 (August 6, 1964)

For while the call of God renews itself and expresses itself in different ways according to changing circumstances of place and time, it nevertheless requires a certain constancy of orientation. The interior impulse which is the response to God's call stirs up in the depth of one's being certain fundamental options. Fidelity to the exigencies of these fundamental options is the touchstone of authenticity in religious life.

—*Evangelica Testificatio*, 12 (June 29, 1971)

Let us not forget that every human institution is prone to become set in its ways and is threatened by formalism. It is continually necessary to revitalize external forms with this interior driving force, without which these external forms would very quickly become an excessive burden.

—*Evangelica Testificatio*, 12 (June 29, 1971)

In this context, therefore, when we speak about reform we are not concerned to change things, but to preserve all the more resolutely the characteristic features which Christ has impressed on His Church. Or rather, we are concerned to restore to the Church that ideal of perfection and beauty that corresponds to its original image, and that is at the same time consistent with its necessary, normal and legitimate growth from its original, embryonic form into its present structure.

—*Ecclesiam Suam*, 47 (August 6, 1964)

There are certain persons concerned with the care of souls who scorn a priori, devotions of piety which, in their correct forms have been recommended by the magisterium, who leave them aside and in this way create a vacuum which they do not fill. They forget that the Council has said that devotions of piety should harmonize with the liturgy, not be suppressed. Secondly there are those who, without wholesome liturgical and pastoral criteria, mix practices of piety and liturgical acts in hybrid celebrations. It sometimes happens that novenas or similar practices of piety are inserted into the very celebration of the Eucharistic Sacrifice. This creates the danger that the Lord's Memorial Rite, instead of being the culmination of the meeting of the Christian community, becomes the occasion, as it were, for devotional practices.

—*Marialis Cultus*, 31 (February 2, 1974)

It is known, besides, that We have encouraged everywhere the use of the vernacular in the Liturgy, acceding willingly to the clear indications of the Council. This attitude was not dictated by a lessening of Our esteem for Latin, but by an acute consciousness of the necessities of the pastoral ministry.

—On the Latin Language (April 26, 1968)[113]

The last Council has in this sense affirmed the legitimate autonomy of culture and particularly of the sciences.[114] Here we are thinking of a true secularism: a concept of the world according to which the latter is self-explanatory, without any need for recourse to God, who thus becomes superfluous and an encumbrance. This sort of secularism, in order to recognize the power of man, therefore ends up by doing without God and even by denying Him.

—*Evangelii Nuntiandi*, 55 (December 8, 1975)

---

[113] Paul VI, "Need for Latin Remains Unchanged." *L'Osservatore Romano*, weekly edition in English, May 9, 1968, archived at https://www.ewtn.com/library/PAPALDOC/P6LATIN.HTM.

[114] Cf. *Gaudium et Spes*, 59.

# Saint Pope Paul VI

First We must lay down a few rules to guide us in the work of reform. Obviously, there can be no question of reforming the essential nature of the Church or its basic and necessary structure. To use the word reform in that context would be to misuse it completely. We cannot brand the holy and beloved Church of God with the mark of infidelity.

—*Ecclesiam Suam*, 46 (August 6, 1964)

The Council had no wish to expound new doctrines concerning her, just as it did not aim to say everything possible about her; but it did present Mary most holy in such a way and with such rules that everyone who is faithful to the Council teachings must not only feel strengthened in professing that Marian devotion which has always been held in such great honor and with such great intensity in the Catholic Church, but must also feel drawn to model his devotion in accordance with the broad, authentic, enchanting visions which the magnificent and meaningful conciliar pages offer for the meditation and devotion of the thus well-provided Catholic.

—General Audience (May 29, 1968)

We wish to encourage those who are seeking the true renewal of the religious life. The boldness of certain arbitrary transformations, an exaggerated distrust of the past—even when it witnesses to the wisdom and vigor of ecclesial traditions—and a mentality excessively preoccupied with hastily conforming to the profound changes which disturb Our times have succeeded in leading some to consider as outmoded the specific forms of religious life. Has not appeal even unjustly been made to the Council to cast doubt on the very principle of religious life? And yet it is well known that the Council recognized "this special gift" as having a choice place in the life of the Church, because it enables those who have received it to be more closely conformed to "that manner of virginal and humble life which Christ the Lord elected for Himself, and which His Virgin Mother also chose."[115] The Council has also indicated the ways for the renewal of religious life in accordance with the Gospel.[116]

—*Evangelica Testificatio*, 2 (June 29, 1971)

Certainly many exterior elements, recommended by founders of orders or religious congregations are seen today to be outmoded. Various encumbrances or rigid forms accumulated over the centuries need to be curtailed. Adaptations must be made. New forms can even be sought and instituted with the approval of the Church. For some years now the greater part of religious institutes have been generously dedicating themselves to the attainment of this goal, experimenting—sometimes too hardily—with new types of constitutions and rules. We know well and We are following with attention this effort at renewal which was desired by the Council.[117]

—*Evangelica Testificatio*, 5 (June 29, 1971)

It will be for the Council, naturally, to decide what reforms are to be introduced into the Church's legislation and discipline. The post-conciliar committees, or commissions—especially the Commission for the Revision of Canon Law, which has already been set up—will concern themselves with the task of formulating in concrete terms the recommendations of the Ecumenical Synod. It will be your duty, therefore, Venerable Brethren, to indicate to us what decisions are required for purifying and rejuvenating the

---

[115] *Lumen Gentium*, 46.

[116] Vatican Council II, Decree on the Adaptation and Renewal of Religious Life *Perfectae Caritatis* (1966).

[117] Cf. Paul VI, Motu Proprio *Ecclesiae Sanctae* (August 6, 1966); Jerome Cardinal Hamer, "Directives on Formation in Religious Institutes *Renovationis Causam*" (January 6, 1969).

Church's image. Let Us, for Our part, give public expression once again to this resolve of Ours to do all We can to sponsor this reform.

—*Ecclesiam Suam*, 14 (August 6, 1964)

No one should deceive himself into thinking that the Church which has now become a vast, magnificent, and majestic temple built to the glory of God, should be reduced to the modest proportions which it had in its earliest days, as though this minimal form were the only one that is genuine and lawful. Nor should one conceive the desire of renewing the whole structure of the Church just by taking account of the special spiritual gifts (charism) of some of its members. Some imagine that the only genuine renewal of the Church is one which is born from the ideas of a few, admittedly zealous, people who not infrequently consider themselves divinely inspired. Their vain dreams of the wrong sort of renewal could easily defile the very shape which the Church ought to have.

—*Ecclesiam Suam*, 47 (August 6, 1964)

Dear sons and daughters, by a free response to the call of the Holy Spirit you have decided to follow Christ, consecrating yourselves totally to Him. The evangelical counsels of chastity vowed to God, of poverty and of obedience have now become the law of your existence. The Council reminds us that "the authority of the Church has taken care, under the inspiration of the Holy Spirit, to interpret these evangelical counsels, to regulate their practice, and also to establish stable forms of living according to them."[118] ...

This teaching of the Council illustrates well the grandeur of this self-giving, freely made by yourselves, after the pattern of Christ's self-giving to His Church; like His, yours is total and irreversible. It is precisely for the sake of the kingdom of heaven that you have

[118] *Lumen Gentium*, 43.

vowed to Christ, generously and without reservation, that capacity to love, that need to possess and that freedom to regulate one's own life, which are so precious to man. Such is your consecration, made within the Church and through her ministry — both that of her representatives who receive your profession and that of the Christian community itself, whose love recognizes, welcomes, sustains and embraces those who within it make an offering of themselves as a living sign "which can and ought to attract all the members of the Church to an effective and prompt fulfillment of the duties of their Christian vocation ... more adequately manifesting to all believers the presence of heavenly goods already possessed in this world."[119]

—*Evangelica Testificatio*, 7 (June 29, 1971)

Thus the Council rightly insists on the obligation of religious to be faithful to the spirit of their founders, to their evangelical intentions and to the example of their sanctity. In this it finds one of the principles for the present renewal and one of the most secure criteria for judging what each institute should undertake.[120] In reality, the charism of the religious life, far from being an impulse born of flesh and blood[121] or one derived from a mentality which conforms itself to the modern world,[122] is the fruit of the Holy Spirit, who is always at work within the Church.

—*Evangelica Testificatio*, 11 (June 29, 1971)

The Council must be known: who really knows it? Many people think they know it by the vague and generic idea they have of it

---

[119] Ibid., 44.
[120] Cf. *Lumen Gentium*, 45; *Perfectae Caritatis*, 2b.
[121] Cf. John 1:13.
[122] Cf. Rom. 12:2.

as being an upheaval, breaking with the complicated and heavy traditions of the past, and authorizing us to assume rash attitudes of thought and of action, as if this were the spirit of the Council.

—General Audience (March 5, 1969)

We wish to repeat here and now before this distinguished assembly, that Latin must continue to be fostered, above all, in our Seminaries and in the houses of formation of the Regular Clergy, because it is essential to the mental formation of their students, as well as to the study of the classics and of the Fathers of the Church and, particularly, it will enable them to appreciate the treasures of the Sacred Liturgy. Without Latin, their higher and complete intellectual, theological and liturgical formation—which the modern world demands of priests—would be minimized.

—On the Latin Language (April 26, 1968)

The first benefit which We trust the Church will reap from a deepened self-awareness, is a renewed discovery of its vital bond of union with Christ. This is something which is perfectly well known, but it is supremely important and absolutely essential. It can never be sufficiently understood, meditated upon and preached. What shall We not say about this truth, which is the principal item, surely, of the whole of our religious heritage? Fortunately, you already have an excellent grasp of this doctrine, and here We would add nothing further except to make a strenuous recommendation that you always attribute maximum importance to it and look upon it as a guiding principle both in your spiritual life and in your preaching of the word of God.

—*Ecclesiam Suam*, 35 (August 6, 1964)

We repeat that it is evident that Latin must be kept in honor in the Church, for the lofty and grave reasons already mentioned. But We must not forget to speak also to those who, by an excessive cult of the past, for purely esthetic motives or opposition to anything new, have criticized the authorized innovations. We must not forget that Latin must also be put in the service of the pastoral ministry, and it is not an end in itself. Whilst defending these claims for the recognition of Latin in the life of the Church, we must avoid the danger of paralyzing or checking the pastoral renewal ordered by the Ecumenical Council. In this field, as in all others, the salvation of souls remains the supreme law.

—On the Latin Language (April 26, 1968)


How does the Church see the world today? The Council defined this vision, studied it and widened it a great deal, so that it modifies not a little the judgment and attitude that we must have with regard to the world. And this has happened because the doctrine of the Church has been enriched by a more complete knowledge of her own being and of her mission.

—General Audience (March 5, 1969)

*Chapter 6*

# Credo of the People of God

On June 30, 1968, Pope Paul VI issued a papal letter (a *motu proprio*) only a few weeks before the promulgation of his prophetic encyclical *Humanae Vitae*. It was a moment of crisis. In 1966, the Dutch bishops had approved the infamous Dutch Catechism, which had departed obstinately from the teachings of the Church and represented one of the lowest points in the era immediately after the Second Vatican Council.

To bolster the faithful in this difficult time, the pope decided to declare a special Year of Faith from 1967 to 1968, dedicating it to the apostles Peter and Paul, to mark the nineteenth centenary of their martyrdom. The Year of Faith ended in St. Peter's Square, on June 30, 1968, with a solemn profession of faith, titled the *Credo of the People of God*.

Paul said in the introduction to the document, "In making this profession, we are aware of the disquiet which agitates certain modern quarters with regard to the faith." The *Credo of the People of God* was meant to be more than a mere restatement of the Nicene Creed. Pope Paul intended it to provide clarity and hope to Catholics dismayed and confused in an age of uncertainty. As Paul added, "we place our unshakable confidence in the Holy Spirit, the soul of the Church, and in theological faith upon which rests the life of the Mystical Body."

# Saint Pope Paul VI

## Credo of the People of God (*Solemni Hac Liturgia*)

1. With this solemn liturgy we end the celebration of the nineteenth centenary of the martyrdom of the holy apostles Peter and Paul, and thus close the Year of Faith. We dedicated it to the commemoration of the holy apostles in order that we might give witness to our steadfast will to be faithful to the deposit of the faith[123] which they transmitted to us, and that we might strengthen our desire to live by it in the historical circumstances in which the Church finds herself in her pilgrimage in the midst of the world.

2. We feel it our duty to give public thanks to all who responded to our invitation by bestowing on the Year of Faith a splendid completeness through the deepening of their personal adhesion to the word of God, through the renewal in various communities of the profession of faith, and through the testimony of a Christian life. To our brothers in the episcopate especially, and to all the faithful of the holy Catholic Church, we express our appreciation and we grant our blessing.

### A Mandate

3. Likewise, we deem that we must fulfill the mandate entrusted by Christ to Peter, whose successor we are, the last in merit; namely, to confirm our brothers in the faith.[124] With the awareness, certainly, of our human weakness, yet with all the strength impressed on our spirit by such a command, we shall accordingly make a profession of faith, pronounce a creed which, without being strictly speaking a dogmatic definition, repeats in substance, with some developments called for by the spiritual condition of our time, the creed of Nicea, the creed of the immortal tradition of the holy Church of God.

[123] Cf. 1 Tim. 6:20.
[124] Cf. Luke 22:32.

4. In making this profession, we are aware of the disquiet which agitates certain modern quarters with regard to the faith. They do not escape the influence of a world being profoundly changed, in which so many certainties are being disputed or discussed. We see even Catholics allowing themselves to be seized by a kind of passion for change and novelty. The Church, most assuredly, has always the duty to carry on the effort to study more deeply and to present, in a manner ever better adapted to successive generations, the unfathomable mysteries of God, rich for all in fruits of salvation. But at the same time the greatest care must be taken, while fulfilling the indispensable duty of research, to do no injury to the teachings of Christian doctrine. For that would be to give rise, as is unfortunately seen in these days, to disturbance and perplexity in many faithful souls.

## Await the Word

5. It is important in this respect to recall that, beyond scientifically verified phenomena, the intellect which God has given us reaches that which is, and not merely the subjective expression of the structures and development of consciousness; and, on the other hand, that the task of interpretation — of hermeneutics — is to try to understand and extricate, while respecting the word expressed, the sense conveyed by a text, and not to recreate, in some fashion, this sense in accordance with arbitrary hypotheses.

6. But above all, we place our unshakable confidence in the Holy Spirit, the soul of the Church, and in theological faith upon which rests the life of the Mystical Body. We know that souls await the word of the Vicar of Christ, and we respond to that expectation with the instructions which we regularly give. But today we are given an opportunity to make a more solemn utterance.

7. On this day which is chosen to close the Year of Faith, on this feast of the blessed apostles Peter and Paul, we have wished to offer to the living God the homage of a profession of faith. And

as once at Caesarea Philippi the apostle Peter spoke on behalf of the twelve to make a true confession, beyond human opinions, of Christ as Son of the living God, so today his humble successor, pastor of the Universal Church, raises his voice to give, on behalf of all the People of God, a firm witness to the divine Truth entrusted to the Church to be announced to all nations.

We have wished our profession of faith to be to a high degree complete and explicit, in order that it may respond in a fitting way to the need of light felt by so many faithful souls, and by all those in the world, to whatever spiritual family they belong, who are in search of the Truth.

To the glory of God most holy and of our Lord Jesus Christ, trusting in the aid of the Blessed Virgin Mary and of the holy apostles Peter and Paul, for the profit and edification of the Church, in the name of all the pastors and all the faithful, we now pronounce this profession of faith, in full spiritual communion with you all, beloved brothers and sons.

## Profession of Faith

8. We believe in one only God, Father, Son and Holy Spirit, creator of things visible such as this world in which our transient life passes, of things invisible such as the pure spirits which are also called angels,[125] and creator in each man of his spiritual and immortal soul.

9. We believe that this only God is absolutely one in His infinitely holy essence as also in all His perfections, in His omnipotence,

---

[125] Cf. Heinrich Denzinger and Adolf Schönmetzer, *Enchiridion symbolorum, definitionum et declarationum de rebus fidei et morum*, 34th ed. (Barcelona: Herber, 1967), 3002. Henceforth, references to the 1967 Denzinger-Schönmetzer *Enchiridion* will be abbreviated Dz.-Sch.

His infinite knowledge, His providence, His will and His love. He is He who is, as He revealed to Moses;[126] and He is love, as the apostle John teaches us:[127] so that these two names, being and love, express ineffably the same divine reality of Him who has wished to make Himself known to us, and who, "dwelling in light inaccessible,"[128] is in Himself above every name, above every thing and above every created intellect. God alone can give us right and full knowledge of this reality by revealing Himself as Father, Son and Holy Spirit, in whose eternal life we are by grace called to share, here below in the obscurity of faith and after death in eternal light. The mutual bonds which eternally constitute the Three Persons, who are each one and the same divine being, are the blessed inmost life of God thrice holy, infinitely beyond all that we can conceive in human measure.[129] We give thanks, however, to the divine goodness that very many believers can testify with us before men to the unity of God, even though they know not the mystery of the most holy Trinity.

## The Father

10. We believe then in the Father who eternally begets the Son; in the Son, the Word of God, who is eternally begotten; in the Holy Spirit, the uncreated Person who proceeds from the Father and the Son as their eternal love. Thus in the Three Divine Persons, *coaeternae sibi et coaequales*,[130] the life and beatitude of God perfectly one superabound and are consummated in the supreme excellence and glory proper to uncreated being, and always

---

[126] Cf. Exod. 3:14.
[127] Cf. 1 John 4:8.
[128] Cf. 1 Tim. 6:16.
[129] Cf. Dz.-Sch., 804.
[130] Cf. ibid., 75.

"there should be venerated unity in the Trinity and Trinity in the unity."[131]

## The Son

11. We believe in our Lord Jesus Christ, who is the Son of God. He is the Eternal Word, born of the Father before time began, and one in substance with the Father, homoousios to Patri,[132] and through Him all things were made. He was incarnate of the Virgin Mary by the power of the Holy Spirit, and was made man: equal therefore to the Father according to His divinity, and inferior to the Father according to His humanity;[133] and Himself one, not by some impossible confusion of His natures, but by the unity of His person.[134]

12. He dwelt among us, full of grace and truth. He proclaimed and established the Kingdom of God and made us know in Himself the Father. He gave us His new commandment to love one another as He loved us. He taught us the way of the beatitudes of the Gospel: poverty in spirit, meekness, suffering borne with patience, thirst after justice, mercy, purity of heart, will for peace, persecution suffered for justice sake. Under Pontius Pilate He suffered—the Lamb of God bearing on Himself the sins of the world, and He died for us on the cross, saving us by His redeeming blood. He was buried, and, of His own power, rose on the third day, raising us by His resurrection to that sharing in the divine life which is the life of grace. He ascended to heaven, and He will come again, this time in glory, to judge the living and the dead: each according to his merits—those who

---

[131] Cf. ibid.
[132] Cf. ibid., 150.
[133] Cf. ibid., 76.
[134] Cf. ibid.

have responded to the love and piety of God going to eternal life, those who have refused them to the end going to the fire that is not extinguished.

And His Kingdom will have no end.

## The Holy Spirit

13. We believe in the Holy Spirit, who is Lord and Giver of life, who is adored and glorified together with the Father and the Son. He spoke to us by the prophets; He was sent by Christ after His resurrection and His ascension to the Father; He illuminates, vivifies, protects and guides the Church; He purifies the Church's members if they do not shun His grace. His action, which penetrates to the inmost of the soul, enables man to respond to the call of Jesus: Be perfect as your Heavenly Father is perfect (Matt. 5:48).

14. We believe that Mary is the Mother, who remained ever a Virgin, of the Incarnate Word, our God and Savior Jesus Christ,[135] and that by reason of this singular election, she was, in consideration of the merits of her Son, redeemed in a more eminent manner,[136] preserved from all stain of original sin[137] and filled with the gift of grace more than all other creatures.[138]

15. Joined by a close and indissoluble bond to the Mysteries of the Incarnation and Redemption,[139] the Blessed Virgin, the Immaculate, was at the end of her earthly life raised body and soul to heavenly glory[140] and likened to her risen Son in anticipation of the future lot of all the just; and we believe that the Blessed

---

[135] Cf. ibid., 251–252.
[136] Cf. *Lumen Gentium*, 53.
[137] Cf. Dz.-Sch., 2803.
[138] Cf. *Lumen Gentium*, 53.
[139] Cf. ibid., 53, 58, 61.
[140] Cf. Dz.-Sch., 3903.

Mother of God, the New Eve, Mother of the Church,[141] continues in heaven her maternal role with regard to Christ's members, cooperating with the birth and growth of divine life in the souls of the redeemed.[142]

## Original Offense

16. We believe that in Adam all have sinned, which means that the original offense committed by him caused human nature, common to all men, to fall to a state in which it bears the consequences of that offense, and which is not the state in which it was at first in our first parents—established as they were in holiness and justice, and in which man knew neither evil nor death. It is human nature so fallen, stripped of the grace that clothed it, injured in its own natural powers and subjected to the dominion of death, that is transmitted to all men, and it is in this sense that every man is born in sin. We therefore hold, with the Council of Trent, that original sin is transmitted with human nature, "not by imitation, but by propagation" and that it is thus "proper to everyone."[143]

## Reborn of the Holy Spirit

17. We believe that our Lord Jesus Christ, by the sacrifice of the cross redeemed us from original sin and all the personal sins committed by each one of us, so that, in accordance with the word of the apostle, "where sin abounded, grace did more abound."[144]

---

[141] Cf. *Lumen Gentium*, 53, 56, 61, 63; Paul VI, address on the closing of the third session of the Second Vatican Council (November 21, 1964); Apostolic Exhortation *Signum Magnum* (1967), introduction.

[142] Cf. *Lumen Gentium*, 62; Paul VI, *Signum Magnum*, I, 1.

[143] Cf. Dz.-Sch., 1513.

[144] Cf. Rom. 5:20.

## Baptism

18. We believe in one Baptism instituted by our Lord Jesus Christ for the remission of sins. Baptism should be administered even to little children who have not yet been able to be guilty of any personal sin, in order that, though born deprived of supernatural grace, they may be reborn "of water and the Holy Spirit" to the divine life in Christ Jesus.[145]

## The Church

19. We believe in one, holy, catholic, and apostolic Church, built by Jesus Christ on that rock which is Peter. She is the Mystical Body of Christ; at the same time a visible society instituted with hierarchical organs, and a spiritual community; the Church on earth, the pilgrim People of God here below, and the Church filled with heavenly blessings; the germ and the first fruits of the Kingdom of God, through which the work and the sufferings of Redemption are continued throughout human history, and which looks for its perfect accomplishment beyond time in glory.[146] In the course of time, the Lord Jesus forms His Church by means of the sacraments emanating from His plenitude.[147] By these she makes her members participants in the Mystery of the Death and Resurrection of Christ, in the grace of the Holy Spirit who gives her life and movement.[148] She is therefore holy, though she has sinners in her bosom, because she herself has no other life but that of grace: it is by living by her life that her members are sanctified;

---

[145] Cf. Dz.-Sch., 1514.

[146] Cf. *Lumen Gentium*, 8, 5.

[147] Cf. ibid., 7, 11.

[148] Cf. Vatican Council II, Constitution on the Sacred Liturgy *Sacrosanctum Concilium* (December 4, 1963), 5, 6; cf. *Lumen Gentium*, 7, 12, 50.

it is by removing themselves from her life that they fall into sins and disorders that prevent the radiation of her sanctity. This is why she suffers and does penance for these offenses, of which she has the power to heal her children through the blood of Christ and the gift of the Holy Spirit.

## The Word

20. Heiress of the divine promises and daughter of Abraham according to the Spirit, through that Israel whose scriptures she lovingly guards, and whose patriarchs and prophets she venerates; founded upon the apostles and handing on from century to century their ever-living word and their powers as pastors in the successor of Peter and the bishops in communion with him; perpetually assisted by the Holy Spirit, she has the charge of guarding, teaching, explaining and spreading the Truth which God revealed in a then veiled manner by the prophets, and fully by the Lord Jesus. We believe all that is contained in the word of God written or handed down, and that the Church proposes for belief as divinely revealed, whether by a solemn judgment or by the ordinary and universal magisterium.[149] We believe in the infallibility enjoyed by the successor of Peter when he teaches ex cathedra as pastor and teacher of all the faithful,[150] and which is assured also to the episcopal body when it exercises with him the supreme magisterium.[151]

21. We believe that the Church founded by Jesus Christ and for which He prayed is indefectibly one in faith, worship and the bond of hierarchical communion. In the bosom of this Church, the rich variety of liturgical rites and the legitimate diversity of

[149] Cf. Dz.-Sch., 3011.
[150] Cf. ibid., 3074.
[151] Cf. *Lumen Gentium*, 25.

theological and spiritual heritages and special disciplines, far from injuring her unity, make it more manifest.[152]

## One Shepherd

22. Recognizing also the existence, outside the organism of the Church of Christ, of numerous elements of truth and sanctification which belong to her as her own and tend to Catholic unity,[153] and believing in the action of the Holy Spirit who stirs up in the heart of the disciples of Christ love of this unity,[154] we entertain the hope that the Christians who are not yet in the full communion of the one only Church will one day be reunited in one flock with one only shepherd.

23. We believe that the Church is necessary for salvation, because Christ, who is the sole mediator and way of salvation, renders Himself present for us in His body which is the Church.[155] But the divine design of salvation embraces all men; and those who without fault on their part do not know the Gospel of Christ and His Church, but seek God sincerely, and under the influence of grace endeavor to do His will as recognized through the promptings of their conscience, they, in a number known only to God, can obtain salvation.[156]

## Sacrifice of Calvary

24. We believe that the Mass, celebrated by the priest representing the person of Christ by virtue of the power received through the

---

[152] Cf. ibid., 23; cf. Vatican Council II, Decree on the Catholic Churches of the Eastern Rite *Orientalium Ecclesiarum* (November 21, 1964), 2, 3, 5, 6.
[153] Cf. *Lumen Gentium*, 8.
[154] Cf. ibid., 15.
[155] Cf. ibid., 14.
[156] Cf. ibid., 16.

Sacrament of Orders, and offered by him in the name of Christ and the members of His Mystical Body, is the sacrifice of Calvary rendered sacramentally present on our altars. We believe that as the bread and wine consecrated by the Lord at the Last Supper were changed into His body and His blood which were to be offered for us on the cross, likewise the bread and wine consecrated by the priest are changed into the body and blood of Christ enthroned gloriously in heaven, and we believe that the mysterious presence of the Lord, under what continues to appear to our senses as before, is a true, real and substantial presence.[157]

## Transubstantiation

25. Christ cannot be thus present in this sacrament except by the change into His body of the reality itself of the bread and the change into His blood of the reality itself of the wine, leaving unchanged only the properties of the bread and wine which our senses perceive. This mysterious change is very appropriately called by the Church transubstantiation. Every theological explanation which seeks some understanding of this mystery must, in order to be in accord with Catholic faith, maintain that in the reality itself, independently of our mind, the bread and wine have ceased to exist after the Consecration, so that it is the adorable body and blood of the Lord Jesus that from then on are really before us under the sacramental species of bread and wine,[158] as the Lord willed it, in order to give Himself to us as food and to associate us with the unity of His Mystical Body.[159]

26. The unique and indivisible existence of the Lord glorious in heaven is not multiplied, but is rendered present by the sacrament

---

[157] Cf. Dz.-Sch., 1651.
[158] Cf. ibid., 1642, 1651–1654; Paul VI, encyclical letter *Mysterium Fidei* (September 3, 1965).
[159] Cf. St. Thomas Aquinas, *Summa Theologica*, III, Q. 73, art. 3.

in the many places on earth where Mass is celebrated. And this existence remains present, after the sacrifice, in the Blessed Sacrament which is, in the tabernacle, the living heart of each of our churches. And it is our very sweet duty to honor and adore in the blessed Host which our eyes see, the Incarnate Word whom they cannot see, and who, without leaving heaven, is made present before us.

## Temporal Concern

27. We confess that the Kingdom of God begun here below in the Church of Christ is not of this world whose form is passing, and that its proper growth cannot be confounded with the progress of civilization, of science or of human technology, but that it consists in an ever more profound knowledge of the unfathomable riches of Christ, an ever stronger hope in eternal blessings, an ever more ardent response to the love of God, and an ever more generous bestowal of grace and holiness among men. But it is this same love which induces the Church to concern herself constantly about the true temporal welfare of men. Without ceasing to recall to her children that they have not here a lasting dwelling, she also urges them to contribute, each according to his vocation and his means, to the welfare of their earthly city, to promote justice, peace and brotherhood among men, to give their aid freely to their brothers, especially to the poorest and most unfortunate. The deep solicitude of the Church, the Spouse of Christ, for the needs of men, for their joys and hopes, their griefs and efforts, is therefore nothing other than her great desire to be present to them, in order to illuminate them with the light of Christ and to gather them all in Him, their only Savior. This solicitude can never mean that the Church conform herself to the things of this world, or that she lessen the ardor of her expectation of her Lord and of the eternal Kingdom.

28. We believe in the life eternal. We believe that the souls of all those who die in the grace of Christ whether they must still be purified in purgatory, or whether from the moment they leave their bodies Jesus takes them to paradise as He did for the Good Thief are the People of God in the eternity beyond death, which will be finally conquered on the day of the Resurrection when these souls will be reunited with their bodies.

## Prospect of Resurrection

29. We believe that the multitude of those gathered around Jesus and Mary in paradise forms the Church of Heaven where in eternal beatitude they see God as He is,[160] and where they also, in different degrees, are associated with the holy angels in the divine rule exercised by Christ in glory, interceding for us and helping our weakness by their brotherly care.[161]

30. We believe in the communion of all the faithful of Christ, those who are pilgrims on earth, the dead who are attaining their purification, and the blessed in heaven, all together forming one Church; and we believe that in this communion the merciful love of God and His saints is ever listening to our prayers, as Jesus told us: Ask and you will receive.[162] Thus it is with faith and in hope that we look forward to the resurrection of the dead, and the life of the world to come.

Blessed be God Thrice Holy. Amen.

PAUL VI

[160] Cf. 1 John 3:2; Dz.-Sch., 1000.
[161] Cf. *Lumen Gentium*, 49.
[162] Cf. Luke 10:9–10; John 16:24.

*Chapter 7*

# The Mass and the Sacraments

One of the greatest controversies surrounding the implementation of the Second Vatican Council was its impact on the Church's Liturgy and the celebration of the sacraments. The *Novus Ordo*—the New Order of the Mass, which has been the ordinary form of the Roman Rite since 1970—has been especially controversial in some quarters.

For Pope Paul VI, the reforms of the council and their implementation were intended to bring renewal to the Church and to deepen the participation and faith of all Catholics. The pontiff thus labored to defend the reforms but also to reiterate that the fundamental teachings of the Church had not changed. That was made manifest in September 1965, when, even as the council continued its deliberations, and as he did with the topic of the Church in the encyclical *Ecclesiam Suam*, Paul issued an encyclical on the Eucharist.

Under the title *Mysterium Fidei* and promulgated on the feast of Pope St. Pius X, the document sought to bolster the love of the Eucharist and to stress that the Church's teachings were being safeguarded—regarding the Real Presence above all. What is especially striking throughout is Paul's deep love for the Eucharist and the Liturgy. He began the encyclical by writing about both:

> The Mystery of Faith, that is, the ineffable gift of the Eucharist that the Catholic Church received from Christ, her

Spouse, as a pledge of His immense love, is something that she has always devoutly guarded as her most precious treasure, and during the Second Vatican Council she professed her faith and veneration in a new and solemn declaration. In dealing with the restoration of the sacred liturgy, the Fathers of the Council were led by their pastoral concern for the whole Church to regard it as a matter of highest importance to urge the faithful to participate actively, with undivided faith and the utmost devotion, in the celebration of this Most Holy Mystery, to offer it to God along with the priest as a sacrifice for their own salvation and that of the whole world, and to use it as spiritual nourishment.

For if the sacred liturgy holds first place in the life of the Church, then the Eucharistic Mystery stands at the heart and center of the liturgy, since it is the font of life that cleanses us and strengthens us to live not for ourselves but for God and to be united to each other by the closest ties of love. (1–2)

Paul took many other opportunities throughout his pontificate to explain and to defend the immense reforms that were taking place in the liturgical life of the Church, including the reforms that were being launched in the celebration of the sacraments. He issued several documents on the sacraments, including *Divinae Consortium Naturae* on the sacrament of Confirmation in 1971. He spoke and wrote directly to priests and men and women religious to assist and encourage them in their lives and service, especially in the face of so many priests leaving active ministry. And he called on the faithful to remember the importance of penance with a 1966 apostolic constitution on the topic, *Paenitemini*.

The Liturgy remained especially important in his thoughts and his teachings. When he promulgated the new Roman Missal in 1969, he wrote, "One ought not to think, however, that this revision of the Roman Missal has been improvident." He continued:

> All this is wisely ordered in such a way that there is developed more and more among the faithful a "hunger for the Word of God,"[163] which, under the guidance of the Holy Spirit, leads the people of the New Covenant to the perfect unity of the Church. We are fully confident that both priests and faithful will prepare their hearts more devoutly and together at the Lord's Supper, meditating more profoundly on Sacred Scripture, and at the same time they will nourish themselves more day by day with the words of the Lord. It will follow then that according to the wishes of the Second Vatican Council, Sacred Scripture will be at the same time a perpetual source of spiritual life, an instrument of prime value for transmitting Christian doctrine and finally the center of all theology.[164]

## The Mass

The Lord is immolated in an unbloody way in the Sacrifice of the Mass and He re-presents the sacrifice of the Cross and applies its salvific power at the moment when he becomes sacramentally present — through the words of consecration — as the spiritual food of the faithful, under the appearances of bread and wine.

—*Mysterium Fidei*, 34 (September 3, 1965)

If we look at the matter properly we shall see that the fundamental outline of the Mass is still the traditional one, not only theologically but also spiritually. Indeed, if the rite is carried out

---

[163] Cf. Amos 8:11.
[164] Paul VI, Apostolic Constitution *Missale Romanum* (April 3, 1969).

as it ought to be, the spiritual aspect will be found to have greater richness. The greater simplicity of the ceremonies, the variety and abundance of scriptural texts, the joint acts of the ministers, the silences which will mark various deeper moments in the rite, will all help to bring this out.

—General Audience (November 26, 1969)[165]

We have to listen with docility to the voice of the teaching and praying Church. Her voice, which constantly echoes the voice of Christ, assures us that the way in which Christ becomes present in this Sacrament is through the conversion of the whole substance of the bread into His body and of the whole substance of the wine into His blood, a unique and truly wonderful conversion that the Catholic Church fittingly and properly calls transubstantiation.[166] As a result of transubstantiation, the species of bread and wine undoubtedly take on a new signification and a new finality, for they are no longer ordinary bread and wine but instead a sign of something sacred and a sign of spiritual food; but they take on this new signification, this new finality, precisely because they contain a new "reality" which we can rightly call ontological. For what now lies beneath the aforementioned species is not what was there before, but something completely different; and not just in the estimation of Church belief but in reality, since once the substance or nature of the bread and wine has been changed into the body and blood of Christ, nothing remains of the bread and the wine except for the species—beneath which Christ is present whole and entire

---

[165] Paul VI, "Changes in Mass for Greater Apostolate," *L'Osservatore Romano*, weekly edition in English, December 4, 1969, archived at http://www.ewtn.com/library/PAPALDOC/P6691126.HTM.

[166] Cf. Council of Trent, Decree on the Most Holy Eucharist, c. 4 and canon 2.

in His physical "reality," corporeally present, although not in the manner in which bodies are in a place.

—*Mysterium Fidei*, 46 (September 3, 1965)

The Eucharist is the commemoration of Jesus Christ and his love for God the Father in heaven, and for all men, a love unto death. This love of Jesus is not a matter of the past; it is meant to remain present and to live in every human heart.

—Address to non-Christians, Bombay, India (December 3, 1964)

No one can fail to see that the divine Eucharist bestows an incomparable dignity upon the Christian people. For it is not just while the Sacrifice is being offered and the Sacrament is being confected, but also after the Sacrifice has been offered and the Sacrament confected—while the Eucharist is reserved in churches or oratories—that Christ is truly Emmanuel, which means "God with us." For He is in the midst of us day and night; He dwells in us with the fullness of grace and of truth.[167]

—*Mysterium Fidei*, 67 (September 3, 1965)

Christ, the victim and the priest, renews and offers up his redeeming sacrifice through the ministry of the Church in the symbolic rite of his last supper. He leaves us his body and blood under the appearances of bread and wine, for our personal and spiritual nourishment, for our fusion in the unity of his redeeming love and his immortal life.

—General Audience (November 26, 1969)

This evangelizing preaching takes on many forms, and zeal will inspire the reshaping of them almost indefinitely. In fact there are innumerable events in life and human situations which offer the

[167] Cf. John 1:14.

opportunity for a discreet but incisive statement of what the Lord has to say in this or that particular circumstance. It suffices to have true spiritual sensitivity for reading God's message in events. But at a time when the liturgy renewed by the Council has given greatly increased value to the Liturgy of the Word, it would be a mistake not to see in the homily an important and very adaptable instrument of evangelization. Of course it is necessary to know and put to good use the exigencies and the possibilities of the homily, so that it can acquire all its pastoral effectiveness. But above all it is necessary to be convinced of this and to devote oneself to it with love. This preaching, inserted in a unique way into the Eucharistic celebration, from which it receives special force and vigor, certainly has a particular role in evangelization, to the extent that it expresses the profound faith of the sacred minister and is impregnated with love. The faithful assembled as a Paschal Church, celebrating the feast of the Lord present in their midst, expect much from this preaching, and will greatly benefit from it provided that it is simple, clear, direct, well-adapted, profoundly dependent on Gospel teaching and faithful to the magisterium, animated by a balanced apostolic ardor coming from its own characteristic nature, full of hope, fostering belief, and productive of peace and unity. Many parochial or other communities live and are held together thanks to the Sunday homily, when it possesses these qualities.

—*Evangelii Nuntiandi*, 43 (December 8, 1975)


Anyone who has a special devotion to the sacred Eucharist and who tries to repay Christ's infinite love for us with an eager and unselfish love of his own, will experience and fully understand—and this will bring great delight and benefit to his soul—just how precious is a life hidden with Christ in God[168] and just how worthwhile

---

[168] Cf. Col. 3:3.

it is to carry on a conversation with Christ, for there is nothing more consoling here on earth, nothing more efficacious for progress along the paths of holiness.

—*Mysterium Fidei*, 67 (September 3, 1965)

It is not permissible to extol the so-called "community" Mass in such a way as to detract from Masses that are celebrated privately; or to concentrate on the notion of sacramental sign as if the symbolism—which no one will deny is certainly present in the Most Blessed Eucharist—fully expressed and exhausted the manner of Christ's presence in this Sacrament; or to discuss the mystery of transubstantiation without mentioning what the Council of Trent had to say about the marvelous conversion of the whole substance of the bread into the Body and the whole substance of the wine into the Blood of Christ, as if they involve nothing more than "transignification," or "transfinalization" as they call it; or, finally, to propose and act upon the opinion that Christ Our Lord is no longer present in the consecrated Hosts that remain after the celebration of the sacrifice of the Mass has been completed.

—*Mysterium Fidei*, 11 (September 3, 1965)

For each and every Mass is not something private, even if a priest celebrates it privately; instead, it is an act of Christ and of the Church. In offering this sacrifice, the Church learns to offer herself as a sacrifice for all and she applies the unique and infinite redemptive power of the sacrifice of the Cross to the salvation of the whole world. For every Mass that is celebrated is being offered not just for the salvation of certain people, but also for the salvation of the whole world.

—*Mysterium Fidei*, 32 (September 3, 1965)

You also realize, Venerable Brothers, that the Eucharist is reserved in churches or oratories to serve as the spiritual center of a religious community or a parish community, indeed of the whole Church and the whole of mankind, since it contains, beneath the veil of the species, Christ the invisible Head of the Church, the Redeemer of the world, the center of all hearts.

—*Mysterium Fidei*, 68 (September 3, 1965)

Therefore let those Institutes and Sodalities, to which is entrusted by special law approved by the Church the duty of manifesting this devotion of adoration in regard to the Sacrament of the Eucharist, be aware that they are carrying out a most important office, and doing so in the name of the Church.... There is no reason, therefore, why those who carry out this most important duty of worship should lose heart in our day as if, as some are wont to say, it were a matter of some "obsolete devotion" and as if they were wasting their time when other work is more pressing.

—Letter to Fr. Roland Huot, Superior General of the
Congregation of Priests of the Blessed Sacrament, "Devotion
to Holy Eucharist outside of Mass" (January 10, 1969)[169]

And so We beseech you, Venerable Brothers, to take this faith, which means nothing less than maintaining complete fidelity to the words of Christ and the Apostles, and preserve it in its purity and integrity among the people entrusted to your care and vigilance, with all false and pernicious opinions being completely rejected; and We beseech you to foster devotion to the Eucharist, which should be the focal point and goal of all other forms of devotion.

—*Mysterium Fidei*, 64 (September 3, 1965)

---

[169] Paul VI, "Devotion to Holy Eucharist Outside Mass," *L'Osservatore Romano*, weekly edition in English, February 6, 1969, archived at https://www.ewtn.com/library/PAPALDOC/P6ADORE.HTM.

## The Mass and the Sacraments

It is desirable to have the faithful in large numbers take an active part in the sacrifice of the Mass each and every day and receive the nourishment of Holy Communion with a pure and holy mind and offer fitting thanks to Christ the Lord for such a great gift.

—*Mysterium Fidei*, 66 (September 3, 1965)

We can see that some of those who are dealing with this Most Holy Mystery in speech and writing are disseminating opinions on Masses celebrated in private or on the dogma of transubstantiation that are disturbing the minds of the faithful and causing them no small measure of confusion about matters of faith, just as if it were all right for someone to take doctrine that has already been defined by the Church and consign it to oblivion or else interpret it in such a way as to weaken the genuine meaning of the words or the recognized force of the concepts involved.

—*Mysterium Fidei*, 10 (September 3, 1965)

The Eucharist, through which we do not cease to proclaim the death and resurrection of the Lord and to prepare ourselves for His coming again in glory, brings back constantly to mind the physical and moral sufferings by which Christ was afflicted, and which He had indeed freely accepted, even to His agony and death on the Cross. May the trials which you encounter be for you an opportunity for bearing in union with the Lord, and of offering to the Father, the many misfortunes and unjust sufferings which weigh upon our brothers and sisters; to these the sacrifice of Christ can alone—in faith—give meaning.

—*Evangelica Testificatio*, 48 (June 29, 1971)

Moreover, the Catholic Church has held firm to this belief in the presence of Christ's Body and Blood in the Eucharist not only in her teaching but in her life as well, since she has at all times paid

this great Sacrament the worship known as "latria," which may
be given to God alone.

—*Mysterium Fidei*, 55 (September 3, 1965)

The most life-giving Sacrament of the Holy Eucharist, which is
so to say the center-point of the life of the Church as being that
in which the very author of grace is truly, really and substantially
contained, so takes possession of the minds of the faithful that, not
by any lengthy investigation but by a certain insight, they realize
that the worship of adoration is to be accorded to it. By this act
of supreme worship the virtue of religion is effectively developed
and steadily increased whereby the faithful soul acknowledges its
Creator, so far transcending nature, recognizes his dominion and
strives humbly to find its own place in relation to Him. Moreover
this adoration is manifested also in the body which is offered as a
"living sacrifice, holy, pleasing to God,"[170] "because," as St. Thomas
Aquinas says, "in all acts of worship, what is external has reference
to what is internal as to its motive, therefore external adoration
is the expression of internal; just as by making use of bodily signs
of humility our desire to submit ourselves to God is aroused."[171]

—Letter to Fr. Roland Huot, Superior General of the
Congregation of Priests of the Blessed Sacrament, "Devotion
to Holy Eucharist outside of Mass" (January 10, 1969)

Because, Venerable Brothers, the Sacrament of the Eucharist is a
sign and cause of the unity of Christ's Mystical Body, and because
it stirs up an active "ecclesial" spirit in those who are more fervent
in their Eucharistic devotion, never stop urging your faithful, as
they approach the Mystery of the Eucharist, to learn to embrace

[170] Cf. Rom. 12:1.
[171] Cf. *Summa Theologica*, II-II, Q. 84, art. 2

the Church's cause as their own, to pray to God without slackening, to offer themselves to God as an acceptable sacrifice for the peace and unity of the Church; so that all the sons of the Church may be united and feel united and there may be no divisions among them but rather unity of mind and intention, as the Apostle commands.[172]

—*Mysterium Fidei*, 70 (September 3, 1965)

The Eucharist is a sign and a bond of unity.[173] It is a sacrament of communion. In the very act whereby the Eucharist puts us in real communion with Christ it puts us in spiritual, mystical, moral and social communion with all those who eat the same bread.[174] It is the sacrament of ecclesial unity. It is the supreme uniting element of the community of the faithful. It is the sacrament which contains the real Body of Christ and which has as its purpose to produce the Mystical Body of Christ, which is the Church.

—Homily for the Mass in Happy Valley, Hong Kong (December 4, 1970)

Understanding of prayer is worth more than the silken garments in which it is royally dressed. Participation by the people is worth more—particularly participation by modern people, so fond of plain language which is easily understood and converted into everyday speech. If the divine Latin language kept us apart from the children, from youth, from the world of labor and of affairs, if it were a dark screen, not a clear window, would it be right for us fishers of souls to maintain it as the exclusive language of prayer and religious intercourse?

—General Audience (November 26, 1969)

[172] Cf. 1 Cor. 1:10.
[173] Cfr. *Summa Theologica*, III, Q. 73, art. 2, 3.
[174] Cf. 1 Cor. 10:17.

# Saint Pope Paul VI

## THE NEW RITE OF THE MASS
## ADDRESS TO A GENERAL AUDIENCE,
## NOVEMBER 19, 1969[175]

Our Dear Sons and Daughters:

We wish to draw your attention to an event about to occur in the Latin Catholic Church: the introduction of the liturgy of the new rite of the Mass. It will become obligatory in Italian dioceses from the First Sunday of Advent, which this year falls on November 30. The Mass will be celebrated in a rather different manner from that in which we have been accustomed to celebrate it in the last four centuries, from the reign of St. Pius V, after the Council of Trent, down to the present.

This change has something astonishing about it, something extraordinary. This is because the Mass is regarded as the traditional and untouchable expression of our religious worship and the authenticity of our faith. We ask ourselves, how could such a change be made? What effect will it have on those who attend Holy Mass? Answers will be given to these questions, and to others like them, arising from this innovation. You will hear the answers in all the Churches. They will be amply repeated there and in all religious publications, in all schools where Christian doctrine is taught. We exhort you to pay attention to them. In that way you will be able to get a clearer and deeper idea of the stupendous and mysterious notion of the Mass.

[175] Paul VI, "The Mass Is the Same," *L'Osservatore Romano*, weekly edition in English, November 27, 1969, archived at http://www.ewtn.com/library/PAPALDOC/P6601119.HTM.

But in this brief and simple discourse We will try only to relieve your minds of the first, spontaneous difficulties which this change arouses. We will do so in relation to the first three questions which immediately occur to mind because of it.

How could such a change be made? Answer: It is due to the will expressed by the Ecumenical Council held not long ago. The Council decreed: "The rite of the Mass is to be revised in such a way that the intrinsic nature and purpose of its several parts, as also the connection between them, can be more clearly manifested, and that devout and active participation by the faithful can be more easily accomplished.

"For this purpose the rites are to be simplified, while due care is taken to preserve their substance. Elements which, with the passage of time, came to be duplicated, or were added with but little advantage, are now to be discarded. Where opportunity allows or necessity demands, other elements which have suffered injury through accidents of history are now to be restored to the earlier norm of the Holy Fathers."[176]

The reform which is about to be brought into being is therefore a response to an authoritative mandate from the Church. It is an act of obedience. It is an act of coherence of the Church with herself. It is a step forward for her authentic tradition. It is a demonstration of fidelity and vitality, to which we all must give prompt assent.

It is not an arbitrary act. It is not a transitory or optional experiment. It is not some dilettante's improvisation. It is a law. It has been thought out by authoritative experts of sacred Liturgy; it has been discussed and meditated upon for a long

---

[176] *Sacrosanctum Concilium*, 50.

time. We shall do well to accept it with joyful interest and put it into practice punctually, unanimously and carefully.

This reform puts an end to uncertainties, to discussions, to arbitrary abuses. It calls us back to that uniformity of rites and feeling proper to the Catholic Church, the heir and continuation of that first Christian community, which was all "one single heart and a single soul."[177] The choral character of the Church's prayer is one of the strengths of her unity and her catholicity. The change about to be made must not break up that choral character or disturb it. It ought to confirm it and make it resound with a new spirit, the spirit of her youth.

The second question is: What exactly are the changes?

You will see for yourselves that they consist of many new directions for celebrating the rites. Especially at the beginning, these will call for a certain amount of attention and care. Personal devotion and community sense will make it easy and pleasant to observe these new rules. But keep this clearly in mind: Nothing has been changed of the substance of our traditional Mass. Perhaps some may allow themselves to be carried away by the impression made by some particular ceremony or additional rubric, and thus think that they conceal some alteration or diminution of truths which were acquired by the Catholic faith for ever, and are sanctioned by it. They might come to believe that the equation between the law of prayer, *lex orandi* and the law of faith, *lex credendi*, is compromised as a result.

It is not so. Absolutely not. Above all, because the rite and the relative rubric are not in themselves a dogmatic definition. Their theological qualification may vary in different

[177] Acts 4:32.

degrees according to the liturgical context to which they refer. They are gestures and terms relating to a religious action — experienced and living — of an indescribable mystery of divine presence, not always expressed in a universal way. Only theological criticism can analyze this action and express it in logically satisfying doctrinal formulas. The Mass of the new rite is and remains the same Mass we have always had. If anything, its sameness has been brought out more clearly in some respects.

The unity of the Lord's Supper, of the Sacrifice on the cross of the re-presentation and the renewal of both in the Mass, is inviolably affirmed and celebrated in the new rite just as they were in the old. The Mass is and remains the memorial of Christ's Last Supper. At that Supper the Lord changed the bread and wine into His Body and His Blood, and instituted the Sacrifice of the New Testament. He willed that the Sacrifice should be identically renewed by the power of His Priesthood, conferred on the Apostles. Only the manner of offering is different, namely, an unbloody and sacramental manner; and it is offered in perennial memory of Himself, until His final return.[178]

In the new rite you will find the relationship between the Liturgy of the Word and the Liturgy of the Eucharist, strictly so called, brought out more clearly, as if the latter were the practical response to the former.[179] You will find how much the assembly of the faithful is called upon to participate in the celebration of the Eucharistic sacrifice, and how in the Mass they are and fully feel themselves "the Church." You

[178] Cf. De la Taille, *Mysterium Fidei*, Elucd. IX.
[179] Cf. Louis Bouyer, CO.

will also see other marvelous features of our Mass. But do not think that these things are aimed at altering its genuine and traditional essence.

Rather try to see how the Church desires to give greater efficacy to her liturgical message through this new and more expansive liturgical language; how she wishes to bring home the message to each of her faithful, and to the whole body of the People of God, in a more direct and pastoral way.

In like manner We reply to the third question: What will be the results of this innovation? The results expected, or rather desired, are that the faithful will participate in the liturgical mystery with more understanding, in a more practical, a more enjoyable and a more sanctifying way. That is, they will hear the Word of God, which lives and echoes down the centuries and in our individual souls; and they will likewise share in the mystical reality of Christ's sacramental and propitiatory sacrifice.

So do not let us talk about "the new Mass." Let us rather speak of the "new epoch" in the Church's life.

The Mystery of Faith, that is, the ineffable gift of the Eucharist that the Catholic Church received from Christ, her Spouse, as a pledge of His immense love, is something that she has always devoutly guarded as her most precious treasure.

—*Mysterium Fidei*, 1 (September 3, 1965)

The Catholic Church has always displayed and still displays this latria that ought to be paid to the Sacrament of the Eucharist, both during Mass and outside of it, by taking the greatest possible care of consecrated Hosts, by exposing them to the solemn veneration of the faithful, and by carrying them about in processions to the joy of great numbers of the people.

—*Mysterium Fidei*, 56 (September 3, 1965)

Understanding of prayer is worth more than the silken garments in which it is royally dressed. Participation by the people is worth more—particularly participation by modern people, so fond of plain language which is easily understood and converted into everyday speech. If the divine Latin language kept us apart from the children, from youth, from the world of labor and of affairs, if it were a dark screen, not a clear window, would it be right for us fishers of souls to maintain it as the exclusive language of prayer and religious intercourse?

—General Audience (November 26, 1969)

May the all-merciful Redeemer, who shortly before His death prayed to the Father that all who were to believe in Him might be one, just as He and the Father are one,[180] deign to hear this most ardent prayer of Ours and of the whole Church as quickly as possible, so that we may all celebrate the Eucharistic Mystery with one voice and one faith, and through sharing in the Body of Christ become one body,[181] joined together by the same bonds that Christ wanted it to have.

—*Mysterium Fidei*, 73 (September 3, 1965)

## The Sacraments

Those who are baptized and by this means incorporated into Christ's Mystical Body, His Church, must attach the greatest importance to

[180] Cf. John 17:20–21.
[181] Cf. 1 Cor. 10:17.

this event. They must be acutely aware of being raised to a higher status, of being reborn to a supernatural life, there to experience the happiness of being God's adopted sons, the special dignity of being Christ's brothers, the blessedness, the grace and the joy of the indwelling Holy Spirit.

—*Ecclesiam Suam*, 39 (August 6, 1964)

This exercise of bodily mortification—far removed from any form of stoicism—does not imply a condemnation of the flesh which sons of God deign to assume.[182] On the contrary mortification aims at the "liberation"[183] of man, who often finds himself, because of concupiscence, almost chained[184] by his own senses.

—*Paenitemini*, II (February 17, 1966)

Jesus Christ the Good Shepherd remains forever the exemplar of all our pastoral activities. We are his disciples, and "it is enough for the disciple to be like his teacher."[185] Our ministry is patterned on his. We have been sent to carry on, in his name and by his power, the work of God's only Son. We have been sent, as apostles, to preach the Gospel of salvation, to proclaim life in Christ, and finally to lead the human family to the fullness of eternal life. Since, in God's plan, the whole person is called to eternal life, and this life is already begun on earth, our ministry necessarily involves service to human life in its entirety.

—Address to the bishops of the United States on
their Ad Limina Visit (May 26, 1978)

---

[182] Cf. Roman Martyrology for the Vigil of Christmas; 1 Tim. 4:1–5; Phil. 4:8; Origen, *Against Celsus* 7:36.

[183] Cf. Lenten Liturgy, throughout.

[184] Cf. Rom. 7:23.

[185] Matt. 10:25.

# The Mass and the Sacraments

Dear brothers, be men of God, proclaiming by your whole conduct the primacy of the supernatural, the uprightness of your faith, the whole-heartedness of your self-giving to the Lord. It is freely that you have offered your whole being to Christ so as to bring to the world the message of salvation.

—Address to the clergy of Australia, Sydney (December 1, 1970)

You are aware that this service of the Gospel can only be understood and lived in faith, prayer, penance and love; you know that it involves struggles and mortification and at times even misunderstanding. We urge you to hold fast with faith and generosity to all these commitments which conform you to the image of Christ the Priest.[186]

—Address to the clergy of Australia, Sydney (December 1, 1970)

Penance therefore—already in the Old Testament—is a religious, personal act which has as its aim love and surrender to God: fasting for the sake of God, not for one's own self.[187]

—*Paenitemini*, I (February 17, 1966)

To be a Christian, to have received holy Baptism, must not be looked upon as something of negligible importance. It must be something which thrills the baptized person to the very core of his being. He must look upon it with the eyes of the Christians of the early Church, as an "illumination" which draws down upon his soul the life-giving radiance of divine truth, opens heaven to him, and sheds upon this mortal life that light which enables him to walk as a child of the light toward the vision of God, the wellspring of eternal happiness.

—*Ecclesiam Suam*, 39 (August 6, 1964)

---

[186] Cfr. Paul VI, Letter to the Cardinal Secretary of State (February 2, 1970).
[187] Cf. Zech. 7:5.

# Saint Pope Paul VI

Those members of the Church who are stricken by infirmities, ill-nesses, poverty or misfortunes, or who are persecuted for the love of justice, are invited to unite their sorrows to the suffering of Christ in such a way that they not only satisfy more thoroughly the precept of penitence but also obtain for the brethren a life of grace and for themselves that beatitude which is promised in the Gospel to those who suffer.[188]

—*Paenitemini*, III (February 17, 1966)

It is strongly recommended to all the faithful that they keep deeply rooted in their hearts a genuine Christian spirit of penitence to spur them to accomplish works of charity and penitence.

—*Paenitemini*, III (February 17, 1966)

When the liturgy turns its gaze either to the primitive Church or to the Church of our own days it always finds Mary. In the primitive Church she is seen praying with the apostles;[189] in our own day she is actively present, and the Church desires to live the mystery of Christ with her.

—*Marialis Cultus*, 11 (February 2, 1974)

Yet, one can never sufficiently stress the fact that evangelization does not consist only of the preaching and teaching of a doctrine. For evangelization must touch life: the natural life to which it gives a new meaning, thanks to the evangelical perspectives that it reveals; and the supernatural life, which is not the negation but the purification and elevation of the natural life.

---

[188] *Lumen Gentium*, 41
[189] Cf. Roman Missal, Common of the Blessed Virgin Mary, 6; *Tempore Paschali*, Collect.

# The Mass and the Sacraments

This supernatural life finds its living expression in the seven sacraments and in the admirable radiation of grace and holiness which they possess....

We must note with sadness that the evangelizing work of the Church is strongly opposed, if not prevented, by certain public powers. Even in our own day it happens that preachers of God's Word are deprived of their rights, persecuted, threatened or eliminated solely for preaching Jesus Christ and His Gospel.

—*Evangelii Nuntiandi*, 48, 50 (December 8, 1975)

Through "corporal fasting"[190] man regains strength and the "wound inflicted on the dignity of our nature by intemperance is cured by the medicine of a salutary abstinence."[191]

—*Paenitemini*, II (February 17, 1966)

Priests of Christ! Bishops, successors of the Apostles! Let us together confess our humbleness and our greatness, just as Mary, the exquisite Mother of God, while proclaiming her humility as His handmaid, exalted the great things which God did to her and with her. You are bearers of peace: how humble and how human is your mission! It is not arms, nor riches, nor pride of conquest and glory that are your strength, but the Word of God, the Gospel!

—Address to new bishops, Bombay, India (December 3, 1964)

The kingdom of God announced by Christ can be entered only by a "change of heart" ("metanoia"), that is to say through that intimate

---

[190] Cf. Roman Missal, Preface for Lent: "*corporali jejunio vitia comprimis, mentem elevas, virtutem largiris . . .*"

[191] Cf. ibid.; Collect for Thursday after First Sunday of the Passion (Passion Sunday).

and total change and renewal of the entire man—of all his opinions, judgments and decisions—which takes place in him in the light of the sanctity and charity of God, the sanctity and charity which was manifested to us in the Son and communicated fully.[192]

—*Paenitemini*, I (February 17, 1966)

If one studies the history of Christian worship, in fact, one notes that both in the East and in the West the highest and purest expressions of devotion to the Blessed Virgin have sprung from the liturgy or have been incorporated into it.

—*Marialis Cultus*, 15 (February 2, 1974)

In the presence of Christ man is illumined with a new light and consequently recognizes the holiness of God and the gravity of sin.[193] Through the word of Christ a message is transmitted to him which invites him to conversion and grants forgiveness of sins.

—*Paenitemini*, I (February 17, 1966)

Shepherds of souls, you have nothing to ask; but you have everything to give: your own selves. Your authority derives from this, that you can call every man you meet your friend; and if he responds to you, you will call him brother and son. Your wisdom will be twofold: divine and human. As your prophecy, you will have the doctrine which the divine Master taught us. You will have the ability to understand the heart of man, his greatness, his folly, his sufferings, his misery; your knowledge and science will be the science of life. Go, then, Shepherds, on all the roads of the earth; go, reveal to the peoples their dignity, their freedom, their mission

---

[192] Cf. Heb. 1:2; Col. 1:19 and throughout; Eph. 1:23 and throughout.
[193] Cf. Luke 5:8 and 7:36–50.

on this earth and in the next world. Your journey will not be an easy one, but do not fear, for the Lord is with you.

—Address to new bishops, Bombay, India (December 3, 1964)

As Bishops of the Church of God, we must humbly ask for strength, so as not to be "tossed here and there, carried about by every wind of doctrine."[194] Let us speak out; let us proclaim the message of the Beatitudes; let us exercise personally with ever greater energy our teaching mission: to teach as Jesus taught. Understanding? Yes. Compassion? Yes. Sensitivity? Yes. But supernatural sensitivity, and fidelity to Jesus Christ and to his Cross and Resurrection.

—Address on the occasion of the canonization of St. John Neumann (June 20, 1977)

The preeminently interior and religious character of penitence and the new wondrous aspects which it assumes "in Christ and in the Church" neither excludes nor lessens in any way the external practice of this virtue, but on the contrary reaffirms its necessity with particular urgency[195] and prompts the Church—always attentive to the signs of the times—to seek, beyond fast and abstinence, new expressions more suitable for the realization, according to the character of various epochs, of the precise goal of penitence.

—*Paenitemini*, II (February 17, 1966)

In the Bishop, Our Lord Jesus Christ is among us. In a word, it is the communication of the fulness of the one supreme Priesthood

---

[194] Eph. 4:14.

[195] For example: (a) with regard to priests, cf. Vatican Council II, Decree Priestly Ministry and Life *Presbyterorum Ordinis* (1965), 16; (b) regarding spouses, cf. *Gaudium et Spes*, 49; also cf. no. 52; cf. Pius XII, speech to cardinals, archbishops, bishops, etc. (Nov. 2, 1950); cf. Justin, *Dialogue with Trypho*, 141:2–3 (MG 6: 797–799).

of Christ Himself, now appropriated to the Bishop, which must occupy our attention, our admiration, our exultation. This is a grandeur which confounds us, for God alone is its cause,[196] and because God gives it to whom He wills, generally choosing the most humble.[197] Yet it is a grandeur which exacts reverence, and which no one can despise with impunity.[198] Let us recognize Christ in the Bishop, and let us praise the Lord!

—Homily at Episcopal Ordination,
Kololo, Uganda (August 1, 1969)

True penitence, however, cannot ever prescind from physical asceticism as well. Our whole being, in fact, body and soul, (indeed the whole of nature, even animals without reason, as Holy Scripture often points out)[199] must participate actively in this religious act whereby the creature recognizes divine holiness and majesty.

—*Paenitemini*, II (February 17, 1966)

The ministry that we are called upon to perform is indeed a service of love: the love of Christ for his Father and his brethren becoming the pattern of our own pastoral charity. This love must be constant expression in our giving to our people the word of God, and in fulfilling their deepest needs for Christ, who is "the way, and the truth, and the life."[200] In particular we owe this love to the poor and suffering.

—Address to a group of bishops from England on
their Ad Limina Visit (November 10, 1977)

[196] Cf. Luke 1:48.
[197] Cf. 1 Cor. 1:27.
[198] Cf. Tit. 2:1–5; Luke 10:16.
[199] Cf. John 3:7–8.
[200] John 14:6.

What has actually taken place by means of the imposition of hands and the formula of consecration? What has happened is that these newly elected ones have been invested with an extraordinary out-pouring of the Holy Spirit. An incomparable dignity—much more interior, indeed, than external—has transfigured them. A fearful power has been conferred upon them; a virtue which comes from on high, and is ratified in heaven,[201] has been communicated to them; a new and deeper assimilation to Christ has stamped upon them a superior personality.[202]

—Homily at Episcopal Ordination,
Kololo, Uganda (August 1, 1969)

For what reason, however, is this preference given to the Bishop by Christ? We know this (and it is Our second consideration today): Christ has so favored the Bishop in order to make him an Apostle. The Bishops, you know, are the successors of the Apostles. And who are the Apostles? They are those whom the Lord chose, and separated, and segregated for a mission in favor of the people.[203] They are those whom He sends forth.[204] Apostle means one sent forth. The Apostles, and hence also the Bishops, their successors, are the representatives, or, rather, the vehicles and instruments of the love of Christ for men. The episcopal ministry is a sign and an instrument of salvation.[205]

—Homily at Episcopal Ordination,
Kololo, Uganda (August 1, 1969)

---

[201] Cf. Luke 24:49; John 20:23.

[202] Cf. Luke 10:16; Gal. 2:20; *Lumen Gentium*, 21.

[203] Cf. Heb. 5:1.

[204] Cf. John 15:16; Matt. 19:29; Luke 18:29; Gal. 1:15; Rom. 1:1; Acts 13:2.

[205] Cf. Matt. 9:38; Luke 6:13; John 20:21.

For the Church, evangelizing means bringing the Good News into all the strata of humanity, and through its influence transforming humanity from within and making it new: "Now I am making the whole of creation new."[206] But there is no new humanity if there are not first of all new persons renewed by Baptism[207] and by lives lived according to the Gospel.[208] The purpose of evangelization is therefore precisely this interior change, and if it had to be expressed in one sentence the best way of stating it would be to say that the Church evangelizes when she seeks to convert,[209] solely through the divine power of the message she proclaims, both the personal and collective consciences of people, the activities in which they engage, and the lives and concrete milieu which are theirs.

—*Evangelii Nuntiandi*, 18 (December 8, 1975)

And because love reaches its perfection in unity, we are called to promote that unity for which Christ prayed, for which he died. Our whole ministry is directed to building up the Church in truth and love. United with us and in the communion of the universal Church, you will find the guarantee of the authenticity of your pastoral initiatives, and the assurance of their supernatural effectiveness for the Kingdom of God.

—Address to a group of bishops from England on their Ad Limina Visit (November 10, 1977)

But is Baptism and a certain amount of faith enough to belong fully to the Church? We have to recall that this fullness, this perfect

---

[206] Rev. 21:5; cf. 2 Cor. 5:17; Gal. 6:15.
[207] Cf. Rom. 6:4.
[208] Cf. Eph. 4:24–25; Col. 3:9–10.
[209] Cf. Rom. 1:16; 1 Cor. 1:18; 2:4.

communion is a profound and inextinguishable requirement of the religious order founded by Christ. If belonging to the Church in at least an initial or partial way is highly valuable, then it is just as desirable for this belonging to reach its full measure. The Church is one and unique.

—General Audience (June 1, 1966)

It is Christ's will, it is the breath of the Holy Spirit which calls the Church to make this change. A prophetic moment is occurring in the mystical body of Christ, which is the Church. This moment is shaking the Church, arousing it, obliging it to renew the mysterious art of its prayer.

—General Audience (November 26, 1969)

Following the Master, every Christian must renounce himself, take up his own cross and participate in the sufferings of Christ. Thus transformed into the image of Christ's death, he is made capable of meditating on the glory of the resurrection.[210]

—*Paenitemini*, I (February 17, 1966)

No longer Latin, but the spoken language will be the principal language of the Mass. The introduction of the vernacular will certainly be a great sacrifice for those who know the beauty, the power and the expressive sacrality of Latin. We are parting with the speech of the Christian centuries; we are becoming like profane intruders in the literary preserve of sacred utterance. We will lose a great part of that stupendous and incomparable artistic and spiritual thing, the Gregorian chant.

—General Audience (November 26, 1969)

---

[210] Cf. Phil. 3:10–11; Rom. 8:17.

Since the Church is closely linked to Christ, the penitence of the individual Christian also has an intimate relationship of its own with the whole ecclesial community. In fact, not only does he receive in the bosom of the Church through baptism the fundamental gift of "metanoia," but this gift is restored and reinvigorated in those members of the Body of Christ who have fallen into sin through the sacrament of penance.

*—Paenitemini*, I (February 17, 1966)

## The Priesthood and Celibacy

In 1967, Pope Paul VI reaffirmed the Church's discipline of priestly celibacy through the encyclical *Sacerdotalis Caelibatus*. The encyclical sought both to meditate on the value of celibacy and to restate the reasons for it in the face of dissent in the period immediately after the end of the council, in 1965. He began the encyclical by declaring, "Priestly celibacy has been guarded by the Church for centuries as a brilliant jewel, and retains its value undiminished even in our time when the outlook of men and the state of the world have undergone such profound changes."

The following are excerpts from the encyclical:

Considering what contemporary scholarly investigation has ascertained, it is not right to continue repeating[211] that celibacy is against nature because it runs counter to lawful physical, psychic and affective needs, or to claim that a completely mature human personality demands fulfillment of these needs. Man, created to God's image and likeness,[212] is not just flesh and blood; the sexual instinct is not all that he has; man has also, and pre-eminently,

[211] See Eph. 5:25–27.
[212] Gen. 1:26–27.

understanding, choice, freedom, and thanks to these powers he is, and must remain, the chief work of creation; they give him mastery over his physical, mental and emotional appetites. (53)

* * *

The choice of celibacy does not connote ignorance of or contempt for the sexual instinct and man's capacity for giving himself in love. That would certainly do damage to his physical and psychological balance. On the contrary, it demands clear understanding, careful self-control and a wise elevation of the mind to higher realities. In this way celibacy sets the whole man on a higher level and makes an effective contribution to his perfection. (55)

* * *

Christ, the only Son of the Father, by the power of the Incarnation itself was made Mediator between heaven and earth, between the Father and the human race. Wholly in accord with this mission, Christ remained throughout His whole life in the state of celibacy, which signified His total dedication to the service of God and men.[213] (21)

* * *

The response to the divine call is an answer of love to the love which Christ has shown us so sublimely.[214] This response is included in the mystery of that special love for souls who have accepted His most urgent appeals.[215] With a divine force, grace increases the longings of love. And love, when it is genuine, is all-embracing, stable and lasting, an irresistible spur to all forms of heroism. (24)

---

[213] See *Presbyterorum Ordinis*, 16.
[214] See John 3:16; 15:13.
[215] See Mark 10:21.

# Saint Pope Paul VI

* * *

The consecrated celibacy of the sacred ministers actually manifests the virginal love of Christ for the Church, and the virginal and supernatural fecundity of this marriage, by which the children of God are born, "not of blood, nor of the will of the flesh."[216]

The priest dedicates himself to the service of the Lord Jesus and of His Mystical Body with complete liberty, which is made easier by his total offering, and thus he depicts more fully the unity and harmony of the priestly life.[217] His ability for listening to the word of God and for prayer increases. Indeed, the word of God, as preserved by the Church, stirs up vibrant and profound echoes in the priest who daily meditates on it, lives it and preaches it to the faithful. (26–27)

* * *

By a daily dying to himself and by giving up the legitimate love of a family of his own for the love of Christ and of His kingdom, the priest will find the glory of an exceedingly rich and fruitful life in Christ, because like Him and in Him, he loves and dedicates himself to all the children of God.

In the community of the faithful committed to his charge, the priest represents Christ. Thus, it is most fitting that in all things he should reproduce the image of Christ and in particular follow His example, both in his personal and in his apostolic life. To his children in Christ, the priest is a sign and a pledge of that sublime and new reality which is the kingdom of God; he dispenses it and he possesses it to a more perfect degree. Thus he nourishes the faith and hope of all Christians, who, as such, are bound to observe chastity according to their proper state of life.

---

[216] John 1:13. See *Lumen Gentium*, 42; *Presbyterorum Ordinis*, 16.
[217] See *Presbyterorum Ordinis*, 14.

# The Mass and the Sacraments

The consecration to Christ under an additional and lofty title like celibacy evidently gives to the priest, even in the practical field, the maximum efficiency and the best disposition of mind, mentally and emotionally, for the continuous exercise of a perfect charity.[218] This charity will permit him to spend himself wholly for the welfare of all, in a fuller and more concrete way.[219] It also obviously guarantees him a greater freedom and flexibility in the pastoral ministry,[220] in his active and living presence in the world, to which Christ has sent him[221] so that he may pay fully to all the children of God the debt due to them.[222] (30–32)

\* \* \*

It is asserted, moreover, that the maintaining of priestly celibacy in the Church does great harm in those regions where the shortage of the clergy—a fact recognized with sadness and deplored by the same Council[223]—gives rise to critical situations: that it prevents the full realization of the divine plan of salvation and at times jeopardizes the very possibility of the initial proclamation of the Gospel. Thus the disquieting decline in the ranks of the clergy is attributed by some to the heavy burden of the obligation of celibacy.

Then there are those who are convinced that a married priesthood would remove the occasions for infidelity, waywardness and

---

[218] See Vatican Council II, Decree on Training for the Priesthood *Optatam Totius* (October 28, 1965), 10.

[219] See 2 Cor. 12:15.

[220] See *Presbyterorum Ordinis*, 16.

[221] See John 17:18.

[222] See Rom. 1:14.

[223] See Vatican Council II, *Christus Dominus*, 35; Decree on the Apostolate of the Laity *Apostolicam Actuositatem* (November 18, 1965), 1; *Presbyterorum Ordinis*, 10ff.; *Ad Gentes*, 19, 38.

distressing defections which hurt and sadden the whole Church. These also maintain that a married priesthood would enable Christ's ministers to witness more fully to Christian living by including the witness of married life, from which they are excluded by their state of life. (8–9)

\* \* \*

Hence We consider that the present law of celibacy should today continue to be linked to the ecclesiastical ministry. This law should support the minister in his exclusive, definitive and total choice of the unique and supreme love of Christ; it should uphold him in the entire dedication of himself to the public worship of God and to the service of the Church; it should distinguish his state of life both among the faithful and in the world at large. (14)

\* \* \*

Consideration of how celibacy is "particularly suited"[224] to God's ministers is not something recent. Even if the explicit reasons have differed with different mentalities and different situations, they were always inspired by specifically Christian considerations; and from these considerations we can get an intuition of the more fundamental motives underlying them.[225] These can be brought into clearer light only under the influence of the Holy Spirit, promised by Christ to His followers for the knowledge of things to come[226] and to enable the People of God to increase in the understanding of the mystery of Christ and of the Church.

The Christian priesthood, being of a new order, can be understood only in the light of the newness of Christ, the Supreme Pontiff

[224] *Presbyterorum Ordinis*, 16.
[225] See *Dei Verbum*, 8.
[226] See John 16:13.

and eternal Priest, who instituted the priesthood of the ministry as a real participation in His own unique priesthood.[227] The minister of Christ and dispenser of the mysteries of God,[228] therefore, looks up to Him directly as his model and supreme ideal. (18–19)

\* \* \*

In any case, the Church of the West cannot weaken her faithful observance of her own tradition. Nor can she be regarded as having followed for centuries a path which instead of favoring the spiritual richness of individual souls and of the People of God, has in some way compromised it, or of having stifled, with arbitrary juridical prescriptions, the free expansion of the most profound realities of nature and of grace. (41)

\* \* \*

We wholeheartedly call on the entire People of God to do their duty in bringing about an increase in priestly vocations.[229] We ask them fervently to beg the Father of all, the divine Spouse of the Church, and the Holy Spirit, her principle of life, through the intercession of the Blessed Virgin Mary, Mother of Christ and of His Church, to pour out, especially at present, this divine gift, which the Father certainly does not wish to give sparingly. They should also fervently pray, in like manner, that souls may dispose themselves to receive this gift by a profound faith and a generous love. (45)

\* \* \*

We are not easily led to believe that the abolition of ecclesiastical celibacy would considerably increase the number of priestly

---

[227] *Lumen Gentium*, 28; *Presbyterorum Ordinis*, 2.
[228] See 1 Cor. 4:1.
[229] See *Optatam Totius*, 2; *Presbyterorum Ordinis*, 11.

vocations: the contemporary experience of those Churches and ecclesial communities which allow their ministers to marry seems to prove the contrary. The causes of the decrease in vocations to the priesthood are to be found elsewhere—for example, in the fact that individuals and families have lost their sense of God and of all that is holy, their esteem for the Church as the institution of salvation through faith and the sacraments. (49)

\* \* \*

The Church cannot and should not fail to realize that the choice of celibacy—provided that it is made with human and Christian prudence and responsibility—is governed by grace which, far from destroying or doing violence to nature, elevates it and imparts to it supernatural powers and vigor. (51)

## Chapter 8

# Joy

Joy is not an attribute that most observers would immediately associate with Pope Paul VI. Introverted and introspective by temperament, he nevertheless spoke frequently of joy, and Paul's confessor, Paolo Dezza, even considered Paul "a man of great joy."[230]

"No one," the pope wrote, seemingly anticipating Pope Francis, "is excluded from the joy brought by the Lord. The great joy announced by the angel on Christmas night is truly for all the people,[231] both for the people of Israel then anxiously awaiting a Savior, and for the numberless people made up of all those who, in time to come, would receive its message and strive to live by it."[232]

This was why, in 1975, on the tenth anniversary of the close of the Second Vatican Council, Pope Paul proclaimed a Holy Year for which he issued the apostolic exhortation *Gaudete in Domino*, "On Christian Joy." The pope wrote:

Rejoice in the Lord always; the Lord is near to all who call upon Him in truth![233]

---

[230] Hebblethwaite, *Paul VI*, p. 339.
[231] Cf. Luke 2:10.
[232] *Gaudete in Domino*, II.
[233] Cf. Phil. 4:4–5; Ps. 145:18.

Dear brothers and sons and daughters in Christ, many times already in the course of this Holy Year we have exhorted the People of God to correspond with joyful enthusiasm to the grace of the Jubilee. As you know, our invitation is essentially an appeal to interior renewal and reconciliation in Christ. It is a question of people's salvation, of their complete happiness. In this time, when throughout the world believers are preparing to celebrate the coming of the Holy Spirit, we invite you to implore from Him the gift of joy....

We have therefore felt it as a happy interior need to address to you in the course of this year of grace, and very fittingly on the occasion of Pentecost, an Apostolic Exhortation whose theme is precisely: Christian joy — joy in the Holy Spirit. It is a sort of hymn to the divine joy that we would like to utter, so that it may awaken an echo in the whole world, and first of all in the Church: may joy be poured out in hearts together with the love of which it is the fruit, by the Holy Spirit that has been given to us.[234] Thus we wish that your voice may be joined with ours, for the spiritual consolation of the Church of God and of all those who are willing to lend their hearts and minds to this celebration.[235]

Pope Paul strove to live the joy of the gospel and to proclaim it to the world, even as he presided over an era in the Church and the world when joy seemed to be in short supply. But this is why it was so important.

\* \* \*

Technological society has succeeded in multiplying the opportunities for pleasure, but it has great difficulty in generating joy. For

---

[234] Cf. Rom. 5:5.
[235] *Gaudete in Domino*, prologue.

# *Joy*

joy comes from another source. It is spiritual. Money, comfort, hygiene and material security are often not lacking; and yet boredom, depression and sadness unhappily remain the lot of many. These feelings sometimes go as far as anguish and despair, which apparent carefreeness, the frenzies of present good fortune and artificial paradises cannot assuage.

—*Gaudete in Domino*, I (May 9, 1975)

No one is excluded from the joy brought by the Lord. The great joy announced by the angel on Christmas night is truly for all the people,[236] both for the people of Israel then anxiously awaiting a Savior, and for the numberless people made up of all those who, in time to come, would receive its message and strive to live by it.

—*Gaudete in Domino*, III (May 9, 1975)

Beloved brethren and sons and daughters, is it not normal that joy should dwell in us, when our hearts contemplate or rediscover, in faith, the fundamental and simple reasons for joy? God has so loved the world that He gave His only begotten Son; through His Spirit, God's presence does not cease to enfold us with His tenderness and to fill us with His life; and we are journeying towards the blessed transfiguration of our life in the path of the resurrection of Jesus. Yes, it would be very strange if this Good News, which evokes the alleluia of the Church, did not give us the look of those who are saved. The joy of being Christian, of being united with the Church, of being "in Christ," and in the state of grace with God, is truly able to fill the human heart. Is it not this profound exultation that gives an overwhelming accent to the Memorial of Pascal: "Joy, joy, joy, tears of joy?" And near to us, how many writers there are who know how to express in a new form—we

---

[236] Cf. Luke 2:10.

are thinking, for example, of Georges Bernanos — this evangelical joy of the humble which shines forth everywhere in the world and which speaks of God's silence!

—*Gaudete in Domino*, conclusion (May 9, 1975)

In essence, Christian joy is the spiritual sharing in the unfathomable joy, both divine and human, which is in the heart of Jesus Christ glorified. As soon as God the Father begins to manifest in history the mystery of His will, according to His purpose which He set forth in Christ as a plan for the fullness of time,[237] this joy is mysteriously announced in the midst of the People of God, before its identity has been unveiled.

—*Gaudete in Domino*, II (May 9, 1975)

Our appeal here is inspired by the fervor of the greatest preachers and evangelizers, whose lives were devoted to the apostolate. Among these we are glad to point out those whom we have proposed to the veneration of the faithful during the course of the Holy Year. They have known how to overcome many obstacles to evangelization.

Such obstacles are also present today, and we shall limit ourself to mentioning the lack of fervor. It is all the more serious because it comes from within. It is manifested in fatigue, disenchantment, compromise, lack of interest and above all lack of joy and hope. We exhort all those who have the task of evangelizing, by whatever title and at whatever level, always to nourish spiritual fervor.[238]

—*Evangelii Nuntiandi*, 80 (December 8, 1975)

[237] Cf. Eph. 1:9–10.
[238] Cf. Rom. 12:11.

# Joy

Gathered in the Holy Spirit, we may experience together the joy of life in Christ, and the joy of being apostles of him who is Life itself. And we pray that, through the power of the Holy Spirit, you will go forth to prepare in your local Churches a fresh outpouring of Christian joy among all your people: a joy based on the keen conviction that God sent his Son to bring eternal life, so that the world might be saved through him.

—Address to the bishops of the United States on
their Ad Limina Visit (May 26, 1978)

Christian joy could not be properly praised if one were to remain indifferent to the outward and inward witness that God the Creator renders to Himself in the midst of His creation: "And God saw that it was good."[239] Raising up man in the setting of a universe that is the work of His power, wisdom and love, and even before manifesting Himself personally according to the mode of revelation, God disposes the mind and heart of His creature to meet joy, at the same time as truth. One should therefore be attentive to the appeal that rises from man's heart, from the age of wondering childhood to serene old age, as a presentiment of the divine mystery.

—*Gaudete in Domino*, I (May 9, 1975)

Man experiences joy when he finds himself in harmony with nature, and especially in the encounter, sharing and communion with other people. All the more does he know spiritual joy or happiness when his spirit enters into possession of God, known and loved as the supreme and immutable good.[240] Poets, artists, thinkers, but also ordinary men and women, simply disposed to a certain inner light, have been able and still are able, in the times before Christ

---

[239] Gen. 1:10, 12, 18, 21, 25, 31.
[240] Cf. *Summa Theologica*, II-II, Q. 28, arts. 1, 4.

and in our own time and among us, to experience something of the joy of God.

—*Gaudete in Domino*, I (May 9, 1975)

Bent over a material that resists his efforts, the worker leaves his imprint on it, at the same time developing his own powers of persistence, inventiveness and concentration. Further, when work is done in common—when hope, hardship, ambition and joy are shared—it brings together and firmly unites the wills, minds and hearts of men. In its accomplishment, men find themselves to be brothers.[241]

—*Populorum Progressio*, 27 (March 26, 1967)

Nor can we overlook the immense ranks of men and women in religious life, of laity and of young people too, united in the faithful observance of perfect chastity. They live in chastity, not out of disdain for the gift of life, but because of a greater love for that new life which springs from the Paschal mystery. They live this life of courageous self-denial and spiritual joyfulness with exemplary fidelity and also with relative facility.

—*Sacerdotalis Caelibatus*, 13 (June 24, 1967)

Paschal joy is not just that of a possible transfiguration: it is the joy of the new presence of the Risen Christ dispensing to His own the Holy Spirit, so that He may dwell with them. The Holy Spirit is given to the Church as the inexhaustible principle of her joy as the bride of the glorified Christ. He recalls to her mind, through the ministry of grace and truth exercised by the successors of the

---

[241] Cf., for example, M. D. Chenu, O.P., *Pour une théologie du travail* (Paris: Editions du Seuil, 1955). English trans., *The Theology of Work* (Dublin: Gill, 1963).

apostles, the very teaching of the Lord. The Holy Spirit stirs up in the Church divine life and the apostolate. And the Christian knows that this Spirit will never be quenched in the course of history.

—*Gaudete in Domino*, III (May 9, 1975)

Let us preserve the delightful and comforting joy of evangelizing, even when it is in tears that we must sow. May it mean for us—as it did for John the Baptist, for Peter and Paul, for the other apostles and for a multitude of splendid evangelizers all through the Church's history—an interior enthusiasm that nobody and nothing can quench. May it be the great joy of our consecrated lives. And may the world of our time, which is searching, sometimes with anguish, sometimes with hope, be enabled to receive the Good News not from evangelizers who are dejected, discouraged, impatient or anxious, but from ministers of the Gospel whose lives glow with fervor, who have first received the joy of Christ, and who are willing to risk their lives so that the kingdom may be proclaimed and the Church established in the midst of the world.

—*Evangelii Nuntiandi*, 80 (December 8, 1975)

The Church—which during the council examined with greater attention its relations not only with the separated brethren but also with non-Christian religions—has noted with joy that almost everywhere and at all times penitence has held a place of great importance, since it is closely linked with the intimate sense of religion which pervades the life of most ancient peoples as well as with the more advanced expressions of the great religions connected with the progress of culture.[242]

—*Paenitemini*, I (February 17, 1966)

[242] Cf. Vatican Council II, Declaration on Church's Relations with Non-Christian Religions *Nostra Aetate* (October 28, 1965), 2, 3.

# Saint Pope Paul VI

The Holy Spirit raises up therein a filial prayer that springs forth from the depths of the soul and is expressed in praise, thanksgiving, reparation and supplication. Then we can experience joy which is properly spiritual, the joy which is a fruit of the Holy Spirit.[243] It consists in the human spirit's finding repose and a deep satisfaction in the possession of the Triune God, known by faith and loved with the charity that comes from Him. Such a joy henceforth characterizes all the Christian virtues.

—*Gaudete in Domino*, III (May 9, 1975)

Joy is the result of a human-divine communion, and aspires to a communion ever more universal. In no way can it encourage the person who enjoys it to have an attitude of preoccupation with self. Joy gives the heart a catholic openness to the world of people, at the same time that it wounds the heart with a longing for eternal bliss. Among the fervent, joy deepens their awareness of being exiles, but it guards them from the temptation to desert the place of their combat for the coming of the kingdom. It makes them hasten actively towards the heavenly consummation of the nuptials of the Lamb.

—*Gaudete in Domino*, IV (May 9, 1975)

Our soul is filled with great joy as We contemplate your belief in the Eucharist, which is ours as well, as we listen to the liturgical prayers you use to celebrate this great mystery, as we behold your Eucharistic devotion, as we read your theological works explaining or defending the doctrine of this most sacred Sacrament.

—*Mysterium Fidei*, 74 (September 3, 1965)

We are pleased to dedicate more expressly to you, the young Christians of the present day, the promise of the Church of tomorrow,

---

[243] Cf. Rom. 14:17; Gal. 5:22.

# Joy

this celebration of spiritual joy. We cordially urge you to be attentive to the inner appeals which come to you. We urge you to raise up your eyes, your hearts, your fresh energies, to the heights, to accept the effort of the soul's yearnings. And we wish to give you this assurance: however debilitating the prejudice diffused everywhere today, of the human spirit's inability to discover permanent and life-giving Truth, equally profound and liberating is the joy of divine Truth finally recognized in the Church: *gaudium de Veritate*.[244] This is the joy which is offered to you.

—*Gaudete in Domino*, VI (May 9, 1975)

Contemplated in the episodes of the Gospels and in the reality which she already possesses in the City of God, the Blessed Virgin Mary offers a calm vision and a reassuring word to modern man, torn as he often is between anguish and hope, defeated by the sense of his own limitations and assailed by limitless aspirations, troubled in his mind and divided in his heart, uncertain before the riddle of death, oppressed by loneliness while yearning for fellowship, a prey to boredom and disgust. She shows forth the victory of hope over anguish, of fellowship over solitude, of peace over anxiety, of joy and beauty over boredom and disgust, of eternal visions over earthly ones, of life over death.

—*Marialis Cultus*, 57 (February 2, 1974)

In the life of the Church's sons and daughters, this sharing in the joy of the Lord cannot be dissociated from the celebration of the Eucharistic mystery, at which they are nourished with His Body and Blood. For being thus sustained like travelers, on the road to eternity, they already receive sacramentally the first fruits of eschatological joy.

—*Gaudete in Domino*, IV (May 9, 1975)

[244] St. Augustine, *Confessions*, X, 23.

# Saint Pope Paul VI

As the kernel and center of His Good News, Christ proclaims salvation, this great gift of God which is liberation from everything that oppresses man but which is above all liberation from sin and the Evil One, in the joy of knowing God and being known by Him, of seeing Him, and of being given over to Him.

—*Evangelii Nuntiandi*, 9 (December 8, 1975)

There is also needed a patient effort to teach people, or teach them once more, how to savor in a simple way the many human joys that the Creator places in our path: the elating joy of existence and of life; the joy of chaste and sanctified love; the peaceful joy of nature and silence; the sometimes austere joy of work well done; the joy and satisfaction of duty performed; the transparent joy of purity, service and sharing; the demanding joy of sacrifice. The Christian will be able to purify, complete and sublimate these joys; he will not be able to disdain them. Christian joy presupposes a person capable of natural joy. These natural joys were often used by Christ as a starting point when He proclaimed the kingdom of God.

—*Gaudete in Domino*, I (May 9, 1975)

## Chapter 9

# Marriage, Life, and Family

At the time of Paul's election in 1963, the culture of the West was accelerating toward the embrace of the sexual revolution, widespread contraception, and abortion on demand. The fathers of the Second Vatican Council understood this and, with the support of the pope, issued the Pastoral Constitution on the Church in the Modern World *Gaudium et Spes*, with its stern call to combat threats to family and the sanctity of life.

Those threats emerged as one of the most pressing concerns of Paul's pontificate, exemplified by the immense pressure placed upon him and the Church by the media, many dissenting theologians, and a culture awash in the sexual revolution to abandon the Church's consistent teaching on contraception, marriage, and the human person. Paul's most important response to this demand was his courageous decision to issue the encyclical *Humanae Vitae* in 1968, reaffirming for a new era the Church's teachings on contraception and authentic motherhood and fatherhood.

He was excoriated for the encyclical, but he never stopped talking about the importance of defending life, promoting marriage, and helping the family in the face of modernity. In fact, Pope Paul used his homily for the feast of Sts. Peter and Paul—one of his last public appearances—for a final declaration on the essential relationship between defending life and defending the Faith.

Twenty-five years after the encyclical was issued, one of the greatest experts on *Humanae Vitae*, Dr. Janet Smith, wrote that Paul had made four major prophecies about the consequences of ignoring the wisdom of the Church's teachings: the rise of infidelity; the loss of respect for women; the abuse of power by public authorities; and the mistaken belief that humanity has unlimited dominion over the body. And she observed just how right he had been.

Now, fifty years after the encyclical was written, we continue to see that Pope Paul was truly a prophet in his time, and for ours.

\* \* \*

Matrimony, according to the will of God, continues the work of the first creation;[245] and considered within the total plan of salvation, it even acquired a new meaning and a new value. Jesus, in fact, has restored its original dignity,[246] has honored it[247] and has raised it to the dignity of a sacrament and of a mysterious symbol of His own union with the Church.[248] Thus, Christian couples walk together toward their heavenly fatherland in the exercise of mutual love, in the fulfillment of their particular obligations, and in striving for the sanctity proper to them.

—*Sacerdotalis Caelibatus*, 20 (June 24, 1967)

Though it is true that sometimes it is lawful to tolerate a lesser moral evil in order to avoid a greater evil or in order to promote a greater good, it is never lawful, even for the gravest reasons, to do evil that good may come of it[249]—in other words, to intend directly

---

[245] See Gen. 2:18.
[246] See Matt. 19:3–8.
[247] See John 2:1–11.
[248] See Eph. 5:32.
[249] See Rom. 3:8.

something which of its very nature contradicts the moral order, and which must therefore be judged unworthy of man, even though the intention is to protect or promote the welfare of an individual, of a family or of society in general. Consequently, it is a serious error to think that a whole married life of otherwise normal relations can justify sexual intercourse which is deliberately contraceptive and so intrinsically wrong.

—*Humanae Vitae*, 14 (July 25, 1968)

We are deeply distressed by what happens to many of these young people. They come to wealthier nations to acquire scientific knowledge, professional training, and a high-quality education that will enable them to serve their own land with greater effectiveness. They do get a fine education, but very often they lose their respect for the priceless cultural heritage of their native land.

—*Populorum Progressio*, 68 (March 26, 1967)

In humble obedience then to her voice, let Christian husbands and wives be mindful of their vocation to the Christian life, a vocation which, deriving from their Baptism, has been confirmed anew and made more explicit by the Sacrament of Matrimony. For by this sacrament they are strengthened and, one might almost say, consecrated to the faithful fulfillment of their duties.

—*Humanae Vitae*, 25 (July 25, 1968)

Peace and Life. They are supreme values in the civil order. They are also values that are interdependent. Do we want Peace? Then let us defend Life!

—Message for the Day of Peace (January 1, 1977)

In preserving intact the whole moral law of marriage, the Church is convinced that she is contributing to the creation of a truly human civilization. She urges man not to betray his personal responsibilities by putting all his faith in technical expedients. In this way she defends the dignity of husband and wife. . . .

The Church, in fact, cannot act differently toward men than did the Redeemer. She knows their weaknesses, she has compassion on the multitude, she welcomes sinners. But at the same time she cannot do otherwise than teach the law. For it is in fact the law of human life restored to its native truth and guided by the Spirit of God.[250]

—*Humanae Vitae*, 18, 19 (July 25, 1968)

Man is not really himself, however, except within the framework of society and there the family plays the basic and most important role. The family's influence may have been excessive at some periods of history and in some places, to the extent that it was exercised to the detriment of the fundamental rights of the individual. Yet time honored social frameworks, proper to the developing nations, are still necessary for a while, even as their excessive strictures are gradually relaxed. The natural family, stable and monogamous—as fashioned by God[251] and sanctified by Christianity—"in which different generations live together, helping each other to acquire greater wisdom and to harmonize personal rights with other social needs, is the basis of society."[252]

—*Populorum Progressio*, 36 (March 26, 1967)

Not much experience is needed to be fully aware of human weakness and to understand that human beings—and especially the young, who are so exposed to temptation—need incentives to

---

[250] See Rom. 8.
[251] Cf. Matt. 19:6.
[252] *Gaudium et Spes*, 52.

keep the moral law, and it is an evil thing to make it easy for them to break that law. Another effect that gives cause for alarm is that a man who grows accustomed to the use of contraceptive methods may forget the reverence due to a woman, and, disregarding her physical and emotional equilibrium, reduce her to being a mere instrument for the satisfaction of his own desires, no longer considering her as his partner whom he should surround with care and affection.

—*Humanae Vitae*, 17 (July 25, 1968)

The phrase "Peace and Life" may seem almost tautological, a rhetorical slogan. It is not so. The combination of the two terms in the phrase represents a hard won conquest in the onward march of human progress—a march still short of its final goal. How many times in the drama of human history the phrase "Peace and Life" has involved a fierce struggle of the two terms, not a fraternal embrace. Peace is sought and won through conflict, like a sad doom necessary for self-defense.

—Message for the Day of Peace (January 1, 1977)

Disregard for the sacred character of life in the womb weakens the very fabric of civilization; it prepares a mentality, and even a public attitude, that can lead to the acceptance of other practices that are against the fundamental rights of the individual. This mentality can, for example, completely undermine concern for those in want, manifesting itself in insensitivity to social needs; it can produce contempt for the elderly, to the point of advocating euthanasia; it can prepare the way for those forms of genetic engineering that go against life, the dangers of which are not yet fully known to the general public.

—Address to the bishops of the United States on their Ad Limina Visit (May 26, 1978)

# Saint Pope Paul VI

Married love is also faithful and exclusive of all other, and this until death. This is how husband and wife understood it on the day on which, fully aware of what they were doing, they freely vowed themselves to one another in marriage. Though this fidelity of husband and wife sometimes presents difficulties, no one has the right to assert that it is impossible; it is, on the contrary, always honorable and meritorious. The example of countless married couples proves not only that fidelity is in accord with the nature of marriage, but also that it is the source of profound and enduring happiness.

—*Humanae Vitae*, 9 (July 25, 1968)

The close relationship between Peace and Life seems to spring from the nature of things, but not always, not yet from the logic of people's thought and conduct.

—Message for the Day of Peace (January 1, 1977)

With regard to physical, economic, psychological and social conditions, responsible parenthood is exercised by those who prudently and generously decide to have more children, and by those who, for serious reasons and with due respect to moral precepts, decide not to have additional children for either a certain or an indefinite period of time.

—*Humanae Vitae*, 10 (July 25, 1968)

In particular, every contribution made to better the moral climate of society, to oppose permissiveness and hedonism, and all assistance to the family, which is the source of new life, effectively uphold the values of life. We know that, in conjunction with the tenth anniversary of "*Humanae Vitae*," various initiatives are being sponsored throughout your country to explain natural family planning, in accordance with the teaching of the Church. These activities honor life directly in the dignity and importance of its origin. In supporting natural family planning programs, the Church gives witness not only to her fidelity to the design of the Creator, but also to her faithful service to the human person.

—Address to the bishops of the United States on
their Ad Limina Visit (May 26, 1978)

Accordingly we cannot fail to disapprove of each and every offence against nascent life, and we must appeal to every Authority, and to everyone who has due competence, to work for the prohibition of procured abortion and for its remedy. The mother's womb and the child's cradle are the first barriers that not only protect Peace as well as Life but also build Peace.[253] The one who chooses Peace in opposition to war and to violence automatically chooses Life and chooses humanity in its profound essential demands; and this is the meaning of this Message that we are again sending with humble yet ardent conviction to those accountable for Peace on earth, and to all our Brethren in the world.

—Message for the Day of Peace (January 1, 1978)

Peace and Life can in practice be dissociated, there looms on the horizon of the future a catastrophe that in our days could be immeasurable and irreparable both for Peace and Life. Hiroshima is a terribly eloquent proof and a frighteningly prophetic example of this. In the reprehensible hypothesis that Peace were thought of in unnatural separation from its relationship with Life, Peace could be imposed as the sad triumph of death.

—Message for the Day of Peace (January 1, 1977)

Just as man does not have unlimited dominion over his body in general, so also, and with more particular reason, he has no such

[253] Cf. Ps. 127:3ff.

dominion over his specifically sexual faculties, for these are concerned by their very nature with the generation of life, of which God is the source.

—*Humanae Vitae*, 13 (July 25, 1968)

The intelligence, especially that of children and young people, needs to learn through systematic religious instruction the fundamental teachings, the living content of the truth which God has wished to convey to us and which the Church has sought to express in an ever richer fashion during the course of her long history. No one will deny that this instruction must be given to form patterns of Christian living and not to remain only notional.

—*Evangelii Nuntiandi*, 44 (December 8, 1975)

The formula is: "If you want Peace, defend Life." Life is the crown of Peace. If we base the logic of our activity on the sacredness of Life, war is virtually disqualified as a normal and habitual means of asserting rights and so of ensuring Peace. Peace is but the incontestable ascendancy of right and, in the final analysis, the joyful celebration of Life.

—Message for the Day of Peace (January 1, 1977)

If therefore there are well-grounded reasons for spacing births, arising from the physical or psychological condition of husband or wife, or from external circumstances, the Church teaches that married people may then take advantage of the natural cycles immanent in the reproductive system and engage in marital intercourse only during those times that are infertile, thus controlling birth in a way which does not in the least offend the moral principles.[254]

—*Humanae Vitae*, 16 (July 25, 1968)

[254] See Pius XII, address to midwives.

# Marriage, Life, and Family

It seems to us in fact that the present world crisis, which is marked by a great confusion among many young people, partly betrays a senile and definitely out-of-date aspect of a commercial, hedonistic and materialistic civilization which is still trying to present itself as the gateway to the future. Even in its very excesses, the instinctive reaction of many young people against this illusion takes on a certain importance. This generation is waiting for something else.

—*Gaudete in Domino*, VI (May 9, 1975)

Peace and Life support enormous and incalculable burdens in order to maintain a Peace founded on a perpetual threat to Life, as also to defend Life by means of a constant threat to Peace. People will say: it is inevitable. This can be true within a concept of civilization that is still so imperfect. But let us at least recognize that this constitutional challenge which the arms race sets up between Life and Peace is a formula that is fallacious in itself and which must be corrected and superseded.

—Message for the Day of Peace (January 1, 1977)

But it is not only war that kills Peace. Every crime against life is a blow to Peace, especially if it strikes at the moral conduct of the people, as often happens today, with horrible and often legal ease, as in the case of the suppression of incipient life, by abortion. The suppression of an incipient life, or one that is already born, violates above all the sacrosanct moral principle to which the concept of human existence must always have reference: human life is sacred from the first moment of its conception and until the last instant of its natural survival in time. It is sacred; what does this mean? It means that life must be exempt from any arbitrary power to suppress it; it must not be touched; it is worthy of all respect, all care, all dutiful sacrifice.

—Message for the Day of Peace (January 1, 1977)

# Saint Pope Paul VI

Neither the Church nor her doctrine is inconsistent when she considers it lawful for married people to take advantage of the infertile period but condemns as always unlawful the use of means which directly prevent conception, even when the reasons given for the later practice may appear to be upright and serious. In reality, these two cases are completely different. In the former the married couple rightly use a faculty provided them by nature. In the later they obstruct the natural development of the generative process.

—*Humanae Vitae*, 16 (July 25, 1968)

In the task of development man finds the family to be the first and most basic social structure; but he is often helped by professional organizations. While such organizations are founded to aid and assist their members, they bear a heavy responsibility for the task of education which they can and must carry out. In training and developing individual men, they do much to cultivate in them an awareness of the common good and of its demands upon all.

—*Populorum Progressio*, 38 (March 26, 1967)

The question of human procreation, like every other question which touches human life, involves more than the limited aspects specific to such disciplines as biology, psychology, demography or sociology. It is the whole man and the whole mission to which he is called that must be considered: both its natural, earthly aspects and its supernatural, eternal aspects.

—*Humanae Vitae*, 7 (July 25, 1968)

We have no less trust in the ministry that has given rise to human life, the ministry of parenthood, in the first place that of motherhood. How delicate, how tender, how affectionate and how strong our words become! Over this field of nascent life Peace spreads

its first protecting shield. It is a shield endowed with the softest
protection, but a shield of defence and love.

—Message for the Day of Peace (January 1, 1978)

Married love particularly reveals its true nature and nobility when
we realize that it takes its origin from God....

Marriage, then, is far from being the effect of chance or the
result of the blind evolution of natural forces. It is in reality the
wise and provident institution of God the Creator, whose purpose
was to effect in man His loving design. As a consequence, husband
and wife, through that mutual gift of themselves, which is specific
and exclusive to them alone, develop that union of two persons
in which they perfect one another, cooperating with God in the
generation and rearing of new lives.

The marriage of those who have been baptized is, in addition,
invested with the dignity of a sacramental sign of grace, for it represents the union of Christ and His Church.

—*Humanae Vitae*, 8 (July 25, 1968)

It is a love which is total—that very special form of personal
friendship in which husband and wife generously share everything,
allowing no unreasonable exceptions and not thinking solely of
their own convenience. Whoever really loves his partner loves not
only for what he receives, but loves that partner for the partner's
own sake, content to be able to enrich the other with the gift of
himself.

—*Humanae Vitae*, 9 (July 25, 1968)

How is it possible to think that a father or a mother will have the
hope of a new and more just society, when a totalitarian ideological education is privileged in schools, and when it is difficult for
families, even in the privacy of the home, to communicate to

their children the values of the spirit which are the foundation of life?

—Address to the Diplomatic Corps (January 14, 1978)

Responsible parenthood, as we use the term here, has one further essential aspect of paramount importance. It concerns the objective moral order which was established by God, and of which a right conscience is the true interpreter. In a word, the exercise of responsible parenthood requires that husband and wife, keeping a right order of priorities, recognize their own duties toward God, themselves, their families and human society.

From this it follows that they are not free to act as they choose in the service of transmitting life, as if it were wholly up to them to decide what is the right course to follow. On the contrary, they are bound to ensure that what they do corresponds to the will of God the Creator. The very nature of marriage and its use makes His will clear, while the constant teaching of the Church spells it out.[255]

—*Humanae Vitae*, 10 (July 25, 1968)

The sexual activity, in which husband and wife are intimately and chastely united with one another, through which human life is transmitted, is, as the recent Council recalled, "noble and worthy."[256] It does not, moreover, cease to be legitimate even when, for reasons independent of their will, it is foreseen to be infertile. For its natural adaptation to the expression and strengthening of the union of husband and wife is not thereby suppressed. The fact is, as experience shows, that new life is not the result of each and every act of sexual intercourse. God has wisely ordered laws of

[255] See *Gaudium et Spes*, 50–51.
[256] See Ibid., 49.

nature and the incidence of fertility in such a way that successive births are already naturally spaced through the inherent operation of these laws. The Church, nevertheless, in urging men to the observance of the precepts of the natural law, which it interprets by its constant doctrine, teaches that each and every marital act must of necessity retain its intrinsic relationship to the procreation of human life.[257]

—*Humanae Vitae*, 11 (July 25, 1968)

The fundamental nature of the marriage act, while uniting husband and wife in the closest intimacy, also renders them capable of generating new life—and this as a result of laws written into the actual nature of man and of woman. And if each of these essential qualities, the unitive and the procreative, is preserved, the use of marriage fully retains its sense of true mutual love and its ordination to the supreme responsibility of parenthood to which man is called. We believe that our contemporaries are particularly capable of seeing that this teaching is in harmony with human reason.

—*Humanae Vitae*, 12 (July 25, 1968)

Men rightly observe that a conjugal act imposed on one's partner without regard to his or her condition or personal and reasonable wishes in the matter, is no true act of love, and therefore offends the moral order in its particular application to the intimate relationship of husband and wife. If they further reflect, they must also recognize that an act of mutual love which impairs the capacity to transmit life which God the Creator, through specific laws, has built into it, frustrates His design which constitutes the norm of

---

[257] See Pius XI, *Casti Connubii*; Pius XII, address to midwives.

marriage, and contradicts the will of the Author of life. Hence to use this divine gift while depriving it, even if only partially, of its meaning and purpose, is equally repugnant to the nature of man and of woman, and is consequently in opposition to the plan of God and His holy will.

—*Humanae Vitae*, 13 (July 25, 1968)

The transmission of human life is a most serious role in which married people collaborate freely and responsibly with God the Creator. It has always been a source of great joy to them, even though it sometimes entails many difficulties and hardships.

The fulfillment of this duty has always posed problems to the conscience of married people, but the recent course of human society and the concomitant changes have provoked new questions. The Church cannot ignore these questions, for they concern matters intimately connected with the life and happiness of human beings.

—*Humanae Vitae*, 1 (July 25, 1968)

Unless we are willing that the responsibility of procreating life should be left to the arbitrary decision of men, we must accept that there are certain limits, beyond which it is wrong to go, to the power of man over his own body and its natural functions—limits, let it be said, which no one, whether as a private individual or as a public authority, can lawfully exceed.

—*Humanae Vitae*, 17 (July 25, 1968)

Young people, in particular, must be given a warm reception; more and more families and hostels must open their doors to them. This must be done, first of all, that they may be shielded from feelings of loneliness, distress and despair that would sap their strength. It is also necessary so that they may be guarded against the corrupting influence of their new surroundings, where the contrast between the dire poverty of their homeland and the lavish luxury of their present surroundings is, as it were, forced upon them. And finally, it must be done so that they may be protected from subversive notions and temptations to violence, which gain headway in their minds when they ponder their "wretched plight."[258] In short, they should be welcomed in the spirit of brotherly love, so that the concrete example of wholesome living may give them a high opinion of authentic Christian charity and of spiritual values.

—*Populorum Progressio*, 67 (March 26, 1967)

Since the Church did not make either of these laws, she cannot be their arbiter—only their guardian and interpreter. It could never be right for her to declare lawful what is in fact unlawful, since that, by its very nature, is always opposed to the true good of man.

—*Humanae Vitae*, 18 (1968)

The teaching of the Church regarding the proper regulation of birth is a promulgation of the law of God Himself. And yet there is no doubt that to many it will appear not merely difficult but even impossible to observe. Now it is true that like all good things which are outstanding for their nobility and for the benefits which they confer on men, so this law demands from individual men and women, from families and from human society, a resolute purpose and great endurance.

—*Humanae Vitae*, 20 (July 25, 1968)

Every crime against life is an attack on peace, especially if it strikes at the moral conduct of people.... But where human rights are truly

[258] Cf. Leo XIII, encyclical letter *Rerum Novarum* (May 15, 1891).

professed and publicly recognized and defended, peace becomes the joyful and operative climate of life in society.

—Message for the Day of Peace (January 1, 1977)

Self-discipline of this kind is a shining witness to the chastity of husband and wife and, far from being a hindrance to their love of one another, transforms it by giving it a more truly human character. And if this self-discipline does demand that they persevere in their purpose and efforts, it has at the same time the salutary effect of enabling husband and wife to develop to their personalities and to be enriched with spiritual blessings. For it brings to family life abundant fruits of tranquility and peace. It helps in solving difficulties of other kinds. It fosters in husband and wife thoughtfulness and loving consideration for one another. It helps them to repel inordinate self-love, which is the opposite of charity. It arouses in them a consciousness of their responsibilities. And finally, it confers upon parents a deeper and more effective influence in the education of their children. As their children grow up, they develop a right sense of values and achieve a serene and harmonious use of their mental and physical powers.

—*Humanae Vitae*, 21 (July 25, 1968)

Among the fruits that ripen if the law of God be resolutely obeyed, the most precious is certainly this, that married couples themselves will often desire to communicate their own experience to others. Thus it comes about that in the fullness of the lay vocation will be included a novel and outstanding form of the apostolate by which, like ministering to like, married couples themselves by the leadership they offer will become apostles to other married couples.

—*Humanae Vitae*, 26 (July 25, 1968)

We are convinced, moreover, that all efforts made to safeguard human rights actually benefit life itself. Everything aimed at banishing discrimination—in law or in fact—which is based on "race, origin, color, culture, sex or religion"[259] is a service to life. When the rights of minorities are fostered, when the mentally or physically handicapped are assisted, when those on the margin of society are given a voice—in all these instances the dignity of human life, the fullness of human life, and the sacredness of human life are furthered.

—Address to the bishops of the United States on
their Ad Limina Visit (May 26, 1978)

We are speaking especially to you who teach moral theology—to spell out clearly and completely the Church's teaching on marriage. In the performance of your ministry you must be the first to give an example of that sincere obedience, inward as well as outward, which is due to the magisterium of the Church.

—*Humanae Vitae*, 28 (July 25, 1968)

Husbands and wives, therefore, when deeply distressed by reason of the difficulties of their life, must find stamped in the heart and voice of their priest the likeness of the voice and the love of our Redeemer.

So speak with full confidence, beloved sons, convinced that while the Holy Spirit of God is present to the magisterium proclaiming sound doctrine, He also illumines from within the hearts of the faithful and invites their assent. Teach married couples the necessary way of prayer and prepare them to approach more often with great faith the Sacraments of the Eucharist and of Penance. Let them never lose heart because of their weakness.

—*Humanae Vitae*, 29 (July 25, 1968)

[259] Paul VI, Apostolic Letter *Octogesima Adveniens* (May 14, 1971), 16.

# Saint Pope Paul VI

The right and lawful ordering of birth demands, first of all, that spouses fully recognize and value the true blessings of family life and that they acquire complete mastery over themselves and their emotions. For if with the aid of reason and of free will they are to control their natural drives, there can be no doubt at all of the need for self-denial. Only then will the expression of love, essential to married life, conform to right order.

—*Humanae Vitae*, 21 (July 25, 1968)

## Chapter 10

# The Human Person

The lifetime of Pope Paul VI—from 1897 to 1978—spanned one of the most painful centuries in human history, including two world wars, the Great Depression, the rise of the Soviet Empire and Nazi Germany, the Cold and Vietnam Wars, the Arab-Israeli conflict, and the immense social, religious, political, and cultural upheavals that transformed society. All of these directly impacted global civilization, but Paul was especially preoccupied with their devastating consequences for the human person and how we think about what it means to be human.

The Second Vatican Council reflected upon the human person in a number of documents—in particular, the Pastoral Constitution on the Church in the Modern World *Gaudium et Spes*. This was not the last word of Paul's pontificate, however, on the human person in the modern world.

Grounded in the Church's intertwined social and moral teachings, Paul discussed the importance of human dignity, the threats of atheism, secularism, and materialism, and the ruinous fruits of the sexual revolution. In his teachings, he anticipated Popes John Paul II, Benedict XVI, and Francis by making lasting contributions to the papal Magisterium with such documents as *Humanae Vitae* and *Populorum Progressio*.

# Saint Pope Paul VI

In an analysis of both *Humanae Vitae* and *Populorum Progressio* in *Crisis Magazine* in 2017, "Paul VI and the Unexpected Lessons of *Populorum Progressio*," Samuel Gregg concluded,

> The vision underpinning *Humanae Vitae* is one of human beings capable of transcending mediocrity, despite our weaknesses and propensity to sin. Few, however, have noted that *Populorum Progressio* articulated precisely the same vision of the person and the flourishing to which we are all called.
>
> The language used by Paul to describe this was that of "self-fulfillment" and "self-development." But fulfillment, according to Paul, wasn't whatever you feel it to be. Man, he stated, is "endowed with intellect and free will" and thus able to "perfect himself." Hence, as a "rational creature" a person can "of his own accord direct his life to God, the first truth and the highest good." Through "this harmonious integration of our human nature" people can realize "a higher state of perfection," one which "bestows new fullness of life." That's one reason why the Church's moral teaching is no mere ideal. It is the way that leads to true life.[260]

This was especially crucial to Paul's frequent declarations against atheism. He presciently saw that atheism and secularism were dire threats not only to faith but also to human flourishing, broadly understood. He defended religious liberty, but he was also extremely blunt—notably for the ever-diplomatic Paul—in assailing the emptiness of the atheist project. "Atheism," he wrote in his encyclical *Ecclesiam Suam*, "is not a liberating force, but a catastrophic one, for it seeks to quench the light of the living God. We shall

---

[260] Samuel Gregg, "Paul VI and the Unexpected Lessons of *Populorum Progressio*," *Crisis Magazine*, March 3, 2017, https://www.crisismaga-zine.com/2017/paul-vi-unexpected-lessons-populorum-progressio.

therefore resist this growing evil with all our strength."[261] For all those caught up today in trendy flirtations with atheist materialism, Paul needs to be heard.

* * *

Racial discrimination possesses at the moment a character of very great relevance by reason of the tension which it stirs up both within countries and on the international level. Men rightly consider unjustifiable and reject as inadmissible the tendency to maintain or introduce legislation or behavior systematically inspired by racialist prejudice. The members of mankind share the same basic rights and duties, as well as the same supernatural destiny. Within a country which belongs to each one, all should be equal before the law, find equal admittance to economic, cultural, civic and social life and benefit from a fair sharing of the nation's riches.

—*Octogesima Adveniens*, 16 (May 14, 1971)

The atheistic political scientist willfully stops short at a certain point in this inevitable process of reasoning, and in doing so shuts out the supreme light which gives intelligibility to the universe. Is there no one among us who could help him to arrive at last at the realization of the objective reality of the cosmic universe which confronts the mind with the presence of God and brings to the lips a healing prayer of tearful humility?

—*Ecclesiam Suam*, 104 (August 6, 1964)

Amid the disturbances and uncertainties of the present hour, the Church has a specific message to proclaim and a support to give to men in their efforts to take in hand and give direction to their future.

—*Octogesima Adveniens*, 5 (May 14, 1971)

[261] *Ecclesiam Suam*, 100.

# Saint Pope Paul VI

Among the vast and complex set of themes which concern the rights of the human person, it seemed to us useful particularly to recall religious freedom, racial equality, and man's right to physical and psychical integrity. We were prompted to make this choice by the fact that these three values are set in the sphere of the relations between persons and the public authorities and today it happens, we have as listeners you, who represent the Governments of so many countries.

— Address to the Diplomatic Corps (January 14, 1978)

Our universal greeting goes out to you, men who do not know us, men who do not understand us, men who do not regard us as useful, necessary or friendly. This greeting goes also to you, men who, while perhaps thinking they are doing good, are opposed to us. A sincere greeting, and unassuming greeting but one filled with hope and, today, please believe that it is filled with esteem and love.

— Homily, closing of the Second
Vatican Council (December 8, 1965)

It is necessary to situate the problems created by the modern economy in the wider context of a new civilization. These problems include human conditions of production, fairness in the exchange of goods and in the division of wealth, the significance of the increased needs of consumption and the sharing of responsibility. In the present changes, which are so profound and so rapid, each day man discovers himself anew, and he questions himself about the meaning of his own being and of his collective survival. Reluctant to gather the lessons of a past that he considers over and done with and too different from the present, man nevertheless needs to have light shed upon his future — a future which he perceives to be as uncertain as it is changing — by permanent eternal truths. These are truths which are certainly greater than man but, if he so wills, he can himself find their traces.[262]

— *Octogesima Adveniens*, 7 (May 14, 1971)

This is our greeting. But please be attentive, you who are listening to us. We ask you to consider how our greeting, differently from what ordinarily happens in day to day conversation, would serve to terminate a relationship of nearness or discourse. Our greeting tends to strengthen and, if necessary, to produce a spiritual relationship whence it draws its meaning and its voice. Ours is a greeting, not of farewell which separates, but of friendship which remains, and which, if so demanded, wishes to be born. It is even precisely in this last expression that our greeting, on the one hand, would desire to reach the heart of every man, to enter therein as a cordial guest and speak in the interior silence of your individual souls, the habitual and ineffable words of the Lord: "My peace I leave with you, my peace I give unto you, but not as the world gives it."[263]

— Homily, closing of the Second
Vatican Council (December 8, 1965)

To arrive at certainty about that ineffable and sovereign existence, it is sufficient, as We have said, to think well. We have a guarantee of that from the First Vatican Council which, summarizing the age-long doctrine of the Church and, We may add, of human philosophy, affirms that "God, beginning and end of all things, can be known with certainty by the natural light of reason through the medium of things created."[264] Why then do so many men, even learned ones, maintain the contrary? Because, We reply, they

[262] Cf. 2 Cor. 4:17.
[263] John 14:27.
[264] Dz.-Sch., 3004.

do not use their minds in accordance with the authentic laws of thought in the search of truth.

—General Audience (June 12, 1968)

People talk and discuss a great deal today about the rights of man. They do so passionately, sometimes angrily, nearly always with a view to greater justice, real or presumed. Not all these claims seem reasonable or feasible, for they are sometimes inspired by individualisms, enthusiasms or anarchical utopia; some are even inadmissible on the moral plane. But, on the whole, as aspiration and straining towards a higher hope, this increased concern for an extent of freedom and responsibility more favorable to the person is a positive fact which must be encouraged. The Church follows it and wishes to continue to follow it with sympathy, while bringing to it, in line with her own mission, the necessary light and clarifications.

—Address to the Diplomatic Corps (January 14, 1978)

Similarly, in many countries a charter for women which would put an end to an actual discrimination and would establish relationships of equality in rights and of respect for their dignity is the object of study and at times of lively demands. We do not have in mind that false equality which would deny the distinction with woman's proper role, which is of such capital importance, at the heart of the family as well as within society. Developments in legislation should on the contrary be directed to protecting her proper vocation and at the same time recognizing her independence as a person, and her equal rights to participate in cultural, economic, social and political life.

—*Octogesima Adveniens*, 13 (May 14, 1971)

For those who believe in God, all human beings, even the least privileged, are sons of the universal Father who created them in his image and guides their destinies with thoughtful love. The father-hood of God means brotherhood among men: this is a strong point of Christian universalism, a common point, too, with other great religions and an axiom of the highest human wisdom of all times, that which involves the promotion of man's dignity.

—Address to the Diplomatic Corps (January 14, 1978)

Though We speak firmly and clearly in defense of religion, and of those human, spiritual values which it proclaims and cherishes, Our pastoral solicitude nevertheless prompts Us to probe into the mind of the modern atheist, in an effort to understand the reasons for his mental turmoil and his denial of God. They are obviously many and complex, and we must come to a prudent decision about them, and answer them effectively. They sometimes spring from the demand for a more profound and purer presentation of religious truth, and an objection to forms of language and worship which somehow fall short of the ideal. These things we must remedy. We must do all we can to purify them and make them express more adequately the sacred reality of which they are the signs.

—*Ecclesiam Suam*, 104 (August 6, 1964)

Egoism and domination are permanent temptations for men. Like-wise an ever finer discernment is needed, in order to strike at the roots of newly arising situations of injustice and to establish pro-gressively a justice which will be less and less imperfect. In indus-trial change, which demands speedy and constant adaptation, those who will find themselves injured will be more numerous and at a greater disadvantage from the point of view of making their voices heard. The Church directs her attention to those new "poor"—the handicapped and the maladjusted, the old, different groups of those on the fringe of society, and so on—in order to recognize them, help them; defend their place and dignity in a society hardened by competition and the attraction of success.

—*Octogesima Adveniens*, 15 (May 14, 1971)

For if We were to speak of "faith" as a true and supernatural knowledge of God, coming from his revelation, then our ordinary powers of thought are indeed necessary and to be used, but they are not enough. They have to be supported by a special help from God Himself, which we call grace. Faith is, in this case, a gift which God Himself grants us; it is that theological virtue which, even in the obscurity that must ever surround God, gives us the certainty and the enjoyment of so many truths about Him.

—General Audience (June 12, 1968)

Christians draw from the faith a particular moral force which commits them, at least as much and even more than others, in favour of a more just and more human society. This is beginning to be recognized even by those who, formerly, were in the habit of describing religious faith as a kind of escape from reality. It seems that one may then ask oneself: can a State fruitfully call for entire trust and collaboration while, by a kind of "negative confessionalism," it proclaims itself atheist and, while declaring that it respects, within a certain framework, individual beliefs, takes up a position against the faith of part of its citizens?

—Address to the Diplomatic Corps (January 14, 1978)

The Church is not identical with civilization. It does however promote it....

Sad to say, this vast circle comprises very many people who profess no religion at all. Many, too, subscribe to atheism in one of its many different forms. They parade their godlessness openly, asserting its claims in education and politics, in the foolish and fatal belief that they are emancipating mankind from false and outworn notions about life and the world and substituting a view that is scientific and up-to-date.

This is the most serious problem of our time.

—*Ecclesiam Suam*, 98, 99–100 (August 6, 1964)

Urban life and industrial change bring strongly to light questions which until now were poorly grasped. What place, for example, in this world being brought to birth, should be given to youth? Everywhere dialogue is proving to be difficult between youth, with its aspirations, renewal and also insecurity for the future, and the adult generations. It is obvious to all that here we have a source of serious conflicts, division and opting out, even within the family, and a questioning of modes of authority, education for freedom and the handing on of values and beliefs, which strikes at the deep roots of society.

—*Octogesima Adveniens*, 13 (May 14, 1971)

It is one thing to state that God exists; it would be another thing to state who He is. We can know with certainty the existence of God, but on the other hand we know always very imperfectly the essence of God, that is to say who He is.[265]

—General Audience (June 12, 1968)

For those who believe in God, human life is a gift that comes from him, a sacred trust which must be preserved in its integrity. The Church feels committed to teaching respect for it in every circumstance and in all stages of existence, from the moment of conception when life begins to form in the mother's womb, to the appointment with our "sister Death." From the cradle to the grave, every human

---

[265] Cf. St. Thomas Aquinas, *Summa contra Gentiles*, I, c. 14.

being, even the weakest and most under-privileged, derived or left aside, possesses an element of nobility which is the image of God and resemblance to him. And Jesus taught his disciples that his own Person is represented, particularly clearly, in the person of these poor people and these little ones.

—Address to the Diplomatic Corps (January 14, 1978)

Atheism, therefore, is not a liberating force, but a catastrophic one, for it seeks to quench the light of the living God. We shall therefore resist this growing evil with all our strength, spurred on by our great zeal for safeguarding the truth, inspired by our social duty of loyally professing Christ and His gospel, and driven on by a burning, unquenchable love, which makes man's good our constant concern. We shall resist in the invincible hope that modern man may recognize the religious ideals which the Catholic faith sets before him and feel himself drawn to seek a form of civilization which will never fail him but will lead on to the natural and supernatural perfection of the human spirit. May the grace of God enable him to possess his temporal goods in peace and honor and to live in the assurance of acquiring those that are eternal.

—*Ecclesiam Suam*, 100 (August 6, 1964)

We know that this is a serious statement to make; but such is the case. An endless discussion could be entered upon as to the duty and art of thinking well, in accordance with the requirements and criteria of true human wisdom and with the logic demanded by science itself and by the honest and correct mode of speech proper to common sense.

Religious thought along those lines, which seems so obvious and ingrained both in man's normal mind and in the relationship of truth which such a mind succeeds in establishing with things known, is today contested as an ingenuous and antiquated pretension, whereas it is and will always be the main path leading the human spirit unfailingly from the world of sense and science to the threshold of the divine world.

—General Audience (June 12, 1968)

It is for these reasons that We are driven to repudiate such ideologies as deny God and oppress the Church—We repudiate them as Our predecessors did, and as everyone must do who firmly believes in the excellence and importance of religion. These ideologies are often identified with economic, social and political regimes; atheistic communism is a glaring instance of this. Yet is it really so much we who condemn them? One might say that it is rather they and their politicians who are clearly repudiating us, and for doctrinaire reasons subjecting us to violent oppression. Truth to tell, the voice we raise against them is more the complaint of a victim than the sentence of a judge.

—*Ecclesiam Suam*, 101 (August 6, 1964)

Is not the rise of an urban civilization which accompanies the advance of industrial civilization a true challenge to the wisdom of man, to his capacity for organization and to his farseeing imagination? Within industrial society urbanization upsets both the ways of life and the habitual structures of existence: the family, the neighborhood, and the very framework of the Christian community. Man is experiencing a new loneliness; it is not in the face of a hostile nature which it has taken him centuries to subdue, but in an anonymous crowd which surrounds him and in which he feels himself a stranger.

—*Octogesima Adveniens*, 10 (May 14, 1971)

How could the Church fail to take up a stern stand as she did towards dueling and still does towards abortion, with regard to torture and to similar acts of violence inflicted on the human person? Those who order them or carry them out commit a crime, really a very serious one for Christian conscience which cannot fail to react and to do everything in its power to get adequate and effective remedies adopted.

—Address to the Diplomatic Corps (January 14, 1978)

There is an urgent need to remake at the level of the street, of the neighborhood or of the great agglomerative dwellings the social fabric whereby man may be able to develop the needs of his personality. Centers of special interest and of culture must be created or developed at the community and parish levels with different forms of associations, recreational centers, and spiritual and community gatherings where the individual can escape from isolation and form a new fraternal relationships.

—*Octogesima Adveniens*, 11 (May 14, 1971)

We are firmly convinced that the basic propositions of atheism are utterly false and irreconcilable with the underlying principles of thought. They strike at the genuine and effective foundation for man's acceptance of a rational order in the universe, and introduce into human life a futile kind of dogmatism which far from solving life's difficulties, only degrades it and saddens it. Any social system based on these principles is doomed to utter destruction.

—*Ecclesiam Suam*, 100 (August 6, 1964)

## Integral Development and the Human Person: *Populorum Progressio*

*Populorum Progressio* has proven a lasting source of papal insight because of its central theme of "integral development"—that is, the fulfillment not just of man's material needs but also of his spiritual needs. Pope Paul argued that the world needed a new humanism:

> If development calls for an ever-growing number of technical experts, even more necessary still is the deep thought and reflection of wise men in search of a new humanism, one which will enable our contemporaries to enjoy the higher values of love and friendship, of prayer and contemplation,[266] and thus find themselves. This is what will guarantee man's authentic development—his transition from less than human conditions to truly human ones. (20)

John Paul II used his 1987 encyclical *Sollicitudo Rei Socialis* to mark the twentieth anniversary of *Populorum Progressio*, and, in his turn, Pope Benedict used *Caritas in Veritate* in 2009 to study integral development.

My venerable predecessor Pope Paul VI illuminated the great theme of the development of peoples with the splendor of truth and the gentle light of Christ's charity. He taught that life in Christ is the first and principal factor of development[267] and he entrusted us with the task of travelling the path of development with all our heart and all our intelligence.[268] (8)

From the start of his pontificate, Pope Francis has included integral development as one of the key elements of his vision for Catholic Social Teaching. In a homily for a Mass celebrating the fiftieth anniversary of the encyclical, for example, Francis's Cardinal Secretary of State, Pietro Parolin, proclaimed:

---

[266] Cf., for example, J. Maritain, *Les conditions spintuelles du progrès et de la paix*, in the anthology *Rencontre des cultures à l'UNESCO sous le signe du Concile Oecuménique Vatican II* (Paris: Mame, 1966), p. 66.

[267] Cf. John XXIII, *Pacem in Terris*, 11.

[268] Cf. ibid., 82.

The treatment proposed by the Holy Father [Blessed Paul] also remains valid and timely: namely, a human development that is both "integral" and "fraternal." The Encyclical sets out the coordinates of an integral development of the human person and a fraternal development of humanity, two themes which can be considered as the axes around which the text is structured. Development consists in the passage from less humane living conditions to more humane living conditions: What are less than human conditions? The material poverty of those who lack the bare necessities of life, and the moral poverty of those who are crushed under the weight of their own self-love; oppressive political structures resulting from the abuse of ownership or the improper exercise of power, from the exploitation of the worker or unjust transactions.[269]

The following are excerpts from *Populorum Progressio*:

The progressive development of peoples is an object of deep interest and concern to the Church. This is particularly true in the case of those peoples who are trying to escape the ravages of hunger, poverty, endemic disease and ignorance; of those who are seeking a larger share in the benefits of civilization and a more active improvement of their human qualities; of those who are consciously striving for fuller growth....

The hungry nations of the world cry out to the peoples blessed with abundance. And the Church, cut to the quick by this cry, asks each and every man to hear his brother's plea and answer it lovingly. (1, 3)

[269] Quoted in Matthew Bunson, "'Populorum Progressio' at 50: Is It Still Relevant?" *National Catholic Register*, April 25, 2017, http://www.ncregister.com/daily-news/populorum-progressio-at-50-is-it-still-relevant.

# The Human Person

\* \* \*

Today we see men trying to secure a sure food supply, cures for diseases, and steady employment. We see them trying to eliminate every ill, to remove every obstacle which offends man's dignity. They are continually striving to exercise greater personal responsibility; to do more, learn more, and have more so that they might increase their personal worth. And yet, at the same time, a large number of them live amid conditions which frustrate these legitimate desires.

Moreover, traditional culture comes into conflict with the advanced techniques of modern industrialization; social structures out of tune with today's demands are threatened with extinction. For the older generation, the rigid structures of traditional culture are the necessary mainstay of one's personal and family life; they cannot be abandoned. The younger generation, on the other hand, regards them as useless obstacles, and rejects them to embrace new forms of societal life. (6)

\* \* \*

The conflict between generations leads to a tragic dilemma: either to preserve traditional beliefs and structures and reject social progress; or to embrace foreign technology and foreign culture, and reject ancestral traditions with their wealth of humanism. The sad fact is that we often see the older moral, spiritual and religious values give way without finding any place in the new scheme of things. (10)

\* \* \*

The Church, which has long experience in human affairs and has no desire to be involved in the political activities of any nation, "seeks but one goal: to carry forward the work of Christ under the lead of the befriending Spirit. And Christ entered this world to give witness to the truth; to save, not to judge; to serve, not to be served."[270] (13)

\* \* \*

The developing nations must choose wisely from among the things that are offered to them. They must test and reject false values that would tarnish a truly human way of life, while accepting noble and useful values in order to develop them in their own distinctive way, along with their own indigenous heritage. (41)

\* \* \*

It is also quite natural for nations with a long-standing cultural tradition to be proud of their traditional heritage. But this commendable attitude should be further ennobled by love, a love for the whole family of man. Haughty pride in one's own nation disunites nations and poses obstacles to their true welfare. It is especially harmful where the weak state of the economy calls for a pooling of information, efforts and financial resources to implement programs of development and to increase commercial and cultural interchange ... and Racism. (62)

\* \* \*

Racism is not the exclusive attribute of young nations, where sometimes it hides beneath the rivalries of clans and political parties, with heavy losses for justice and at the risk of civil war. (63)

\* \* \*

During the colonial period it often flared up between the colonists and the indigenous population, and stood in the way of mutually profitable understanding, often giving rise to bitterness in the wake of genuine injustices. It is still an obstacle to collaboration among

[270] Cf. *Gaudium et Spes*, 3.

disadvantaged nations and a cause of division and hatred within countries whenever individuals and families see the inviolable rights of the human person held in scorn, as they themselves are unjustly subjected to a regime of discrimination because of their race or their color. (63)

\* \* \*

The ultimate goal is a full-bodied humanism.[271] And does this not mean the fulfillment of the whole man and of every man? A narrow humanism, closed in on itself and not open to the values of the spirit and to God who is their source, could achieve apparent success, for man can set about organizing terrestrial realities without God. But "closed off from God, they will end up being directed against man. A humanism closed off from other realities becomes inhuman."[272] (42)

\* \* \*

True humanism points the way toward God and acknowledges the task to which we are called, the task which offers us the real meaning of human life. Man is not the ultimate measure of man. Man becomes truly man only by passing beyond himself. In the words of Pascal: "Man infinitely surpasses man."[273] (42)

\* \* \*

It is not just a question of eliminating hunger and reducing poverty. It is not just a question of fighting wretched conditions,

---

[271] Cf., for example, J. Maritain, *L'humanisme intégral* (Paris: Aubier, 1936). English trans., *True Humanism* (New York: Charles Scribner's Sons, 1938).

[272] Cf. H. de Lubac, S.J., *Le drame de l'humanisme athée*, 3rd ed. (Paris: Spes, 1945), 10. English trans., *The Drama of Atheistic Humanism* (London: Sheed and Ward, 1949), 7.

[273] *Pensées*, ed. Brunschvicg, 434; cf. Maurice Zundel, *L'homme passe l'home* (Le Caire: Editions du lien, 1944).

though this is an urgent and necessary task. It involves building a human community where men can live truly human lives, free from discrimination on account of race, religion or nationality, free from servitude to other men or to natural forces which they cannot yet control satisfactorily. It involves building a human community where liberty is not an idle word, where the needy Lazarus can sit down with the rich man at the same banquet table.[274] (47)

\* \* \*

Every country, rich or poor, has a cultural tradition handed down from past generations. This tradition includes institutions required by life in the world, and higher manifestations — artistic, intellectual and religious — of the life of the spirit. When the latter embody truly human values, it would be a great mistake to sacrifice them for the sake of the former. Any group of people who would consent to let this happen, would be giving up the better portion of their heritage; in order to live, they would be giving up their reason for living. Christ's question is directed to nations also: "What does it profit a man, if he gain the whole world but suffer the loss of his own soul?"[275] (40)

\* \* \*

At birth a human being possesses certain aptitudes and abilities in germinal form, and these qualities are to be cultivated so that they may bear fruit. By developing these traits through formal education or personal effort, the individual works his way toward the goal set for him by the Creator. (15)

---

[274] Cf. Luke 16:19–31.
[275] Matt. 16:26.

# The Human Person

\* \* \*

Endowed with intellect and free will, each man is responsible for his self-fulfillment even as he is for his salvation. He is helped, and sometimes hindered, by his teachers and those around him; yet whatever be the outside influences exerted on him, he is the chief architect of his own success or failure. Utilizing only his talent and willpower, each man can grow in humanity, enhance his personal worth, and perfect himself. (15)

\* \* \*

Self-development, however, is not left up to man's option. Just as the whole of creation is ordered toward its Creator, so too the rational creature should of his own accord direct his life to God, the first truth and the highest good. Thus human self-fulfillment may be said to sum up our obligations. (16)

\* \* \*

Moreover, this harmonious integration of our human nature, carried through by personal effort and responsible activity, is destined for a higher state of perfection. United with the life-giving Christ, man's life is newly enhanced; it acquires a transcendent humanism which surpasses its nature and bestows new fullness of life. This is the highest goal of human self-fulfillment. (16)

\* \* \*

Each man is also a member of society; hence he belongs to the community of man. It is not just certain individuals but all men who are called to further the development of human society as a whole. Civilizations spring up, flourish and die. As the waves of the sea gradually creep farther and farther in along the shoreline, so the human race inches its way forward through history. (17)

# Saint Pope Paul VI

\* \* \*

Neither individuals nor nations should regard the possession of more and more goods as the ultimate objective. Every kind of progress is a two-edged sword. It is necessary if man is to grow as a human being; yet it can also enslave him, if he comes to regard it as the supreme good and cannot look beyond it. When this happens, men harden their hearts, shut out others from their minds and gather together solely for reasons of self-interest rather than out of friendship; dissension and disunity follow soon after. (19)

\* \* \*

What are truly human conditions? The rise from poverty to the acquisition of life's necessities; the elimination of social ills; broadening the horizons of knowledge; acquiring refinement and culture. From there one can go on to acquire a growing awareness of other people's dignity, a taste for the spirit of poverty,[276] an active interest in the common good, and a desire for peace. Then man can acknowledge the highest values and God Himself, their author and end. Finally and above all, there is faith—God's gift to men of good will—and our loving unity in Christ, who calls all men to share God's life as sons of the living God, the Father of all men. (21)

\* \* \*

May the day come when international relationships will be characterized by respect and friendship, when mutual cooperation will be the hallmark of collaborative efforts, and when concerted effort for the betterment of all nations will be regarded as a duty by every nation. The developing nations now emerging are asking that they be allowed to take part in the construction of a better world,

[276] Cf. Matt. 5:3.

a world which would provide better protection for every man's rights and duties. It is certainly a legitimate demand, so everyone must heed and fulfill it. (65)

\* \* \*

Human society is sorely ill. The cause is not so much the depletion of natural resources, nor their monopolistic control by a privileged few; it is rather the weakening of brotherly ties between individuals and nations. (66)

\* \* \*

We cannot insist too much on the duty of giving foreigners a hospitable reception. It is a duty imposed by human solidarity and by Christian charity, and it is incumbent upon families and educational institutions in the host nations. (66)

# Saint Pope Paul VI

## PRAYER OF POPE PAUL VI FOR PRISONERS[277]

This prayer was composed by Pope Paul VI for the inmates of Rome's Regina Coeli prison as part of his visit in April 1964:

Lord, they tell me I must pray; but how can I pray when I am so unhappy? How can I speak to you in the conditions in which I find myself? I am sad; I am angry. Sometimes I am desperate. I would like to curse rather than pray. I suffer deeply because everyone is against me and criticizes me because I am here, away from my own family and from my activities. I am without peace, and how can I pray, O Lord?

I know you were good, you were wise, you were innocent. Yet they slandered you, they dishonored you, they tried you, they beat you, they crucified you, they put you to death? But why? Where is justice? And you were able to forgive those who treated you so unjustly and so cruelly. You were able to pray for them. Indeed, they tell me that you allowed yourself to be put to death in that manner in order to save your executioners, to save all us sinful men. And also to save me?

If this is so, Lord, it means that one may be good at heart even though the condemnation of the courts of men weighs on one's shoulders. I too, Lord, feel at the bottom of my heart that I am better than others would believe. I know what justice is, what honesty is, what honor is, and what goodness is. Before you,

---

[277] *Rituale Romanum* (Roman Ritual), 1964 edition, pt. XI, chap. III, 10.

these thoughts stir in me. Do you see them? Do you see how disgusted I am with my miseries? Do you see that I would like to cry out and weep? Do you understand me, Lord? Is this my prayer?

Yes, this is my prayer. From the depths of my bitterness I raise my voice to you. Do not reject it. You at least, who have suffered as I have, more than I have, you at least, Lord, listen to me. I have so many things to ask of you. Give me, Lord, peace of heart. Give me a tranquil conscience, a new conscience capable of good thoughts.

Indeed, Lord, to you I say it. If I have been remiss, forgive me. We all have need of forgiveness and mercy. I am praying to you for myself. And then, Lord, I pray to you for my loved ones, who are still so dear to me. Lord, assist them. Lord, console them. Lord, tell them to remember me and to love me still. I have so much need to know that somebody is still thinking of me and loves me. And also on these companions in misfortune and affliction, together here in this prison, Lord, have mercy. Mercy on everyone. Yes, also on those who make me suffer, on all. We are all men of this unhappy world. But we are, Lord, your creatures, your likeness, your brothers, O Christ. Have pity on us.

To our poor voice we add the sweet and innocent voice of the Madonna, of the most blessed Mary, who is your Mother, and who is for us also a Mother of intercession and consolation. Lord, give us your peace; give us hope. Amen.

*Chapter 11*

# The Modern World

The Second Vatican Council was convoked by Pope St. John XXIII to help the Church communicate the unchanging truths of the Faith to a world convulsed by traumatic change and upheaval in virtually every sphere of life. The Pastoral Constitution on the Church in the Modern World *Gaudium et Spes* had emerged from the very floor of the council and had been approved by Paul precisely because of his and the Church's abiding worry for the dignity of the human person within the specific context of modernity. The council had much to say to the modern world, and so did Paul.

In his many years in the Vatican, Paul had witnessed the efforts of the Holy See to assist humanity in the grips of world wars, the ascendancy of atheism, and the emergence of new, murderous ideologies—including national socialism and fascism and communism. As archbishop of Milan, he confronted the toxic allure of communists in the great city of the Italian north, which was long a hotbed of communist and Marxist ideology. He applied his pastoral zeal to preaching to the workers of the archdiocese that was, and remains, the largest in Europe to prevent their departure into the Marxist embrace.

As pope, he became a powerful and prophetic voice in an era of massive change and uncertainty, dedicating some of his most important teaching documents to articulating the Faith in new and profound ways in order to evangelize and transform the modern world.

In 1964, he issued the encyclical *Ecclesiam Suam*, which exclaimed, "We believe that it is a duty of the Church at the present time to strive toward a clearer and deeper awareness of itself and its mission in the world, and of the treasury of truth of which it is heir and custodian."[278] But he was also aware of the risks and problems facing Catholics in the modern era.

> As we know, the Church does not exist in isolation from the world. It lives in the world, and its members are consequently influenced and guided by the world. They imbibe its culture, are subject to its laws and adopt its customs. This intimate contact with the world is continually creating problems for the Church and at the present time these problems are extremely acute. (42)

In 1967, he released his contribution to Catholic social teaching, *Populorum Progressio*. The very next year he spoke powerfully to the world about married life, human sexuality, responsible parenthood, and the threats being posed by a contraceptive culture in the *Humanae Vitae*. He wrote, with great foresight,

> Who will blame a government which in its attempt to resolve the problems affecting an entire country resorts to the same measures as are regarded as lawful by married people in the solution of a particular family difficulty?... It could well happen, therefore, that when people, either individually or in family or social life, experience the inherent difficulties of the divine law and are determined to avoid them, they may give into the hands of public authorities the power to

[278] *Ecclesiam Suam*, 18.

intervene in the most personal and intimate responsibility of husband and wife. (17)

In 1974, Paul issued the apostolic exhortation *Evangelii Nuntiandi*, on evangelization in the modern world. It remains even in this new century a blueprint for proclaiming the gospel in the modern era and was a foundational document for the grand project of the New Evangelization that came into full flower under Popes St. John Paul II and Benedict XVI.

In *Evangelii Nuntiandi*, Paul addressed the phenomena of indifferentism and lukewarmness among the faithful, which is today—even more than it was forty years ago—a mounting crisis.

Today there is a very large number of baptized people who for the most part have not formally renounced their Baptism but who are entirely indifferent to it and not living in accordance with it ... the non-practicing Christians of today, more so than those of previous periods, seek to explain and justify their position in the name of an interior religion, of personal independence or authenticity. (56)

Of particular note is a 1971 apostolic letter, *Octogesima Adveniens*, on the eightieth anniversary of Pope Leo XIII's groundbreaking encyclical *Rerum Novarum*. The letter was addressed to Cardinal Maurice Roy, president of the Council of the Laity and of the Pontifical Commission for Justice and Peace.

The eightieth anniversary of the publication of the encyclical *Rerum Novarum*, the message of which continues to inspire action for social justice, prompts us to take up again and to extend the teaching of our predecessors, in response to the new needs of a changing world. The Church, in fact, travels forward with humanity and shares its lot in the setting of history. At the same time that she announces to men the Good News of God's love and of salvation in Christ she clarifies their activity in the light of the Gospel and in this way helps them to correspond to God's plan of love and to realize the fullness of their aspirations. (1)

An almost forgotten contribution to social teachings and Catholic political thought, Paul's letter reflected on a variety of the world's problems in 1971 that are just as urgent today: urbanization, the crises facing youth, the role of women, the rights of workers, the plight of immigrants, the influence of the media, and risks to the environment. These are all themes that have been picked up by subsequent popes.

Much as he did when he was in Milan, the pope spoke also of the allure of the false utopian visions of communism, atheism, bureaucratic socialism, and scientism as the answer to everything—as well as the dangers of unrestrained and dehumanizing forms of capitalism. Only the Church, Paul concluded, can provide answers to the problems of the modern world. "In the face of so many new questions," he writes in the apostolic letter, "the Church makes an effort to reflect in order to give an answer, in its own sphere, to men's expectations. If today the problems seem original in their breadth and their urgency, is man without the means of solving them? It is with all its dynamism that the social teaching of the Church accompanies men in their search." (42)

\* \* \*

How does the Church see the world today? The Council defined this vision, studied it and widened it a great deal, so that it modifies not a little the judgment and attitude that we must have with regard to the world. And this has happened because the doctrine of the Church has been enriched by a more complete knowledge of her own being and of her mission.

—General Audience (March 5, 1969)

# The Modern World

One part of this world, as everyone knows, has in recent years detached itself and broken away from the Christian foundations of its culture, although formerly it had been so imbued with Christianity and had drawn from it such strength and vigor that the people of these nations in many cases owe to Christianity all that is best in their own tradition—a fact that is not always fully appreciated. Another and larger part of the world covers the vast territories of the so-called emerging nations. Taken as a whole, it is a world which offers to the Church not one but a hundred forms of possible contacts, some of which are open and easy, others difficult and problematic, and many, unfortunately, wholly unfavorable to friendly dialogue.

—*Ecclesiam Suam*, 13 (August 6, 1964)

It is with all its dynamism that the social teaching of the Church accompanies men in their search. If it does not intervene to authenticate a given structure or to propose a ready-made model, it does not thereby limit itself to recalling general principles. It develops through reflection applied to the changing situations of this world, under the driving force of the Gospel as the source of renewal when its message is accepted in its totality and with all its demands. It also develops with the sensitivity proper to the Church which is characterized by a disinterested will to serve and by attention to the poorest.

—*Octogesima Adveniens*, 42 (May 14, 1971)

To put it in a word, the edifice of modern civilization has to be built on spiritual principles, for they are the only ones capable not only of supporting it, but of shedding light on it and inspiring it. And we are convinced, as you know, that these indispensable principles of higher wisdom cannot rest on anything but faith in God.

—Address to the United Nations, New York (October 4, 1965)

Political power, which is the natural and necessary link for ensuring the cohesion of the social body, must have as its aim the achievement of the common good. While respecting the legitimate liberties of individuals, families and subsidiary groups, it acts in such a way as to create, effectively and for the well-being of all, the conditions required for attaining man's true and complete good, including his spiritual end. It acts within the limits of its competence, which can vary from people to people and from country to country. It always intervenes with care for justice and with devotion to the common good, for which: it holds final responsibility.

—*Octogesima Adveniens*, 46 (May 14, 1971)

Thus, at the very moment that human love is more than ever threatened by a "ravaging eroticism,"[279] consecrated chastity must be today more than ever understood and lived with uprightness and generosity. Chastity is decisively positive, it witnesses to preferential love for the Lord and symbolizes in the most eminent and absolute way the mystery of the union of the Mystical Body with its Head, the union of the Bride with her eternal Bridegroom. Finally, it reaches, transforms and imbues with a mysterious likeness to Christ man's being in its most hidden depths.

—*Evangelica Testificatio*, 13 (June 29, 1971)

Today men yearn to free themselves from need and dependence. But this liberation starts with the interior freedom that men must find again with regard to their goods and their powers; they will never reach it except through a transcendent love for man, and, in consequence, through a genuine readiness to serve. Otherwise, as one can see only too clearly, the most revolutionary

[279] Cf. Address to the Equipes Notre-Dame Movement (May 4, 1970).

ideologies lead only to a change of masters; once installed in power in their turn, these new masters surround themselves with privileges, limit freedom and allow other forms of injustice to become established.

—*Octogesima Adveniens*, 45 (May 14, 1971)

The Church cannot accept violence, especially the force of arms—which is uncontrollable once it is let loose—and indiscriminate death as the path to liberation, because she knows that violence always provokes violence and irresistibly engenders new forms of oppression and enslavement which are often harder to bear than those from which they claimed to bring freedom.

—*Evangelii Nuntiandi*, 37 (December 8, 1975)

Who will blame a government which in its attempt to resolve the problems affecting an entire country resorts to the same measures as are regarded as lawful by married people in the solution of a particular family difficulty? Who will prevent public authorities from favoring those contraceptive methods which they consider more effective? Should they regard this as necessary, they may even impose their use on everyone. It could well happen, therefore, that when people, either individually or in family or social life, experience the inherent difficulties of the divine law and are determined to avoid them, they may give into the hands of public authorities the power to intervene in the most personal and intimate responsibility of husband and wife.

—*Humanae Vitae*, 17 (July 25, 1968)

While recognizing the autonomy of the reality of politics, Christians who are invited to take up political activity should try to make their choices consistent with the Gospel and, in the framework of a legitimate plurality, to give both personal collective witness to the seriousness of their faith by effective and disinterested service of men.

—*Octogesima Adveniens*, 46 (May 14, 1971)

It is not enough to increase the general fund of wealth and then distribute it more fairly. It is not enough to develop technology so that the earth may become a more suitable living place for human beings. The mistakes of those who led the way should help those now on the road to development to avoid certain dangers. The reign of technology—technocracy, as it is called—can cause as much harm to the world of tomorrow as liberalism did to the world of yesteryear. Economics and technology are meaningless if they do not benefit man, for it is he they are to serve. Man is truly human only if he is the master of his own actions and the judge of their worth, only if he is the architect of his own progress. He must act according to his God-given nature, freely accepting its potentials and its claims upon him.

—*Populorum Progressio*, 34 (March 26, 1967)

Bureaucratic socialism, technocratic capitalism and authoritarian democracy are showing how difficult it is to solve the great human problem of living together in justice and equality. How in fact could they escape the materialism, egoism or constraint which inevitably go with them? This is the source of a protest which is springing up more or less everywhere, as a sign of a deep-seated sickness, while at the same time we are witnessing the rebirth of what it is agreed to call "utopias". These claim to resolve the political problem of modern societies better than the ideologies. It would be dangerous to disregard this. The appeal to a utopia is often a convenient excuse for those who wish to escape from concrete tasks in order to take refuge in an imaginary world.

—*Octogesima Adveniens*, 37 (May 14, 1971)

# The Modern World

It must be admitted that all or nearly all the Constitutions in the world, not to mention several solemn international documents, contain guarantees—often ample and detailed—in favor of freedom of religion and conscience, and of the equality of citizens regardless of religious faith. But one cannot help noting the limitations and prohibitions imposed in various countries, on the legislative and administrative plane, or merely in practice, on many manifestations of religious life, individual profession of faith, the education of the young, the pastoral action of priests or bishops, the internal autonomy of religious communities, the faculty of evangelizing, use of the press, access to the mass media, and so on.

— Address to the Diplomatic Corps (January 14, 1978)

Permit us to say that we have a message, and a happy one, to hand over to each one of you. Our message is meant to be first of all a solemn moral ratification of this lofty Institution, and it comes from our experience of history. It is as an "expert on humanity" that we bring this Organization the support and approval of our recent predecessors, that of the Catholic hierarchy, and our own, convinced as we are that this Organization represents the obligatory path of modern civilization and world peace.

— Address to the United Nations, New York (October 4, 1965)

New forms of atheism seem to flow from it: a man centered atheism, no longer abstract and metaphysical but pragmatic, systematic and militant. Hand in hand with this atheistic secularism, we are daily faced, under the most diverse forms, with a consumer society, the pursuit of pleasure set up as the supreme value, a desire for power and domination, and discrimination of every kind: the inhuman tendencies of this "humanism."

— *Evangelii Nuntiandi*, 55 (December 8, 1975)

# Saint Pope Paul VI

Since the nineteenth century, western societies and, as a result, many others have put their hopes in ceaselessly renewed and indefinite progress. They saw this progress as man's effort to free himself in face of the demands of nature and of social constraints; progress was the condition for and the yardstick of human freedom. Progress, spread by the modern media of information and by the demand for wider knowledge and greater consumption, has become an omnipresent ideology. Yet a doubt arises today regarding both its value and its result. What is the meaning of this never-ending, breathless pursuit of a progress that always eludes one just when one believes one has conquered it sufficiently in order to enjoy it in peace? If it is not attained, it leaves one dissatisfied.

—*Octogesima Adveniens*, 41 (May 14, 1971)

The hour has come when a pause, a moment of recollection, reflection, you might say of prayer, is absolutely needed so that we may think back over our common origin, our history, our common destiny. The appeal to the moral conscience of man has never before been as necessary as it is today, in an age marked by such great human progress. For the danger comes neither from progress nor from science; if these are used well they can, on the contrary, help to solve a great number of the serious problems besetting mankind. The real danger comes from man, who has at his disposal ever more powerful instruments that are as well fitted to bring about ruin as they are to achieve lofty conquests.

—Address to the United Nations, New York (October 4, 1965)

As we all know, the Church is deeply rooted in the world. It exists in the world and draws its members from the world. It derives from it a wealth of human culture. It shares its vicissitudes and promotes its prosperity. But we also know that the modern world is in the grip of change and upheaval. It is undergoing developments which are having a profound influence on its outward way of life and habits of thought. The great advances made in science, technology, and social life, and the various currents of philosophical and political thought pervading modern society, are greatly influencing men's opinions and their spiritual and cultural pursuits.

—*Ecclesiam Suam*, 26 (August 6, 1964)

Overcoming the temptation to wish to measure everything in terms of efficiency and of trade, and in terms of the interplay of forces and interests, man today wishes to replace these quantitative criteria with the intensity of communication, the spread of knowledge and culture, mutual service and a combining of efforts for a common task. Is not genuine progress to be found in the development of moral consciousness, which will lead man to exercise a wider solidarity and to open himself freely to others and to God? For a Christian, progress necessarily comes up against the eschatological mystery of death. The death of Christ and his resurrection and the outpouring of the Spirit of the Lord help man to place his freedom, in creativity and gratitude, within the context of the truth of all progress and the only hope which does not deceive.[280]

—*Octogesima Adveniens*, 41 (May 14, 1971)

Everyone must lend a ready hand to this task, particularly those who can do most by reason of their education, their office, or their authority. They should set a good example by contributing part of their own goods, as several of Our brother bishops have done.[281] In this way they will be responsive to men's longings and faithful

---

[280] Cf. Rom. 5:5.
[281] Cf., for example, Emmanuel Larrain Errázuriz, *Lettre pastorale sur le développement et la paix* (Paris: Pax Christi, 1965).

to the Holy Spirit, because the ferment of the Gospel, too, has aroused and continues to arouse in man's heart the irresistible requirements of his dignity.[282]

—*Populorum Progressio*, 32 (March 26, 1967)

The Church itself is being engulfed and shaken by this tidal wave of change, for however much men may be committed to the Church, they are deeply affected by the climate of the world. They run the risk of becoming confused, bewildered and alarmed, and this is a state of affairs which strikes at the very roots of the Church. It drives many people to adopt the most outlandish views. They imagine that the Church should abdicate its proper role, and adopt an entirely new and unprecedented mode of existence. Modernism might be cited as an example. This is an error which is still making its appearance under various new guises, wholly inconsistent with any genuine religious expression. It is surely an attempt on the part of secular philosophies and secular trends to vitiate the true teaching and discipline of the Church of Christ.

—*Ecclesiam Suam*, 26 (August 6, 1964)

Sincere dialogue between cultures, as between individuals, paves the way for ties of brotherhood. Plans proposed for man's betterment will unite all nations in the joint effort to be undertaken, if every citizen—be he a government leader, a public official, or a simple workman—is motivated by brotherly love and is truly anxious to build one universal human civilization that spans the globe. Then we shall see the start of a dialogue on man rather than on the products of the soil or of technology.

—*Populorum Progressio*, 73 (March 26, 1967)

[282] *Gaudium et Spes*, 26.

# The Modern World

The Christian who wishes to live his faith in a political activity which he thinks of as service cannot without contradicting himself adhere to ideological systems which radically or substantially go against his faith and his concept of man. He cannot adhere to the Marxist ideology, to its atheistic materialism, to its dialectic of violence and to the way it absorbs individual freedom in the collectivity, at the same time denying all transcendence to man and his personal and collective history; nor can he adhere to the liberal ideology which believes it exalts individual freedom by withdrawing it from every limitation, by stimulating it through exclusive seeking of interest and power, and by considering social solidarities as more or less automatic consequences of individual initiatives, not as an aim and a major criterion of the value of the social organization.

—*Octogesima Adveniens*, 26 (May 14, 1971)

Here our message reaches its culmination and we will speak first of all negatively. These are the words you are looking for us to say and the words we cannot utter without feeling aware of their seriousness and solemnity: never again one against the other, never, never again!

—Address to the United Nations, New York (October 4, 1965)

In the developing nations and in other countries lay people must consider it their task to improve the temporal order. While the hierarchy has the role of teaching and authoritatively interpreting the moral laws and precepts that apply in this matter, the laity have the duty of using their own initiative and taking action in this area—without waiting passively for directives and precepts from others. They must try to infuse a Christian spirit into people's mental outlook and daily behavior, into the laws and structures of the civil community.[283] Changes must be made; present conditions

---

[283] Cf. *Apostolicam Actuositatem*, 7, 13, 24.

must be improved. And the transformations must be permeated with the spirit of the Gospel.

—*Populorum Progressio*, 81 (March 26, 1967)

We must come closer together, not only through the modern means of communication, through press and radio, through steamships and jet planes, —we must come together with our hearts, in mutual understanding, esteem and love. We must meet not merely as tourists, but as pilgrims who set out to find God—not in buildings of stone but in human hearts. Man must meet man, nation meet nation, as brothers and sisters, as children of God. In this mutual understanding and friendship, in this sacred communion, we must also begin to work together to build the common future of the human race. We must find the concrete and practical ways of organization and cooperation, so that all resources be pooled, and all efforts united towards achieving a true communion among all nations. Such a union cannot be built on a universal terror or fear of mutual destruction; it must be built on the common love that embraces all and has its roots in God, who is love.

—Address to Non-Christians, Bombay, India (December 3, 1964)

The poorer nations can never be too much on guard against the temptation posed by the wealthier nations. For these nations, with their favorable results from a highly technical and culturally developed civilization, provide an example of work and diligence with temporal prosperity the main pursuit. Not that temporal prosperity of itself precludes the activity of the human spirit. Indeed, with it, "the human spirit, being less subjected to material things, can be more easily drawn to the worship and contemplation of the Creator."[284] On the other hand, "modern civilization itself often

[284] *Gaudium et Spes*, 57.

complicates the approach to God, not for any essential reason, but because it is so much engrossed in worldly affairs."[285]

—*Populorum Progressio*, 41 (March 26, 1967)

If you want to be brothers, let the arms fall from your hands. A person cannot love with offensive weapons in his hands. Arms, and especially the terrible arms that modern science has provided you, engender bad dreams, feed evil sentiments, create nightmares, hostilities, and dark resolutions even before they cause any victims and ruins. They call for enormous expenses. They interrupt projects of solidarity and of useful labor. They warp the outlook of nations. So long as man remains the weak, changeable, and even wicked being that he so often shows himself to be, defensive arms will, alas, be necessary. But your courage and good qualities urge you on to a study of means that can guarantee the security of international life without any recourse to arms.

—Address to the United Nations, New York (October 4, 1965)

But it is not enough to feed the hungry. Each man must also be assured a life in keeping with his dignity.

—Address to the United Nations, New York (October 4, 1965)

Everything therefore in the modern means of social communication which arouses men's baser passions and encourages low moral standards, as well as every obscenity in the written word and every form of indecency on the stage and screen, should be condemned publicly and unanimously by all those who have at heart the advance of civilization and the safeguarding of the outstanding values of the human spirit. It is quite absurd to defend this kind of

[285] Ibid., 19.

depravity in the name of art or culture[286] or by pleading the liberty which may be allowed in this field by the public authorities.

—*Humanae Vitae*, 22 (July 25, 1968)

That is, the discovery of the "signs of the times" takes place to make us notice where they spontaneously meet higher plans, which we know to be Christian and divine (such as the pursuit of unity, of peace, of justice), and where any charitable or apostolic action of ours coincides with a development of favorable circumstances, indicating that the time has come for a simultaneous step forward of the kingdom of God in the human kingdom.

—General Audience (April 16, 1969)

We want to be clearly understood on this point: The present state of affairs must be confronted boldly, and its concomitant injustices must be challenged and overcome. Continuing development calls for bold innovations that will work profound changes. The critical state of affairs must be corrected for the better without delay.

—*Populorum Progressio*, 32 (March 26, 1967)

Prompted by the same scientific demands and the desire to know man better, but at the same time enlightened by their faith, Christians who devote themselves to the human sciences will begin a dialogue between the Church and this new field of discovery, a dialogue which promises to be fruitful. Of course, each individual scientific discipline will be able, in its own particular sphere, to grasp only a partial—yet true—aspect of man; the complete picture and the full meaning will escape it. But within these limits the human

---

[286] See Vatican Council II, Decree on the Media of Social Communication *Inter Mirifica* (1963), 6–7.

sciences give promise of a positive function that the Church willingly recognizes. They can even widen the horizons of human liberty to a greater extent than the conditioning circumstances perceived enable one to foresee. They could thus assist Christian social morality, which no doubt will see its field restricted when it comes to suggesting certain models of society, while its function of making a critical judgment and taking an overall view will be strengthened by its showing the relative character of the behavior and values presented by such and such a society as definitive and inherent in the very nature of man.

—*Octogesima Adveniens*, 40 (May 14, 1971)

The Church accepts, recognizes, and serves the world as it presents itself to her today. She does not regret the formulas of the Church-world synthesis of the past, nor does she dream of the formulas of a Utopian future. The Church adheres to present historical reality; she does not identify herself with it, she does not become a convert to the world (as some people today think they are authorized to do). But she recognizes in the present social reality the setting of her own life, the object of her love and service, the conditions of her language, the drama of her alluring temptations and of her pastoral attempts. In a word, the Church, in Christ and like Christ, loves the world of today and lives, speaks, operates for it, ready to understand it, attend to it, and offer herself.

—General Audience (March 5, 1969)

The discovery of the "signs of the times" is a fact of Christian conscience. It results from a comparison of faith with life; not to superimpose, artificially and superficially, a devout thought on the cases of our experience, but rather to see where these cases postulate, by their intrinsic dynamism, by their very obscurity, and sometimes by their very immorality, a ray of faith, an evangelical word, that classifies them, that redeems them.

—General Audience (April 16, 1969)

This method seems to Us indispensable to prevent certain dangers, to which the fascinating search for the "signs of the times" might expose us. The first danger is that of a charismatic prophetism, which often degenerates into bigoted fancy, conferring miraculous interpretations on chance and often insignificant coincidences. Eagerness to discover easily "the signs of the times" may make us forget the ambiguity, in many cases, of evaluation of observed facts, all the more so if we are, to attribute to the "People of God", that is, to every believer, a possible capacity to decipher "signs of God's presence and purpose."[287] The "sensus fidei" may confer this gift of wise insight, but the assistance of the hierarchical magisterium will always be provident and decisive, when the ambiguity of the interpretation deserves to be solved either in the certainty of truth or to the benefit of the common good.

—General Audience (April 16, 1969)

Is it not too difficult for us, this effort for which the modern mentality has so brain-washed us as to accustom us to the blasphemous cry of our blindness: "God is dead"? Difficult it is. But now comes the Master who adds: "Believe also in Me." Christ enables us to believe, with both natural and supernatural faith.

—General Audience (June 12, 1968)

Men must come together and get down to sincere negotiations. Things must be settled now, even at the cost of some loss of inconvenience, for later they may have to be settled at the cost of

---

[287] *Gaudium et Spes*, 11.

immense harm and enormous slaughter that cannot even be imagined now. But this peace must be based on justice and freedom for mankind, and must take into account the rights of individuals and communities. Otherwise it will be fluid and unstable.

—*Christi Matri*, 6 (September 15, 1966)

When he awakens to the world, does not man feel, in addition to the natural desire to understand and take possession of it, the desire to find within it his fulfillment and happiness? As everyone knows, there are several degrees of this "happiness." Its most noble expression is joy, or "happiness" in the strict sense, when man, on the level of his higher faculties, finds his peace and satisfaction in the possession of a known and loved good.[288] Thus, man experiences joy when he finds himself in harmony with nature, and especially in the encounter, sharing and communion with other people. All the more does he know spiritual joy or happiness when his spirit enters into possession of God, known and loved as the supreme and immutable good.[289] Poets, artists, thinkers, but also ordinary men and women, simply disposed to a certain inner light, have been able and still are able, in the times before Christ and in our own time and among us, to experience something of the joy of God.

—*Gaudete in Domino*, I (May 9, 1975)

This attitude must become characteristic of the Church of today, which is awakening and drawing new apostolic energies from her heart, mobilizing every son of hers to awareness of a common duty of mission and holiness. She does not escape, she does not live estranged from the existential situation of the world, but is grafted upon it spiritually with her message, with her patient and

---

[288] Cf. *Summa Theologica*, I-II, Q. 31, art. 3.
[289] Cf. ibid., II-II, Q. 28, arts. 1, 4.

benign charity (not revolutionary and bellicose; another deviation of the present times), but "patient, kind;... (she) sustains, believes, hopes, endures, to the last."[290]

—General Audience (March 5, 1969)

But how can we ignore the additional fact that joy is always imperfect, fragile and threatened? By a strange paradox, the consciousness of that which, beyond all passing pleasure, would constitute true happiness, also includes the certainty that there is no perfect happiness. The experience of finiteness, felt by each generation in its turn, obliges one to acknowledge and to plumb the immense gap that always exists between reality and the desire for the infinite.

—*Gaudete in Domino*, I (May 9, 1975)

Our life, today, is very busy with the continual vision of the outside world. The media of communication have grown so much, and are so aggressive, that they keep us busy, distract us, take us out of ourselves, empty us of our personal conscience. This is where we must be careful. We can pass from the position of mere observers to that of critics, thinkers, judges. This attitude of reflective knowledge is of the greatest importance for the modern soul, if it wishes to remain a living soul, and not just a screen for the thousand impressions to which it is subject.

—General Audience (April 16, 1969)

A greater spread of education and culture is becoming possible. Nevertheless, by their very action the media of social communication are reaching the point of representing as it were a new power. One cannot but ask about those who really hold this power, the aims that they pursue and the means they use, and finally, about the

---

[290] Cf. 1 Cor. 13:4–7.

effect of their activity on the exercise of individual liberty, both in the political and ideological spheres and in social, economic and cultural life. The men who hold this power have a grave moral responsibility with respect to the truth of the information that they spread, the needs and the reactions that they generate and the values which they put forward.

—*Octogesima Adveniens*, 20 (May 14, 1971)

This first proclamation is addressed especially to those who have never heard the Good News of Jesus, or to children. But, as a result of the frequent situations of dechristianization in our day, it also proves equally necessary for innumerable people who have been baptized but who live quite outside Christian life, for simple people who have a certain faith but an imperfect knowledge of the foundations of that faith, for intellectuals who feel the need to know Jesus Christ in a light different from the instruction they received as children, and for many others.

—*Evangelii Nuntiandi*, 52 (December 8, 1975)

How dark is the tempest that rages today against faith in God? So much so that We can reduce it all to one question: Is it still possible today to believe in God? That is a formidable question and it would require volumes to answer it. But We put the question here not so much to discuss it as would be done in an adequate treatise on the subject, but in order to remind you again of the words of Christ already mentioned: Have no fear. Have faith. That is to say, it is sufficient now for us to reassure you with that exhortation of our divine Master: Yes; it is still possible today to have faith in God and in Christ.

—General Audience (June 12, 1968)

It is disquieting in this regard to note a kind of fatalism which is gaining a hold even on people in positions of responsibility. This feeling sometimes leads to Malthusian solutions inculcated by active propaganda for contraception and abortion. In this critical situation, it must on the contrary be affirmed that the family, without which no society can stand, has a right to the assistance which will assure it of the conditions for a healthy development.

—*Octogesima Adveniens*, 18 (May 14, 1971)

How then will the cry of the poor find an echo in your lives? That cry must, first of all, bar you from whatever would be a compromise with any form of social injustice. It obliges you also to awaken consciences to the drama of misery and to the demands of social justice made by the Gospel and the Church. It leads some of you to join the poor in their situation and to share their bitter cares. Furthermore, it calls many of your institutes to rededicate for the good of the poor some of their works — something which many have already done with generosity. Finally, it enjoins on you a use of goods limited to what is required for the fulfillment of the functions to which you are called. It is necessary that in your daily lives you should give proof, even externally, of authentic poverty.

—*Evangelica Testificatio*, 18 (June 29, 1971)

Some widespread ideologies also wish to catalogue faith in God among the signs of human weakness and alienation. And yet, rarely so much as in these last few decades, have believers more shown themselves to be free men, independent in their moral judgment, resistant in hardships, fearless under pressure and oppression and when faced with death. We have as proof the testimonies of those who shared prison or internment with them. We have also the sacrifices borne serenely, on the plane of civil life, work, studies and career, by a multitude of believers who are willing to undergo discrimination against themselves or their children, provided that it does not impinge on their own convictions.

—Address to the Diplomatic Corps (January 14, 1978)

Today better than yesterday it is possible to have faith in God, if it be true that today the human intelligence is more developed, more educated in thinking, more inclined to look for the inner and the ultimate reasons of everything. For everything lies in this—the ability to think well. When We say this, it is necessary to remember that in the great question which We put, the word "faith" is understood by Us in its primary meaning of natural knowledge of God, that is to say, knowledge of the divinity which can be had through our ordinary powers of thought.

—General Audience (June 12, 1968)

One must be no less attentive to the action which the human sciences can instigate, giving rise to the elaboration of models of society to be subsequently imposed on men as scientifically tested types of behavior. Man can then become the object of manipulations directing his desires and needs and modifying his behavior and even his system of values. There is no doubt that there exists here a grave danger for the societies of tomorrow and for man himself. For even if all agree to build a new society at the service of men, it is still essential to know what sort of man is in question.

—*Octogesima Adveniens*, 39 (May 14, 1971)

This first proclamation is also addressed to the immense sections of mankind who practice non-Christian religions. The Church respects and esteems these non-Christian religions because they are the living expression of the soul of vast groups of people. They carry within them the echo of thousands of years of searching for God, a quest which is incomplete but often made with great sincerity and righteousness of heart. They possess an impressive patrimony of deeply religious texts. They have taught generations of people how to pray. They are all impregnated with innumerable "seeds of the Word"[291] and can constitute a true "preparation for the Gospel,"[292] to quote a felicitous term used by the Second Vatican Council and borrowed from Eusebius of Caesarea.

—*Evangelii Nuntiandi*, 53 (December 8, 1975)

A burning question of the present day preoccupies Us: how can the message of the Gospel penetrate the world? What can be done at those levels in which a new culture is unfolding, where a new type of man is emerging, a man who no longer believes he needs redemption?

—*Evangelica Testificatio*, 52 (June 29, 1971)

Methodological necessity and ideological presuppositions too often lead the human sciences to isolate, in the various situations, certain aspects of man, and yet to give these an explanation which claims to be complete or at least an interpretation which is meant to be all-embracing from a purely quantitative or phenomenological point of view. This scientific reduction betrays a dangerous presupposition. To give a privileged position in this way to such an aspect of analysis is to mutilate man and, under the pretext of a scientific procedure, to make it impossible to understand man in his totality.

—*Octogesima Adveniens*, 38 (May 14, 1971)

---

[291] Cf. Saint Justin, *First Apology* 46, 1–4; *Second Apology* 7, 1–4; 10, 1–3; 13, 3–4; *Florilegium Patristicum II* (Bonn: G. Rauschen, 1911), pp. 81, 125, 129, 133; Clement of Alexandria, *Stromata I*, 19, 91; 94; cf. *Ad Gentes*; cf. *Lumen Gentium*, 17.

[292] Eusebius of Caesarea, *Praeparatio Evangelica*, I, 1; cf. *Lumen Gentium*, 16.

Such a situation certainly raises complex and delicate questions that must be studied in the light of Christian Tradition and the Church's magisterium, in order to offer to the missionaries of today and of tomorrow new horizons in their contacts with non-Christian religions. We wish to point out, above all today, that neither respect and esteem for these religions nor the complexity of the questions raised is an invitation to the Church to withhold from these non-Christians the proclamation of Jesus Christ. On the contrary the Church holds that these multitudes have the right to know the riches of the mystery of Christ[293] — riches in which we believe that the whole of humanity can find, in unsuspected fullness, everything that it is gropingly searching for concerning God, man and his destiny, life and death, and truth.

—*Evangelii Nuntiandi*, 53 (December 8, 1975)

The Church, conscious of human aspirations towards dignity and well-being, pained by the unjust inequalities which still exist and often become more acute between nations and within nations, while respecting the competence of States, must offer her assistance for promoting "a fuller humanism," that is to say "the full development of the whole man and of every man."[294]

—Address to the bishops of Asia in Manila, Philippines (November 28, 1970)

Those in whose hands rests the safety of the human race should realize that in this day and age they have a very grave obligation in conscience. Mindful of their own nation, of the world, of God and history, let them examine their own consciences. Let them

[293] Cf. Eph. 3:8.
[294] *Populorum Progressio*, 42.

realize that in the future their names will be blessed if they wisely succeed in complying with this exhortation.

—*Christi Matri*, 5 (September 15, 1966)

The Church considers it to be undoubtedly important to build up structures which are more human, more just, more respectful of the rights of the person and less oppressive and less enslaving, but she is conscious that the best structures and the most idealized systems soon become inhuman if the inhuman inclinations of the human heart are not made wholesome, if those who live in these structures or who rule them do not undergo a conversion of heart and of outlook.

—*Evangelii Nuntiandi*, 36 (December 8, 1975)

Some Christians are today attracted by socialist currents and their various developments. They try to recognize therein a certain number of aspirations which they carry within themselves in the name of their faith. They feel that they are part of that historical current and wish to play a part within it. Now this historical current takes on, under the same name, different forms according to different continents and cultures, even if it drew its inspiration, and still does in many cases, from ideologies incompatible with faith. Careful judgment is called for. Too often Christians attracted by socialism tend to idealize it in terms which, apart from anything else, are very general: a will for justice, solidarity and equality. They refuse to recognize the limitations of the historical socialist movements, which remain conditioned by the ideologies from which they originated.

—*Octogesima Adveniens*, 31 (May 14, 1971)

Christ has His own special way of speaking in the secrets of hearts —and on the other hand, our greeting wants to be a different and higher relationship because it is not only a two-sided exchange of words among us people of this earth, but it also brings into the picture another present one, the Lord Himself, invisible but working in the framework of human relationships. It invites Him and begs of Him to arouse in him who greets and in him who is greeted new gifts of which the first and highest is charity.

—Homily, closing of the Second
Vatican Council (December 8, 1965)

From the spiritual point of view, the modern world seems to be forever immersed in what a modern author has termed "the drama of atheistic humanism."[295]

On the one hand one is forced to note in the very heart of this contemporary world the phenomenon which is becoming almost its most striking characteristic: secularism. We are not speaking of secularization, which is the effort, in itself just and legitimate and in no way incompatible with faith or religion, to discover in creation, in each thing or each happening in the universe, the laws which regulate them with a certain autonomy, but with the inner conviction that the Creator has placed these laws there.

—*Evangelii Nuntiandi*, 55 (December 8, 1975)

One of the characteristics of our secularized society is, without any doubt, the tendency to relegate religious faith to the level of a private option. And yet, never so much as in our time has freedom of religion and conscience, wherever it is oppressed or limited, been involved and clamed so insistently, even passionately, as a value of existence calling for an exterior and community dimension.

—Address to the Diplomatic Corps (January 14, 1978)

[295] Cf. Henri de Lubac, *Le drame de l'humanisme athee* (Paris: Ed. Spes, 1945).

# Saint Pope Paul VI

We must make haste. Too many people are suffering. While some make progress, others stand still or move backwards; and the gap between them is widening. However, the work must proceed in measured steps if the proper equilibrium is to be maintained. Make-shift agrarian reforms may fall short of their goal. Hasty industrialization can undermine vital institutions and produce social evils, causing a setback to true human values.

—Populorum Progressio, 29 (March 26, 1967)

There is also needed a patient effort to teach people, or teach them once more, how to savor in a simple way the many human joys that the Creator places in our path: the elating joy of existence and of life; the joy of chaste and sanctified love; the peaceful joy of nature and silence; the sometimes austere joy of work well done; the joy and satisfaction of duty performed; the transparent joy of purity, service and sharing; the demanding joy of sacrifice. The Christian will be able to purify, complete and sublimate these joys; he will not be able to disdain them. Christian joy presupposes a person capable of natural joy. These natural joys were often used by Christ as a starting point when He proclaimed the kingdom of God.

—Gaudete in Domino, I (May 9, 1975)

In a civilization and a world marked by a prodigious movement of almost indefinite material growth, what witness would be offered by a religious who let himself be carried away by an uncurbed seeking for his own ease, and who considered it normal to allow himself without discernment or restraint everything that is offered him? At a time when there is an increased danger for many of being enticed by the alluring security of possessions, knowledge and power, the call of God places you at the pinnacle of the Christian conscience. You are to remind men that their true and complete progress consists in responding to their calling "to share as sons in the life of the living God, the Father of all men."[296]

—*Evangelica Testificatio*, 31 (June 29, 1971)

Hope, and the value of individuals, are no longer sufficiently ensured. God seems to him abstract and useless. Without his being able to express it, God's silence weighs heavily on him. Yes, cold and darkness are first in the heart of the man who knows sadness. One can speak here of the sadness of non-believers, when the human spirit, created in the image and likeness of God, and therefore instinctively oriented towards Him as its sole and supreme good, remains without knowing Him clearly, without loving Him, and therefore without experiencing the happiness, even though imperfect, that is brought by the knowledge of God and by the certainty of having a link with Him that even death cannot break.

—*Gaudete in Domino*, I (May 9, 1975)

With demographic growth, which is particularly pronounced in the young nations, the number of those failing to find work and driven to misery or parasitism will grow in the coming years unless the conscience of man rouses itself and gives rise to a general movement of solidarity through an effective policy of investment and of organization of production and trade, as well as of education. We know the attention given to these problems within international organizations, and it is our lively wish that their members will not delay bringing their actions into line with their declarations.

—*Octogesima Adveniens*, 18 (May 14, 1971)

Man is suddenly becoming aware that by an ill-considered exploitation of nature he risks destroying it and becoming in his turn the

---

[296] *Populorum Progressio*, 21.

victim of this degradation. Not only is the material environment becoming a permanent menace—pollution and refuse, new illness and absolute destructive capacity—but the human framework is no longer under man's control, thus creating an environment for tomorrow which may well be intolerable. This is a wide-ranging social problem which concerns the entire human family.

—*Octogesima Adveniens*, 21 (May 14, 1971)

Technical expertise is necessary, but it must be accompanied by concrete signs of genuine love. Untainted by overbearing nationalistic pride or any trace of racial discrimination, experts should learn how to work in collaboration with everyone. They must realize that their expert knowledge does not give them superiority in every sphere of life. The culture which shaped their living habits does contain certain universal human elements; but it cannot be regarded as the only culture, nor can it regard other cultures with haughty disdain. If it is introduced into foreign lands, it must undergo adaptation.

—*Populorum Progressio*, 72 (March 26, 1967)

In this world dominated by scientific and technological change, which threatens to drag it towards a new posivitism, another more fundamental doubt is raised. Having subdued nature by using his reason, man now finds that he himself is as it were imprisoned within his own rationality; he in turn becomes the object of science.

—*Octogesima Adveniens*, 38 (May 14, 1971)

The introduction of industrialization, which is necessary for economic growth and human progress, is both a sign of development and a spur to it. By dint of intelligent thought and hard work, man gradually uncovers the hidden laws of nature and learns to make better use of natural resources. As he takes control over his way of life, he is stimulated to undertake new investigations and fresh discoveries, to take prudent risks and launch new ventures, to act responsibly and give of himself unselfishly.

—*Populorum Progressio*, 25 (March 26, 1967)

Only the love of God—it must be repeated—calls in a decisive way to religious chastity. This love moreover makes so uncompromising a demand for fraternal charity that the religious will live more profoundly with his contemporaries in the heart of Christ. On this condition, the gift of self, made to God and to others, will be the source of deep peace. Without in any way undervaluing human love and marriage—is not the latter, according to faith, the image and sharing of the union of love joining Christ and the Church?[297]—consecrated chastity evokes this union in a more immediate way and brings that surpassing excellence to which all human love should tend.

—*Evangelica Testificatio*, 13 (June 29, 1971)

The Church remains in the world when the Lord of glory returns to the Father. She remains as a sign—simultaneously obscure and luminous—of a new presence of Jesus, of His departure and of His permanent presence. She prolongs and continues Him.

—*Evangelii Nuntiandi*, 15 (December 8, 1975)

The concept of work can turn into an exaggerated mystique. Yet, for all that, it is something willed and approved by God. Fashioned in the image of his Creator, "man must cooperate with Him in completing the work of creation and engraving on the earth the spiritual imprint which he himself has received."[298] God gave

[297] Cf. *Gaudium et Spes*, 48; cf. Eph. 5:25, 32.
[298] *Gaudium et Spes*, 65.

man intelligence, sensitivity and the power of thought—tools with which to finish and perfect the work He began. Every worker is, to some extent, a creator—be he artist, craftsman, executive, laborer or farmer.

—*Populorum Progressio*, 27 (March 26, 1967)

You hear rising up, more pressing than ever, from their personal distress and collective misery, "the cry of the poor."[299] Was it not in order to respond to their appeal as God's privileged ones that Christ came,[300] even going as far as to identify Himself with them?[301] In a world experiencing the full flood of development this persistence of poverty-stricken masses and individuals constitutes a pressing call for "a conversion of minds and attitudes,"[302] especially for you who follow Christ more closely in this earthly condition of self-emptying.[303]

—*Evangelica Testificatio*, 17 (June 29, 1971)

Work, too, has a double edge. Since it promises money, pleasure and power, it stirs up selfishness in some and incites others to revolt. On the other hand, it also fosters a professional outlook, a sense of duty, and love of neighbor. Even though it is now being organized more scientifically and efficiently, it still can threaten man's dignity and enslave him; for work is human only if it results from man's use of intellect and free will.

—*Populorum Progressio*, 28 (March 26, 1967)

---

[299] Cf. Ps. 9:13; Job 34:28; Prov. 21:13.
[300] Cf. Luke 4:18; 6:20.
[301] Cf. Matt. 25:35–40.
[302] *Gaudium et Spes*, 63.
[303] Cf. Matt. 19:21; 2 Cor. 8:9.

# The Modern World

Atheistic secularism and the absence of religious practice are found among adults and among the young, among the leaders of society and among the ordinary people, at all levels of education, and in both the old Churches and the young ones. The Church's evangelizing action cannot ignore these two worlds, nor must it come to a standstill when faced with them; it must constantly seek the proper means and language for presenting, or representing, to them God's revelation and faith in Jesus Christ.

—*Evangelii Nuntiandi*, 56 (December 8, 1975)

*Chapter 12*

# Peace

In 1965, Pope Paul VI became the first pope to visit the United States. He was given an enthusiastic welcome not just by American Catholics but by Americans from every walk of life. The center-piece of the papal visit was on October 4, 1965, when the pope gave an unprecedented address to the United Nations. The pontiff told the assembled diplomats and UN officials:

> It is enough to recall that the blood of millions, countless unheard-of sufferings, useless massacres and frightening ru-ins have sanctioned the agreement that unites you with an oath that ought to change the future history of the world: never again war, never again war! It is peace, peace, that has to guide the destiny of the nations of all mankind![304]

This was a plea repeated throughout his pontificate, and it was made in an era in which the world was convulsed not just with the bitter conflict between the free world and the Soviet Union, but also with related conflicts such as the Vietnam War, as well as the terrible Arab-Israeli Wars. Paul was aware of the immense risk to human civilization from nuclear war and the existential and

---

[304] Paul VI, address to the United Nations, New York (October 4, 1965).

spiritual threat of atheistic communism behind the Iron Curtain. He called on the nations of the world to seek authentic peace and made himself a witness of peace to a world living under the threat of nuclear annihilation.

He began with his monumental 1964 trip to Jerusalem, where he met with Ecumenical Patriarch Athenagoras, taking a major step toward healing the schism that had separated the Catholic and Orthodox churches since 1054. He also used his global journeys to India, America, and Oceania to call for peace. On January 1, 1968, he inaugurated the World Day for Peace, writing:

> We address Ourself to all men of good will to exhort them to celebrate "The Day of Peace," throughout the world, on the first day of the year, January 1, 1968. It is Our desire that then, every year, this commemoration be repeated as a hope and as a promise, at the beginning of the calendar which measures and outlines the path of human life in time, that Peace with its just and beneficent equilibrium may dominate the development of events to come.... The Catholic Church, with the intention of service and of example, simply wishes to "launch the idea," in the hope that it may not only receive the widest consent of the civilized world, but that such an idea may find everywhere numerous promoters, able and capable of impressing on the "Day of Peace," to be celebrated on the first day of every new year, that sincere and strong character of conscious humanity, redeemed from its sad and fatal bellicose conflicts, which will give to the history of the world a more happy, ordered and civilized development."[305]

It was not an accident that he chose January 1 for the annual Day of Peace. It is the solemnity of Mary, Mother of God, a holy

---

[305] Paul VI, Message for the World Day of Peace, 1968.

day of obligation. The pope thus called for Catholics and people of goodwill to begin the New Year with a commitment to authentic peace. He issued the Message for the Day of Peace every year after, and the tradition remains today.

Key to his teaching was that authentic peace must be more than merely the absence of war. Authentic peace means *authentic justice*. In 1972, he dedicated his Message for the Day of Peace to the theme, "If you want Peace, work for Justice." As he wrote in his 1967 social encyclical *Populorum Progressio*,

> When we fight poverty and oppose the unfair conditions of the present, we are not just promoting human well-being; we are also furthering man's spiritual and moral development, and hence we are benefiting the whole human race. For peace is not simply the absence of warfare, based on a precarious balance of power; it is fashioned by efforts directed day after day toward the establishment of the ordered universe willed by God, with a more perfect form of justice among men.[306] (76)

Paul was powerfully committed to the teaching that authentic peace means also the defense of life. He wrote in Message for Peace in 1977: "Peace and Life. They are supreme values in the civil order. They are also values that are interdependent. Do we want Peace? Then let us defend Life!"

\* \* \*

Peace is one of the supreme benefits of man's life on earth, an interest of the first order, a common aspiration, an ideal worthy of mankind, master of itself and of the world, a necessity in order to maintain the conquests achieved and to achieve others, a fundamental law for the free circulation of thought, culture, economy,

---

[306] Cf. *Pacem in Terris*.

art, and a demand which can no longer be suppressed in view of human destiny. This is so because Peace is security, Peace is order. A just and dynamic order, We add, which must continually be built up. Without Peace there is no trust, without trust there is no progress. And that trust, We declare, must be rooted in justice and fairness. Only in a climate of Peace can right be recognized, can justice advance, can freedom breathe.

—Message for the Day of Peace (January 1, 1969)

The voice of innocent blood cries out with heartrending insistence in the heart of the person who killed it. Inner Peace is not possible through selfish sophistries! And even if it is, a blow at Peace—that is, at the general system that protects order, safe living in society, in a word, at Peace—has been perpetrated: the individual Life and Peace in general are always linked by an unbreakable relationship. If we wish progressive social order to be based upon intangible principles, let us not offend against it in the heart of its essential system: respect for human life. Even under this aspect Peace and Life are closely bound together at the basis of order and civilization.

—Message for the Day of Peace (January 1, 1977)

For us Christians, Peace is not only an external equilibrium, a juridical order, a complex of disciplined public relationships; for us, Peace is above all the result of the implementation of that design of wisdom and love, through which God willed to enter into supernatural relations with mankind. Peace is the first effect of that new divine economy which we call grace—"Grace and peace", as the Apostle says—it is a gift of God which becomes the style of Christian life; it is a Messianic phase which reflects its light and hope upon the temporal city also, strengthening with its superior motives those reasons upon which that city bases its own Peace.

—Message for the Day of Peace (January 1, 1969)

# Peace

It is difficult, but essential, to form a genuine idea of Peace. It is difficult for one who closes his eyes to his innate intuition of it, which tells him that Peace is something very human. This is the right way to come to the genuine discovery of Peace: if we look for its true source, we find that it is rooted in a sincere feeling for man. A Peace that is not the result of true respect for man is not true Peace. And what do we call this sincere feeling for man? We call it Justice.

—Message for the Day of Peace (January 1, 1972)

As you know very well, peace is not built merely by means of politics and a balance of power and interests. It is built with the mind, with ideas, with the works of peace. You are working at this great endeavor, but you are only at the beginning of your labors. Will the world ever come to change the selfish and bellicose outlook that has spun out such a great part of its history up to now? It is hard to foresee the future, but easy to assert that the world has to set out resolutely on the path toward a new history, a peaceful history, one that will be truly and fully human, the one that God promised to men of good will. The pathways are marked out before you and the first one is disarmament.

—Address to the United Nations, New York (October 4, 1965)

Civilization walks in the footsteps of Peace armed only with an olive branch. Civilization is followed by the Doctors with the weighty volumes on the Law which will lead to the ideal human society; there follow the Politicians, expert not so much in the calculation of all-conquering armies for winning wars and repressing the defeated and demoralized, but rather in assessing the resources of the psychology of goodness and friendship. Justice too moves in this ordered procession, now no longer proud and cruel but completely intent on defending the weak, punishing the violent and ensuring an order which is extremely difficult to achieve but which alone is worthy of that divine name: order in freedom and conscious duty. Let us rejoice: this procession, though interrupted by hostile attacks and by unexpected accidents, continues along its way before our eyes in this tragic time of ours. Its step is perhaps a little slow, but it is nonetheless sure and beneficial for the whole world. It is a procession intent on using the real weapons of peace.

—Message for the Day of Peace (January 1, 1976)

For those who believe in God, it is spontaneous and instinctive and indeed a duty through the law of religion. And even for those who do not have this good fortune of admitting the protecting and vindicating hand of God upon all human beings, this same sense of the sacred—that is, the untouchable and inviolable element proper to a living human existence—is and must be something sensed by virtue of human dignity.

—Message for the Day of Peace (January 1, 1977)

Nations are the architects of their own development, and they must bear the burden of this work; but they cannot accomplish it if they live in isolation from others. Regional mutual aid agreements among the poorer nations, broader based programs of support for these nations, major alliances between nations to coordinate these activities—these are the road signs that point the way to national development and world peace.

—*Populorum Progressio*, 77 (March 26, 1967)

The Christian's hope comes primarily from the fact that he knows that the Lord is working with us in the world, continuing in his Body which is the Church—and, through the Church, in the whole of mankind—the Redemption which was accomplished on the Cross and which burst forth in victory on the morning of the Resurrection.[307] This hope springs also from the fact that the Christian knows that other men are at work, to undertake actions of justice and peace working for the same ends. For beneath an outward appearance of indifference, in the heart of every man there is a will to live in brotherhood and a thirst for justice and peace, which is to be expanded.

—*Octogesima Adveniens*, 48 (May 14, 1971)

It is enough to recall that the blood of millions, countless unheard-of sufferings, useless massacres and frightening ruins have sanctioned the agreement that unites you with an oath that ought to change the future history of the world: never again war, never again war! It is peace, peace, that has to guide the destiny of the nations of all mankind!

—Address to the United Nations, New York (October 4, 1965)

When we fight poverty and oppose the unfair conditions of the present, we are not just promoting human well-being; we are also furthering man's spiritual and moral development, and hence we are benefiting the whole human race. For peace is not simply the absence of warfare, based on a precarious balance of power; it is fashioned by efforts directed day after day toward the establishment of the ordered universe willed by God, with a more perfect form of justice among men.[308]

—*Populorum Progressio*, 76 (March 26, 1967)

There is no civilization without Peace. But in reality Peace is never complete, never secure. You have seen how the very achievements of progress can be the cause of conflicts, and what conflicts!

—Message for the Day of Peace (January 1, 1977)

[307] Cf. Matt. 28:30; Phil. 2:8–11.
[308] Cf. *Pacem in Terris*.

# Saint Pope Paul VI

Peace does not generate itself, even though the deepest impulses of human nature tend towards Peace. Peace is order, and order is what everything, every reality, aspires to as its destiny and the justification for its existence. Order is a pre-established destiny and justification for existence, but it is brought about together with and in collaboration with many factors. Thus Peace is a pinnacle that presupposes a complex inner supporting framework. Peace is like a flexible body that needs a stout skeleton to give it strength. The stability and beauty of the structure of Peace depend on the support of various causes and conditions. These are often absent. Even when they exist, they are not always strong enough for their function of ensuring that the pyramid of Peace should have a solid base and a lofty summit.

—Message for the Day of Peace (January 1, 1977)

The subjective foundation of Peace is a new spirit which must animate coexistence between peoples, a new outlook on man, his duties and his destiny. Much progress must still be made to render this outlook universal and effective; a new training must educate the new generations to reciprocal respect between nations, to brotherhood between peoples, to collaboration between races, with a view also to their progress and development.

—Message for the Day of Peace (January 1, 1968)

Peace is a duty, Peace is possible. This is the message we keep repeating, a message that makes its own the ideal of civilization, echoes the aspirations of peoples, strengthens the hope of the lowly and weak, and ennobles with justice the security of the strong.

—Message for the Day of Peace (January 1, 1977)

Peace is no dream, no utopia, no illusion. Nor is it a labour of Sisyphus. No, Peace can be prolonged and strengthened. Peace can write the finest pages of history, inscribing them not only with the magnificence of power and glory but also with the greater magnificence of human virtue, people's goodness, collective prosperity, and true civilization: the civilization of love.

—Message for the Day of Peace (January 1, 1977)

Government leaders, your task is to draw your communities into closer ties of solidarity with all men, and to convince them that they must accept the necessary taxes on their luxuries and their wasteful expenditures in order to promote the development of nations and the preservation of peace. Delegates to international organizations, it is largely your task to see to it that senseless arms races and dangerous power plays give way to mutual collaboration between nations, a collaboration that is friendly, peace oriented, and divested of self-interest, a collaboration that contributes greatly to the common development of mankind and allows the individual to find fulfillment.

—*Populorum Progressio*, 84 (March 26, 1967)

Is Peace possible? Yes, it is. It must be. But let us be sincere: Peace, as we have already said, is a duty and is possible, but it is so only with the concourse of many and not easy conditions. We are aware that to discuss the conditions for Peace is a very long and very difficult task.

—Message for the Day of Peace (January 1, 1977)

We recognize that Peace, in historical reality, is a work of continual therapy. Its health is by its very nature frail, consisting as it does in the establishment of relationships between overbearing and fickle men. Peace demands a wise and unceasing effort on the part of that higher creative imagination which we call diplomacy, international order or the dynamic of negotiations. Poor Peace!

—Message for the Day of Peace (January 1, 1976)

The policy of massive armaments is immediately called into question. The ancient saying, which has taught politics and still does so — "if you want peace, prepare for war" (*si vis pacem, para bellum*) — is not acceptable without radical reservation.[309] With the forthright boldness of our principles, we thus denounce the false and dangerous programme of the "arms race", of the secret rivalry between peoples for military superiority.

—Message for the Day of Peace (January 1, 1977)

Peace and Life support enormous and incalculable burdens in order to maintain a Peace founded on a perpetual threat to Life, as also to defend Life by means of a constant threat to Peace. People will say: it is inevitable. This can be true within a concept of civilization that is still so imperfect. But let us at least recognize that this constitutional challenge which the arms race sets up between Life and Peace is a formula that is fallacious in itself and which must be corrected and superseded.

—Message for the Day of Peace (January 1, 1977)

Peace is not a stagnant condition of life which finds in it at the same time both its perfection and its death. Life is movement, growth, work, effort and conquest, things such as these. Is that what Peace is like? Yes, for the very reason that it coincides with the supreme good of man as he makes his way through time, and this good is never attained totally, but is always being newly and inexhaustibly acquired. Peace is thus the central idea giving its driving force to the most active enthusiasm.

—Message for the Day of Peace (January 1, 1972)

[309] Cf. Luke 14:31.

# Peace

There is a direct relation between human rights and peace. It is impossible to have true and lasting peace where human rights are unrecognized, violated and trampled upon.

—Message to His Excellency Emilio Arenales Catalan, president of the Twenty-Third General Assembly of the United Nations (December 4, 1968)

Peace cannot be based on a false rhetoric of words which are welcomed because they answer to the deep, genuine aspirations of humanity, but which can also serve, and unfortunately have sometimes served, to hide the lack of true spirit and of real intentions for peace, if not indeed to mask sentiments and actions of oppression and party interests. Nor can one rightly speak of peace where no recognition or respect is given to its solid foundations: namely, sincerity, justice and love in the relations between states, and, within the limits of each nation, in the relations of citizens with each other and with their rulers; freedom of individuals and of peoples, in all its expressions, civic, cultural, moral, and religious; otherwise, it is not peace which will exist—even if, perchance, oppression is able to create the external appearance of order and legality—but an unceasing and insuppressible growth of revolt and war.

—Message for the Day of Peace (January 1, 1968)

Whoever works to educate the rising generations in the conviction that every man is our brother, is building from the foundation the edifice of peace. Whoever implants in public opinion the sentiment of human brotherhood without reserve, is preparing better days for the world. Whoever conceives of the protection of political interests without the incitement of hate and of combat amongst men, as a logical and indispensable necessity of social life, is opening to human society the ever effective advancement of the common good. Whoever helps in discovering in every man, beyond his physical, ethnic and racial characteristics, the existence of a being equal to his own, is transforming the earth from an epicenter of division, antagonism, treachery and revenge into a field of vital work for civil collaboration. Where brotherhood amongst men is at root disregarded, peace is at root destroyed. And yet peace is the mirror of the real, authentic, modern humanity, victorious over every anachronistic self-injury. Peace is the great concept extolling love amongst men who discover that they are brothers and decide to live as such.

—Message for the Day of Peace (January 1, 1971)

We believe that the idea of Peace still is, and still must be, dominant in human affairs, and that it becomes all the more urgent whenever and wherever it is contradicted by opposite ideas or deeds. It is a necessary idea, an imperative idea, an inspiring idea. It polarizes human aspirations, endeavors and hopes. Its nature is that of an aim, and as such it is at the base and at the goal of our activities, be they individual or collective.

—Message for the Day of Peace (January 1, 1972)

Chapter 13

# Prayer, Holiness, and the Life of Faith

Pope Paul VI was a man of prayer. He studied the so-called French school of spirituality that flourished from the seventeenth century and included such giants as St. Louis Marie de Montfort, Cardinal Pierre de Bérulle, Jean-Jacques Olier, and Jean Eudes, and he had a lifelong devotion to St. Francis de Sales, the bishop of Geneva, Doctor of the Church, and one of the Church's greatest apologists.

As a man of prayer, he was also deeply concerned about its decline in the modern world. It was a concern that — as with the labors of the Second Vatican Council — anticipated the immense crisis of belief today. He called on the faithful to resist the loss of faith and hope, and throughout his pontificate he tried to use Holy Years to bolster the response of Catholics to cultural decline and the crises within the Church. He also issued the *Credo of the People of God*, the drafting of which was shaped heavily by the great philosopher Jacques Maritain.

Paul's preoccupation with the loss of faith and spirituality was exemplified by his address to the bishops of Asia in 1970:

In our day we are witnessing the decline of prayer, and you know the causes of this. Yet in favor of prayer we have two great — though different — resources: the first is the liturgical reform promoted by the recent Council. The Council has not only renewed the outward form of ritual, always according to certain traditional norms, but it has also given fresh life to the sources—doctrinal, sacramental, communal and pastoral—of the Church's prayer.

In addition to his contributions through preaching and writing, Pope Paul offered the Church and the world the example of the saints to remind everyone of the council's universal call to holiness. He canonized eighty-four saints, including multiple groups of martyrs and more recent figures, such as the Americans Elizabeth Ann Seton and John Neumann.

The pope also repeatedly reminded Catholics everywhere of the holiness of the Church. In his 1964 encyclical on the Church, *Ecclesiam Suam*, Paul wrote:

> A vivid and lively self-awareness on the part of the Church inevitably leads to a comparison between the ideal image of the Church as Christ envisaged it, His holy and spotless bride,[310] and the actual image which the Church presents to the world today. This actual image does indeed, thank God, truly bear those characteristics impressed on it by its divine Founder; and in the course of the centuries the Holy Spirit has accentuated and enhanced these traits so as to make the Church conform more and more to the original intention of its Founder and to the particular genius of human society which it is continually striving to win over to itself through the preaching of the gospel of salvation. (10)

He was not naïve, though, adding that "the actual image of the Church will never attain to such a degree of perfection, beauty, holiness and splendor that it can be said to correspond perfectly

---

[310] Cf. Eph. 5:27.

with the original conception in the mind of Him who fashioned it."[311] The imitation of Christ, devotion to the Blessed Mother, the perfection of the virtues, the sacraments, and the joy of a life of prayer: Striving to grow in these, and thus in holiness, was and is essential for the members of the Body of Christ—the Church—in order to spark authentic reform and to proclaim Christ Jesus to a world longing for hope and yearning for the eternal.

\* \* \*

Religion of its very nature is a certain relationship between God and man. It finds its expression in prayer; and prayer is a dialogue. Revelation, too, that supernatural link which God has established with man, can likewise be looked upon as a dialogue. In the Incarnation and in the Gospel it is God's Word that speaks to us. That fatherly, sacred dialogue between God and man, broken off at the time of Adam's unhappy fall, has since, in the course of history, been restored. Indeed, the whole history of man's salvation is one long, varied dialogue, which marvelously begins with God and which He prolongs with men in so many different ways.

—*Ecclesiam Suam*, 70 (August 6, 1964)

Imitation of Jesus Christ is undoubtedly the regal way to be followed to attain sanctity and reproduce in ourselves, according to our forces, the absolute perfection of the heavenly Father. But while the Catholic Church has always proclaimed a truth so sacrosanct, it has also affirmed that imitation of the Virgin Mary, far from distracting the souls from the faithful following of Christ, makes it more pleasant and easier for them.

—*Signum Magnum*, II, 1 (May 13, 1967)

[311] *Ecclesiam Suam*, 10.

# Saint Pope Paul VI

Mary is also the Virgin in prayer. She appears as such in the visit to the mother of the precursor, when she pours out her soul in expressions glorifying God, and expressions of humility, faith and hope. This prayer is the Magnificat,[312] Mary's prayer par excellence, the song of the messianic times in which there mingles the joy of the ancient and the new Israel.

—*Marialis Cultus*, 18 (February 2, 1974)

So we know that this dark disturbing being exists and that he is still at work with his treacherous cunning; he is the hidden enemy who sows errors and misfortunes in human history. It is worth recalling the revealing Gospel parable of the good seed and the cockle, for it synthesizes and explains the lack of logic that seems to preside over our contradictory experiences: "An enemy has done this."[313] He is "a murderer from the beginning, ... and the father of lies," as Christ defines him.[314] He undermines man's moral equilibrium with his sophistry. He is the malign, clever seducer who knows how to make his way into us through the senses, the imagination and the libido, through utopian logic, or through disordered social contacts in the give and take of our activities, so that he can bring about in us deviations that are all the more harmful because they seem to conform to our physical or mental makeup, or to our profound, instinctive aspirations.

—General Audience (November 15, 1972)[315]

---

[312] Cf. Luke 1:46–55.
[313] Matt. 13:28.
[314] See John 8:44–45.
[315] Paul VI, "Confronting the Devil's Power" General Audience, November 15, 1972; translation found at http://www.ewtn.com/library/PAPALDOC/P6DEVIL.HTM.

*Prayer, Holiness, and the Life of Faith*

But it seems to Us that the sort of relationship for the Church to establish with the world should be more in the nature of a dialogue, though theoretically other methods are not excluded. We do not mean unrealistic dialogue. It must be adapted to the intelligences of those to whom it is addressed, and it must take account of the circumstances. Dialogue with children is not the same as dialogue with adults, nor is dialogue with Christians the same as dialogue with non-believers. But this method of approach is demanded nowadays by the prevalent understanding of the relationship between the sacred and the profane. It is demanded by the dynamic course of action which is changing the face of modern society. It is demanded by the pluralism of society, and by the maturity man has reached in this day and age. Be he religious or not, his secular education has enabled him to think and speak, and conduct a dialogue with dignity.
—*Ecclesiam Suam*, 78 (August 6, 1964)

People are afraid of falling back into old Manichean theories, or into frightening deviations of fancy and superstition. Nowadays they prefer to appear strong and unprejudiced to pose as positivists, while at the same time lending faith to many unfounded magical or popular superstitions or, worse still, exposing their souls—their baptized souls, visited so often by the Eucharistic Presence and inhabited by the Holy Spirit!—to licentious sensual experiences and to harmful drugs, as well as to the ideological seductions of fashionable errors. These are cracks through which the Evil One can easily penetrate and change the human mind.
—General Audience (November 15, 1972)

Are We not right in saying that charity is the goal of the Church's practice of the spiritual life? Is it not true to say that the more perfect and more joyful realization of charity is the goal of all theological study and of the practice of Christian piety? Both these things

encourage Us to meditate on the scriptural and sacramental treasures of which the Church is heir, guardian, mistress, and minister.

—*Ecclesiam Suam*, 56 (August 6, 1964)

The discovery of intimacy with God, the necessity for adoration,
the need for intercession—the experience of Christian holiness
shows us the fruitfulness of prayer, in which God reveals Himself
to the spirit and heart of His servants. The Lord gives us this
knowledge of Himself in the fervor of love. The gifts of the Spirit
are many, but they always grant us a taste of that true and intimate
knowledge of the Lord. Without it we shall not succeed either in
understanding the value of the Christian and religious life or in
gaining the strength to advance in it with the joy of a hope that
does not deceive.

—*Evangelica Testificatio*, 43 (June 29, 1971)

We must love and serve the Church as it is, wisely seeking to understand its history and to discover with humility the will of God
who guides and assists it, even when He permits human weakness
to eclipse the splendor of its countenance and the holiness of its
activity. It is precisely this holiness and splendor which we are
endeavoring to discover and promote.

—*Ecclesiam Suam*, 47 (August 6, 1964)

There are many things we do know, however, about this diabolical
world, things that touch on our lives and on the whole history of
mankind. The Devil is at the origin of mankind's first misfortune,
he was the wily, fatal tempter involved in the first sin, the original
sin.[316] That fall of Adam gave the Devil a certain dominion over
man, from which only Christ's Redemption can free us. It is a

---

[316] Gen. 3; Wisd. 1:24.

history that is still going on: let us recall the exorcisms at Baptism, and the frequent references in Sacred Scripture and in the liturgy to the aggressive and oppressive "power of darkness."[317] The Devil is the number one enemy, the preeminent tempter.

—General Audience (November 15, 1972)

Even though the Church, in the reliance which it places on the liberty of the modern Christian with his increased awareness of his duties and his greater maturity and practical wisdom in fulfilling them, may make certain of its laws or precepts easier to observe, nevertheless the law retains its essential binding force. The Christian way of life as set forth and interpreted by the Church in its prudent legislation, demands a not inconsiderable degree of loyalty, perseverance and self-sacrifice. It constrains us, as it were, to take the "narrow way" recommended by Our Savior.[318] It will not require less of us modern Christians than in the past; it may very well require more. It will require a prompt obedience, no less necessary and difficult now than formerly, but it will be all the more meritorious in that it is inspired more by supernatural motives than by natural ones.

—*Ecclesiam Suam*, 51 (August 6, 1964)

Conformity to the spirit of the world, the rejection of the rules of Christian asceticism, indifference in the face of the laxity of contemporary morals, emancipation from the authority of wise and lawful superiors, apathy concerning the contradictory forms of modern thought—these are not the things that can give vigor to the Church and fit it to receive the power and strength of the Holy Spirit's gifts. These are not the things which strengthen the

---

[317] See Luke 22:53; Col. 1:13.
[318] Cf. Matt. 7:13.

Church in its true following of Christ. They neither inject into the Church the watchful spirit of brotherly love, nor do they increase its ability to communicate its message. The only things which can bring these blessings on the Church are the following: the determination to live in accordance with divine grace, faithfulness to the Gospel of Christ, unity in the ranks of the sacred hierarchy and among Christian communities. The follower of Christ is not pliant and cowardly, but loyal and strong.

—*Ecclesiam Suam*, 51 (August 6, 1964)

Many passages in the Gospel show us that we are dealing not just with one Devil, but with many.[319] But the principal one is Satan, which means the adversary, the enemy; and along with him are many others, all of them creatures of God, but fallen because they rebelled and were damned[320]—a whole mysterious world, convulsed by a most unfortunate drama about which we know very little.

—General Audience (November 15, 1972)

The spirit of poverty is a special mark of Christ's Gospel. This passing reference to its necessity and excellence does not, however, relieve Us of Our obligation of pointing out that zeal for poverty is no obstacle to the proper understanding and rightful application of the important laws of economics. This is a subject which has made great strides within recent years. It has been responsible for the progress of civilization, especially in its human and social aspects. But We consider that the inner freedom which results from zeal for evangelical poverty makes us in fact more sensitive to the human aspects of economic questions, and better fitted to

[319] Luke 11:21; Mark 5:9.
[320] See Dz-Sch., 428.

understand them. We can pass, where necessary, a calm and often severe judgment on wealth and on the luxuries of life.

—*Ecclesiam Suam*, 55 (August 6, 1964)

In full agreement with Our predecessors, with those saints whom our age has given to the Church on earth and in heaven, and with the devout instincts of the faithful, We are convinced that charity should today assume its rightful, foremost position in the scale of religious and moral values—and not just in theory, but in the practice of the Christian life. And this applies not only to the charity we show toward God who has poured out the abundance of His love upon us, but also to the charity which we in turn should lavish on our brothers, the whole human race.

—*Ecclesiam Suam*, 56 (August 6, 1964)

At Cana, Mary appears once more as the Virgin in prayer: when she tactfully told her Son of a temporal need she also obtained an effect of grace, namely, that Jesus, in working the first of His "signs," confirmed His disciples' faith in Him.[321]

—*Marialis Cultus*, 18 (February 2, 1974)

It is a departure from the picture provided by biblical Church teaching to refuse to acknowledge the Devil's existence; to regard him as a self-sustaining principle who, unlike other creatures, does not owe his origin to God; or to explain the Devil as a pseudo-reality, a conceptual, fanciful personification of the unknown causes of our misfortunes. When the problem of evil is seen in all its complexity and in its absurdity from the point of view of our limited minds, it becomes an obsession. It poses the greatest single obstacle to our religious understanding of the universe. It is no accident that St.

---

[321] Cf. John 2:1–12.

Augustine was bothered by this for years: "I sought the source of evil, and I found no explanation."[322]

— General Audience (November 15, 1972)

Charity is the key to everything. It sets all to rights. There is nothing which charity cannot achieve and renew. Charity "beareth all things, believeth all things, hopeth all things, endureth all things."[323] Who is there among us who does not realize this? And since we realize it, is not this the time to put it into practice?

— *Ecclesiam Suam*, 56 (August 6, 1964)

In our day we are witnessing the decline of prayer, and you know the causes of this. Yet in favor of prayer we have two great — though different — resources: the first is the liturgical reform promoted by the recent Council. The Council has not only renewed the outward form of ritual, always according to certain traditional norms, but it has also given fresh life to the sources — doctrinal, sacramental, communal and pastoral — of the Church's prayer.

— Address to the bishops of Asia in Manila,

Philippines (November 28, 1970)

This matter of the Devil and of the influence he can exert on individuals as well as on communities, entire societies or events, is a very important chapter of Catholic doctrine which should be studied again, although it is given little attention today. Some think a sufficient compensation can be found in psychoanalytic and psychiatric studies or in spiritualistic experiences, which are unfortunately so widespread in some countries today.

— General Audience (November 15, 1972)

[322] *Confessions* VII, 5, 7, 11, etc.
[323] 1 Cor. 13:7.

## Prayer, Holiness, and the Life of Faith

The Christian must be a militant; he must be vigilant and strong;[324] and he must at times make use of special ascetical practices to escape from certain diabolical attacks. Jesus teaches us this by pointing to "prayer and fasting" as the remedy.[325]

—General Audience (November 15, 1972)

We exhort the laity: Christian families, youth, adults, all those who exercise a trade or profession, leaders, without forgetting the poor who are often rich in faith and hope—all lay people who are conscious of their evangelizing role in the service of their Church or in the midst of society and the world. We say to all of them: our evangelizing zeal must spring from true holiness of life, and, as the Second Vatican Council suggests, preaching must in its turn make the preacher grow in holiness, which is nourished by prayer and above all by love for the Eucharist.[326]

—*Evangelii Nuntiandi*, 76 (December 8, 1975)

Everything has a meaning, a purpose, an order; and everything gives us a glimpse of a Transcendent Presence, a Thought, a Life and ultimately a Love, so that the universe, both by reason of what it is and of what it is not, offers us an inspiring, joyful preparation for something even more beautiful and more perfect.[327] The Christian vision of the universe and of life is therefore triumphantly optimistic; and this vision fully justifies our joy and gratitude for being alive, so that we sing forth our happiness in celebrating God's glory.[328]

—General Audience (November 15, 1972)

[324] 1 Pet. 5:8.
[325] Mark 9:29.
[326] Cf. *Presbyterorum Ordinis*, 13.
[327] See 1 Cor. 2:9; 13:12; Rom. 8:19–23.
[328] See the Gloria of the Mass.

If you have lost the taste for prayer, you will regain the desire for it by returning humbly to its practice. Do not forget, moreover, the witness of history: faithfulness to prayer or its abandonment are the test of the vitality or decadence of the religious life.

—*Evangelica Testificatio*, 42 (June 29, 1971)

Now the Christian life may be defined as a continual search for perfection. This definition is not complete, because it is purely subjective, and omits many other aspects of the Christian life. It is exact, however, in the sense that the kingdom of God, the economy of salvation, the relationship established by Christianity between our littleness and the greatness of God, His ineffable transcendence, His infinite goodness demands a transformation, a purification, a moral and spiritual elevation of man called to so great a destiny. It requires the search for, and the effort toward a personal state of feeling, thought and mentality, a way of conduct, and a wealth of grace and gifts that we call perfection.

—General Audience (August 7, 1968)

We come face to face with sin which is a perversion of human freedom and the profound cause of death because it involves detachment from God, the source of life. And then sin in its turn becomes the occasion and the effect of interference in us and our work by a dark, hostile agent, the Devil. Evil is not merely an absence of something but an active force, a living, spiritual being that is perverted and that perverts others. It is a terrible reality, mysterious and frightening.

—General Audience (November 15, 1972)

Indeed, the cultivation of Christian perfection must still be regarded as the richest source of the Church's spiritual strength. It is the means, so peculiarly its own, whereby the Church basks in the sunlight of Christ's Spirit. It is the Church's natural and necessary way of expressing its religious and social activity. It is the Church's surest defense and the cause of its constant renewal of strength amid the difficulties of the secular world.

—*Ecclesiam Suam,* 38 (August 6, 1964)

The world which, paradoxically, despite innumerable signs of the denial of God, is nevertheless searching for Him in unexpected ways and painfully experiencing the need of Him—the world is calling for evangelizers to speak to it of a God whom the evangelists themselves should know and be familiar with as if they could see the invisible.[329]

—*Evangelii Nuntiandi,* 76 (December 8, 1975)

Our intense desire is to see the Church become what Christ intended it to be: one, holy, and entirely dedicated to the pursuit of that perfection to which Christ called it and for which He qualified it. In its pilgrimage through the world the Church must really strive to manifest that ideal of perfection envisaged for it by the divine Redeemer. Here, therefore, we have the greatest problem confronting the living Church. It is a problem which shows how powerful and effective the Church really is. It goads it into action, submits it to searching criticism and keeps it true to its purpose. It engenders in the Church prayer and compunction, repentance and hope, toil and confidence, the spirit of adventure and achievement.

—*Ecclesiam Suam,* 41 (August 6, 1964)

The Holy Spirit also gives you the grace to discover the image of the Lord in the hearts of men, and teaches you to love them as brothers and sisters. Again, He helps you to see the manifestations

[329] Cf. Heb. 11:27.

of His love in events. If we are humbly attentive to men and things, the Spirit of Jesus enlightens us and enriches us with His wisdom, provided that we are imbued with the spirit of prayer.

—*Evangelica Testificatio*, 44 (June 29, 1971)

It is through faith that we gain this awareness of the mystery of the Church—mature faith, a faith lived out in our lives. Faith such as this gives us a *sensus Ecclesiae*, an awareness of the Church, and this is something with which the genuine Christian should be deeply imbued. He has been raised in the school of the divine word, nourished by the grace of the sacraments and the Paraclete's heavenly inspiration, trained in the practice of the virtues of the Gospel, and influenced by the Church's culture and community life. He has, moreover, the tremendous joy of sharing in the dignity of the royal priesthood granted to the people of God.[330]

—*Ecclesiam Suam*, 36 (August 6, 1964)

Every evangelizer is expected to have a reverence for truth, especially since the truth that he studies and communicates is none other than revealed truth and hence, more than any other, a sharing in the first truth which is God Himself. The preacher of the Gospel will therefore be a person who even at the price of personal renunciation and suffering always seeks the truth that he must transmit to others.

—*Evangelii Nuntiandi*, 78 (December 8, 1975)

The Christian ideal begins with the known premise of the dignity of man and his perfectibility, but based at the same time on a two-fold negative observation: the one derives from his inheritance of original sin which has weakened the very nature of man, giving

---

[330] Cf. 1 Pet. 2:9.

rise to a lack of balance, deficiencies and weakness of his faculties. The other denies the ability of human power alone to reach the true perfection which is necessary to man's salvation, namely his sharing in the life of God through grace. And from these premises the concept of Christian perfection unfolds itself as a victory achieved through grace and a patient practice of the natural and supernatural virtues. Perfection becomes possible, progressive and certain of final fulfilment.

—General Audience (August 7, 1968)

The mystery of the Church is not a truth to be confined to the realms of speculative theology. It must be lived, so that the faithful may have a kind of intuitive experience of it, even before they come to understand it clearly. And the faithful as a community will indeed recognize that they belong to Christ's Mystical Body when they realize that a part of the ministry of the Church's hierarchy is to initiate men into the Christian way of life, to beget them,[331] teach them, sanctify them, and be their leaders. The hierarchy is a sort of instrument fashioned by Christ, which He Himself uses to communicate to His mystical members the marvelous gifts of truth and grace. He uses it, too, to impart an external, visible structure to the Mystical Body in its pilgrimage through the world, and to give it its sublime unity, its ability to perform its various tasks, its concerted multiplicity of form, and its spiritual beauty.

—*Ecclesiam Suam*, 37 (August 6, 1964)

The Lord's spiritual testament tells us that unity among His followers is not only the proof that we are His but also the proof that He is sent by the Father. It is the test of the credibility of Christians and of Christ Himself. As evangelizers, we must offer Christ's faithful not

[331] Cf. Gal. 4:19; 1 Cor. 4:15.

the image of people divided and separated by unedifying quarrels, but the image of people who are mature in faith and capable of finding a meeting-point beyond the real tensions, thanks to a shared, sincere and disinterested search for truth. Yes, the destiny of evangelization is certainly bound up with the witness of unity given by the Church.

— *Evangelii Nuntiandi*, 77 (December 8, 1975)

The Christian life, as encouraged and preserved by the Church, must resist every possible source of deception, contamination, or restriction of its freedom. It must guard against these things as it would guard against contamination by error or evil. Yet at the same time it must not only adapt itself to the forms of thought and living which a temporal environment induces, one might almost say imposes, on it—provided, of course, such forms are not incompatible with the basic principles of its religious and moral teaching-but it must also strive to approach these forms and to correct, ennoble, encourage, and sanctify them. And this demands of the Church a continual process of self-examination and re-appraisal of its external conduct. This in fact is what the present era is demanding of the Church with such insistence and earnestness.

— *Ecclesiam Suam*, 42 (August 6, 1964)

Are the defects in the world of no account?... We find evil in the realm of nature, where so many of its expressions seem to speak to us of some sort of disorder. Then we find it among human beings, in the form of weakness, frailty, suffering, death and something worse: the tension between two laws—one reaching for the good, the other directed toward evil.

— General Audience (November 15, 1972)

If you truly do the work of God, you will of your own accord feel the need for times of retreat which, together with your brothers and sisters in religion, you will transform into times of fullness. In view of the hectic pace and tensions of modern life it is appropriate to give particular importance — over and above the daily rhythm of prayer — to those more prolonged moments of prayer, which can be variously spread out in the different periods of the day, according to the possibilities and the nature of your vocation. If according to your constitutions the houses to which you belong widely practice fraternal hospitality, it will be for you to regulate the frequency and mode of that hospitality, so that all unnecessary disturbance is avoided, and so that your guests are helped to attain close union with God.

—*Evangelica Testificatio*, 35 (June 29, 1971)

## POPE PAUL VI ON THE ROSARY

The Rosary draws from the Gospel the presentation of the mysteries and its main formulas. As it moves from the angel's joyful greeting and the Virgin's pious assent, the Rosary takes its inspiration from the Gospel to suggest the attitude with which the faithful should recite it. In the harmonious succession of Hail Marys, the Rosary puts before us once more a fundamental mystery of the Gospel—the Incarnation of the Word, contemplated at the decisive moment of the Annunciation to Mary. The Rosary is thus a Gospel prayer....

As a Gospel prayer, centered on the mystery of the redemptive Incarnation, the Rosary is therefore a prayer with a clearly Christological orientation. Its most characteristic element, in fact, the litany-like succession of Hail Mary's, becomes in itself an unceasing praise of Christ, who is the ultimate object both of the angel's announcement and of the greeting of the mother of John the Baptist: "Blessed is the fruit of your womb."[332] ...

The Christian family is thus seen to be a domestic Church[333] if its members, each according to his proper place and tasks, all together promote justice, practice works of mercy, devote themselves to helping their brethren, take part in the apostolate of the wider local community and play their part in its liturgical worship.[334] This will be all the more true if together they offer up prayers to God. If this element of common prayer were missing, the family would lack its very character as a domestic Church. Thus there must logically

---

[332] Luke 1:42.

[333] *Lumen Gentium*, 11.

[334] Cf. *Apostolicam Actuositatem*, 11.

follow a concrete effort to reinstate communal prayer in family life if there is to be a restoration of the theological concept of the family as the domestic Church....

After the celebration of the Liturgy of the Hours, the high point which family prayer can reach, the Rosary should be considered as one of the best and most efficacious prayers in common that the Christian family is invited to recite. We like to think, and sincerely hope, that when the family gathering becomes a time of prayer, the Rosary is a frequent and favored manner of praying. We are well aware that the changed conditions of life today do not make family gatherings easy, and that even when such a gathering is possible many circumstances make it difficult to turn it into an occasion of prayer. There is no doubt of the difficulty. But it is characteristic of the Christian in his manner of life not to give in to circumstances but to overcome them, not to succumb but to make an effort. Families which want to live in full measure the vocation and spirituality proper to the Christian family must therefore devote all their energies to overcoming the pressures that hinder family gatherings and prayer in common.

—*Marialis Cultus*, 44, 46, 52, 54 (February 2, 1974)

*Chapter 14*

# The Testament of Pope Paul VI

Four days after the death of Pope Paul VI, on August 10, 1978, the members of the Sacred College of Cardinals heard the pope's last will and testament. It had been known previously only to the members of Paul's family. The last will and testament was originally written, by hand, by Pope Paul and dated on June 30, 1965. The pope added two codicils in 1972 and 1973.

The following is the text of the last will and testament:

In the name of the Father and of the Son and of the Holy Spirit. Amen.

1 — I am fixing my gaze on the mystery of death and of what follows thereafter, in the light of Christ which alone sheds a light upon it; and therefore with humble and serene confidence. I am deeply aware of the truth, which for me is ever reflected from this mystery on the present life; and I thank the conqueror of death for having dispelled the darkness and revealed the light thereof.

Therefore, in the presence of death, of the total and definitive separation from the present life, I deem it my duty to exalt the gift, the good fortune, the beauty, the destiny of this same fleeting existence: Lord, I thank thee for having called me into life, and even more so, making me a Christian, for having regenerated and destined me to the fullness of life.

# Saint Pope Paul VI

Likewise, I feel obliged to thank and to bless those who were the means of conveying to me the gifts of life received from thee O Lord: those who brought me into life (Oh! blessed be my most worthy parents!), those who educated me, loved me, did good to me, helped me, surrounded me with good examples, with care, affection, trust, goodness, kindness, friendship, fidelity and deference. I look with gratitude on the natural and spiritual relationships which have given origin, assistance, support, significance to my humble existence: how many gifts, how many beautiful and noble things, how much hope have I received in this world! Now that my day is drawing to a close, and all of this stupendous and dramatic temporal and earthly scene is ending and dissolving, how can I further thank thee, O Lord, after the gift of natural life, also for the higher gift of faith and grace, in which alone at the end my surviving existence finds refuge? How can I worthily praise thy goodness, O Lord, for the fact that as soon as I entered this world, I was introduced into the ineffable world of the Catholic Church? For having been called and initiated into the priesthood of Christ? For having had the joy and the mission of serving souls, brothers, the young, the poor, the people of God? And for having had the unmerited honour of being a minister of holy Church, especially at Rome, near the Pope, then later at Milan as Archbishop in the See, for me too elevated and venerable, of Saints Ambrose and Charles, and finally in this supreme, formidable and most Holy See of St. Peter? I shall sing forever the mercies of the Lord.

I wish to greet and bless all those whom I met in my earthly pilgrimage; those who were my collaborators, counsellors and friends — and they were so many and so good and generous and dear! — blessed be those to whom I ministered and who were my sons and brothers in Our Lord!

To you, Lodovico and Francesco, brothers by blood and in the spirit, and to all you dear ones of my family who have never asked anything from me, nor received any worldly favour from me, and who have always given me an example of human and Christian virtues, who have understood me with so much discretion and heartfelt feeling, and who above all have helped me to seek in the present life the path to the life to come, to all of you my peace and my blessing.

My thought turns backwards and becomes more encompassing; and well do I know that this would not be a happy farewell if I should not remember to ask forgiveness of all those I may have offended, failed to serve and love enough; and besides to forgive those who should have desired forgiveness from me. May the peace of the Lord be with us!

I feel the Church all around me: O holy Church, one, catholic and apostolic, receive with my blessing and greeting my final act of love.

To you, Rome, the diocese of St. Peter and of the Vicar of Christ, most beloved to this least servant of the servants of God, my most paternal and fullest blessing, so that you, the City of the World, may ever be mindful of your mysterious vocation, and that you may be able to fulfil, with human virtue and with Christian faith, your spiritual and universal mission, however long may be the history of the world.

And to all of you, reverend Brothers in the Episcopate, my heartfelt and respectful greeting. I am with you in the one faith, in the same charity, in the common apostolic commitment, in the joint service of the Gospel, for the building up of the Church of Christ and for the salvation of the whole of mankind. To all priests, to all men and women religious, to the students of our seminaries, to the faithful and militant Catholics, to the young, to the suffering, to the poor, to those who seek truth and justice, to all, the blessing of the Pope as he dies.

And thus, with special reverence and gratitude, to the Cardinals and to the entire Roman Curia: in the presence of you who have been closer to me, I solemnly profess our Faith, I declare our Hope, I exalt the Charity that does not die, humbly accepting from the divine will the death in store for me, calling upon the great mercy of the Lord, imploring the clement intercession of the most holy Virgin Mary, of the angels and the saints, and commending my soul to the prayers of the faithful!

2 — I appoint the Holy See my universal heir: to this I am bound by duty, gratitude and love. Except for the dispositions indicated below.

3 — My private secretary shall be the executor of my will. He shall take advice from the Secretariat of State, and follow the juridical rules in force and the recognized ecclesiastical customs.

4 — As regards the goods of this world: I wish to die poor and thus to facilitate everything in this regard.

As regards movable and immovable possessions which have come to me from my family, they shall freely be disposed of by my brothers Lodovico and Francesco; I request their prayers for my soul and for our deceased relatives. Let them give alms to people in need or to charitable works. They may keep for themselves, and give to those who deserve and desire it, some souvenirs from the things or from the religious objects or from the books that belong to me. My personal notes, copybooks, correspondence and writings are to be destroyed.

As regards other things which can be regarded as my own: they shall be disposed of by my private secretary as the executor of my will and he may keep some souvenirs for himself, and give to my closer friends some small things as a token of remembrance. I should like that manuscripts and handwritten notes of mine should be destroyed, and that correspondence received by me, of a spiritual or personal character and not destined for the knowledge of others, should be burned.

In case that the executor of my will cannot carry out these instructions, let them be carried out by the Secretariat of State.

5 — I earnestly request that arrangements be made for suitable suffrages and generous alms, as far as possible.

As regards my funeral: let it be simple and animated by religious piety (I do not wish to have the catafalque, as is the custom for the funerals of Popes; instead let things be carried out in a humble and becoming manner).

As regards my tomb: I would like to be buried in the earth with a simple stone to indicate the place and invite a prayer of Christian piety. No monument for me.

6 — And most important of all, on taking my leave of this earthly scene, and going to face the judgment and mercy of God, there are so many things I should say, indeed so many. On the state of the Church; let her give ear to some words of ours which we uttered on her behalf seriously and lovingly. On the Council: let it be brought to a good conclusion, and let its prescriptions be put into effect. As regards ecumenism: the approach to the separated Brethren must go on, with great understanding and patience, with great love; but without deflecting from the true Catholic doctrine. As regards the world: one must not think to help it by following its ways of thought, its habits and tastes, but by studying it, loving it and serving it.

I close my eyes on this sorrowful, dramatic and magnificent world, invoking once again on her behalf the divine goodness. Again I bless everyone, especially Rome, Milan and Brescia. For the Holy Land, the land of Jesus, where I went as a pilgrim of faith and peace, a special greeting and blessing.

To the Church, the most beloved Catholic Church, to all mankind, my apostolic blessing.

Then—into thy hands, O Lord, I commend my Spirit.

I, Pope Paul VI

*Given at Rome, at St Peter's, the 30th June 1965; the third year of our Pontificate.*

# Saint Pope Paul VI

*Additional Notes to my Testament*

Into thy hands, O Lord, I commend my Spirit.

My soul magnifies the Lord. Mary!

I believe. I hope. I love.

I thank all those who have done good to me.

I ask pardon of those to whom I may not have done good.

To all I give peace in the Lord.

Greetings to my most beloved brother Lodovico, and to all my family, relations and friends, and to all to whom I have ministered. Thanks to all my collaborators. To the Secretariat of State in particular.

With particular charity I bless Brescia, Milan, Rome, the whole Church. How lovely is thy dwelling place, O Lord!

All my possessions I leave to the Holy See.

Let my private secretary, the dear Don Pasquale Macchi, arrange for suffrages and works of charity and let him keep for himself and give to persons dear to me some souvenirs from among the books and things belonging to me.

I do not desire any special tomb. Just some prayers to obtain God's mercy.

In thee, O Lord, have I hoped. Amen, alleluia.

My blessing to all, in the name of the Lord.

POPE PAUL VI

*Castel Gandolfo, 16 September 1972, 7.30 a.m.*

*Addition to my testamentary dispositions*

I wish to have a very simple funeral, and I do not wish to have either a special tomb or any monument. Just some suffrages (some works of charity and prayers).

POPE PAUL VI

*14 July 1973*

# Selected Writings of Pope St. Paul VI

## Encyclicals

*Humanae Vitae* (July 25, 1968)

*Sacerdotalis Caelibatus* (June 24, 1967)

*Populorum Progressio* (March 26, 1967)

*Christi Matri* (September 15, 1966)

*Mysterium Fidei* (September 3, 1965)

*Mense Maio* (April 29, 1965)

*Ecclesiam Suam* (August 6, 1964)

## Apostolic Constitutions

*Romano Pontifici Eligendo* (October 1, 1975)

*Constans Nobis* (July 11, 1975)

*Sacram Unctionem Infirmorum* (November 30, 1972)

*Divinae Consortium Naturae* (August 15, 1971)

*Indulgentiarum Doctrina* (January 1, 1967)

*Paenitemini* (February 17, 1966)

## Saint Pope Paul VI

## Apostolic Exhortations

*Evangelii Nuntiandi* (December 8, 1975)

*Gaudete in Domino* (May 9, 1975)

*Paterna cum benevolentia* (December 8, 1974)

*Nobis in Animo* (March 25, 1974)

*Marialis Cultus* (February 2, 1974)

*Evangelica Testificatio* (June 29, 1971)

*Quinque iam anni* (December 8, 1970)

*Recurrens mensis october* (October 7, 1969)

*Signum Magnum* (May 13, 1967)

*Petrum et Paulum Apostolos* (February 22, 1967)

*Postrema Sessio* (November 4, 1965)

*Quarta Sessio* (August 28, 1965)

## Motu Proprio

*Inter eximia* (May, 11 1978)

*Iustitiam et pacem* (December 10, 1976)

*Apostolatus peragendi* (December 10, 1976)

*Catholica ecclesia* (October 23, 1976)

*Firma in traditione* (June 13, 1974)

*Con matrimonialium causarum* (September 8, 1973)

*Magisterium vitae* (May 24, 1973)

*Quo aptius* (February 27, 1973)

*Ministeria quaedam* (August 15, 1972)

*Ad Pascendum* (August 15, 1972)

*Sedula cura* (June 27, 1971)

*Causas matrimoniales* (March 28, 1971)

## Selected Writings of Pope St. Paul VI

*Ingravescentem Aetatem* (November 20, 1970)

*Matrimonia mixta* (March 31, 1970)

*Apostolicae caritatis* (March 19, 1970)

*Pastoralis migratorum cura* (August 15, 1969)

*Inclita toto*— apostolic letter in the form of a motu proprio (August 8, 1969)

*Sollicitudo omnium Ecclesiarum* (June 24, 1969)

*Ad hoc usque tempus* (April 15, 1969)

*Sanctitas clarior* (March 19, 1969)

*Mysterii Paschalis* (February 14, 1969)

*Romanae Dioecesis* (June 30, 1968)

*Solemni Hac Liturgia* (*Credo of the People of God*) (June 30, 1968)

*Pontificalia Insignia* (June 21, 1968)

*Pontificalis Domus* (March 28, 1968)

*Pro comperto sane* (August 6, 1967)

*Sacrum Diaconatus Ordinem* (June 18, 1967)

*Episcopalis Potestatis* (May 2, 1967)

*Catholicam Christi Ecclesiam* (January 6, 1967)

*Ecclesiae Sanctae* (August 6, 1966)

*De Episcoporum Muneribus* (June 15, 1966)

*Munus apostolicum* (June 10, 1966)

*Summi Dei beneficio* (May 3, 1966)

*Equestres Ordines*— apostolic letter in the form of a motu proprio (April 15, 1966)

*Peculiare ius*— apostolic letter in the form of a motu proprio (February 8, 1966)

*Romanae Urbis*—apostolic letter in the form of a motu proprio (February 2, 1966)

# Saint Pope Paul VI

*Verbi Dei*—apostolic letter in the form of a motu proprio (January 25, 1966)

*Motu proprio* for the other postconciliar commissions (January 3, 1966)

*Altissimi cantus*—apostolic letter in the form of a motu proprio (December 7, 1965)

*Integrae servandae* (December 7, 1965)

*Apostolica sollicitudo* (September 15, 1965)

*Sacro Cardinalium Consilio* (February 26, 1965)

*Ad purpuratorum Patrum Collegium* (February 11, 1965)

*Progrediente Concilio* (May 19, 1964)

*Studia latinitatis* (February 22, 1964)

*Sacram Liturgiam* (January 25, 1964)

*Pastorale munus* (November 30, 1963)

# About the Author

Matthew Bunson is Senior Contributor for EWTN and Senior Editor for the *National Catholic Register*. He is a senior fellow of the St. Paul Center for Biblical Theology and the author or co-author of more than fifty books, including *OSV's Encyclopedia of Catholic History*, *The Pope Encyclopedia*, *We Have a Pope! Benedict XVI*, and the *Encyclopedia of Saints*. His *Encyclopedia of American Catholic History* was named Reference Book of the Year by the Catholic Press Association, and his book *Pope Francis* was named Biography of the Year by the Association of Catholic Publishers. Bunson is also host of the EWTN series *The Doctors of the Church*.